MAR – – 2020

CAPTAIN AMERICA · NAMOR · WINTER SOLDIER

INVADERS

DEAD IN THE WATER

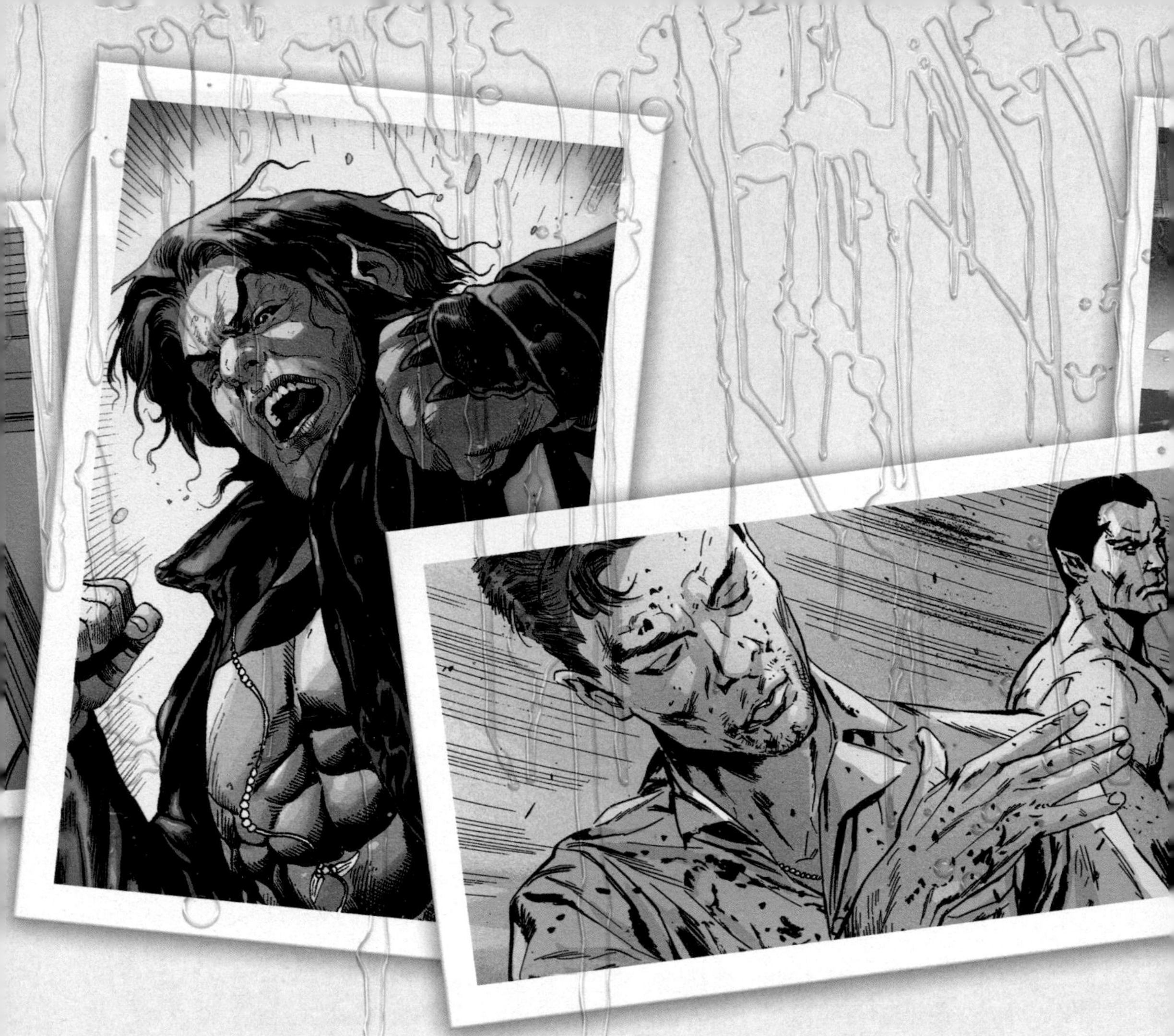

CAPTAIN AMERICA AND BUCKY BARNES! NAMOR THE SUB-MARINER! THE ORIGINAL HUMAN TORCH, JIM HAMMOND! During the darkest hours of World War II, these four banded together as THE INVADERS — to battle the Axis Powers to the death in the name of freedom!

But now the Invaders are locked in battle with one of their own comrades: King Namor of Atlantis. Driven by a psychic projection of Tommy Machan, his deceased friend from the war, Namor has launched several offensives on the surface world — most recently in the form of a missile, which transformed all humans in a small coastal town in Maine into water breathers, gasping to survive!

Namor moved the ocean to cover the city so that its inhabitants could survive underwater. But can the damage be undone?

★★★

COLLECTION EDITOR **KATERI WOODY** — **CAITLIN O'CONNELL** ASSISTANT EDITOR
ASSISTANT MANAGING EDITOR **MAIA LOY** — **MARK D. BEAZLEY** EDITOR, SPECIAL PROJECTS
SENIOR EDITOR, SPECIAL PROJECTS **JENNIFER GRÜNWALD** — **JEFF YOUNGQUIST** VP PRODUCTION & SPECIAL PROJECTS
SVP PRINT, SALES & MARKETING **DAVID GABRIEL** — **C.B. CEBULSKI** EDITOR IN CHIEF
ADAM DEL RE WITH **JAY BOWEN** BOOK DESIGNERS

INVADERS VOL. 2: DEAD IN THE WATER. Contains material originally published in magazine form as INVADERS (2018) #7-12. First printing 2020. ISBN 978-1-302-91750-0. Published by MARVEL WORLDWIDE, INC., a subsidiary of MARVEL ENTERTAINMENT, LLC. OFFICE OF PUBLICATION: 1290 Avenue of the Americas, New York, NY 10104.

Printed in Canada. KEVIN FEIGE, Chief Creative Officer; DAN BUCKLEY, President, Marvel Entertainment; JOHN NEE, Publisher; JOE QUESADA, EVP & Creative Director; TOM BREVOORT, SVP of Publishing; DAVID BOGART, Associate Publisher & SVP of Talent Affairs; Publishing & Partnership; DAVID GABRIEL, VP of Print & Digital Publishing; JEFF YOUNGQUIST, VP of Production & Special Projects; DAN CARR, Executive Director of Publishing Technology; ALEX MORALES, Director of Publishing Operations; DAN EDINGTON, Managing Editor; SUSAN CRESPI, Production Manager; STAN LEE, Chairman Emeritus. For information regarding advertising in Marvel Comics or on Marvel.com, please contact Vit DeBellis, Custom Solutions & Integrated Advertising Manager, at vdebellis@marvel.com. For Marvel subscription inquiries, please call 888-511-5480. **Manufactured between 1/3/2020 and 2/4/2020 by SOLISCO PRINTERS, SCOTT, QC, CANADA.**

10 9 8 7 6 5 4 3 2 1

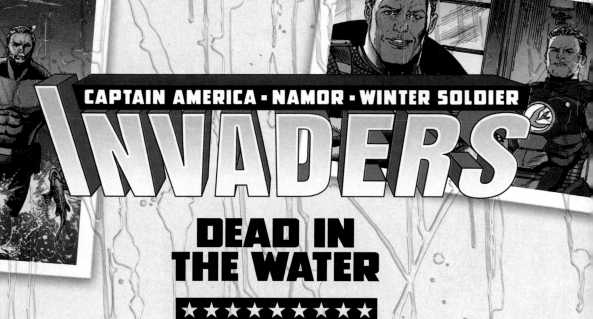

CAPTAIN AMERICA · NAMOR · WINTER SOLDIER

INVADERS

DEAD IN THE WATER

★★★★★★★★★★★

CHIP ZDARSKY
WRITER

CARLOS MAGNO & BUTCH GUICE
ARTISTS

ALEX GUIMARÃES (#7-12) WITH
DONO SÁNCHEZ-ALMARA (#8)
COLOR ARTISTS

BUTCH GUICE & ROMULO FAJARDO JR.
COVER ART

VC's TRAVIS LANHAM
LETTERER

★★★★★★★★★★★

SHANNON ANDREWS BALLESTEROS
ASSISTANT EDITOR

ALANNA SMITH
ASSOCIATE EDITOR

TOM BREVOORT
EDITOR

★★★★★★★★★★★

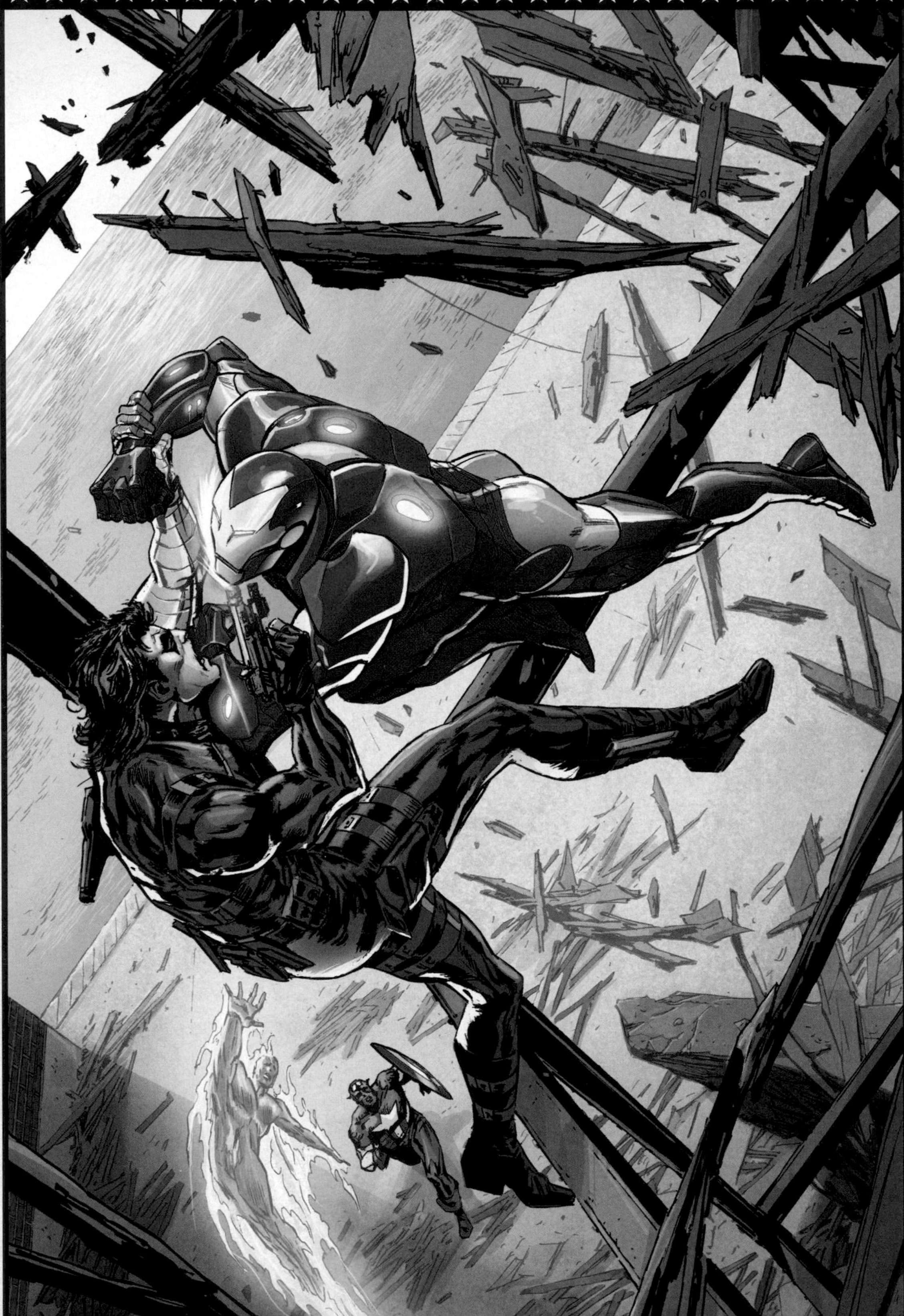

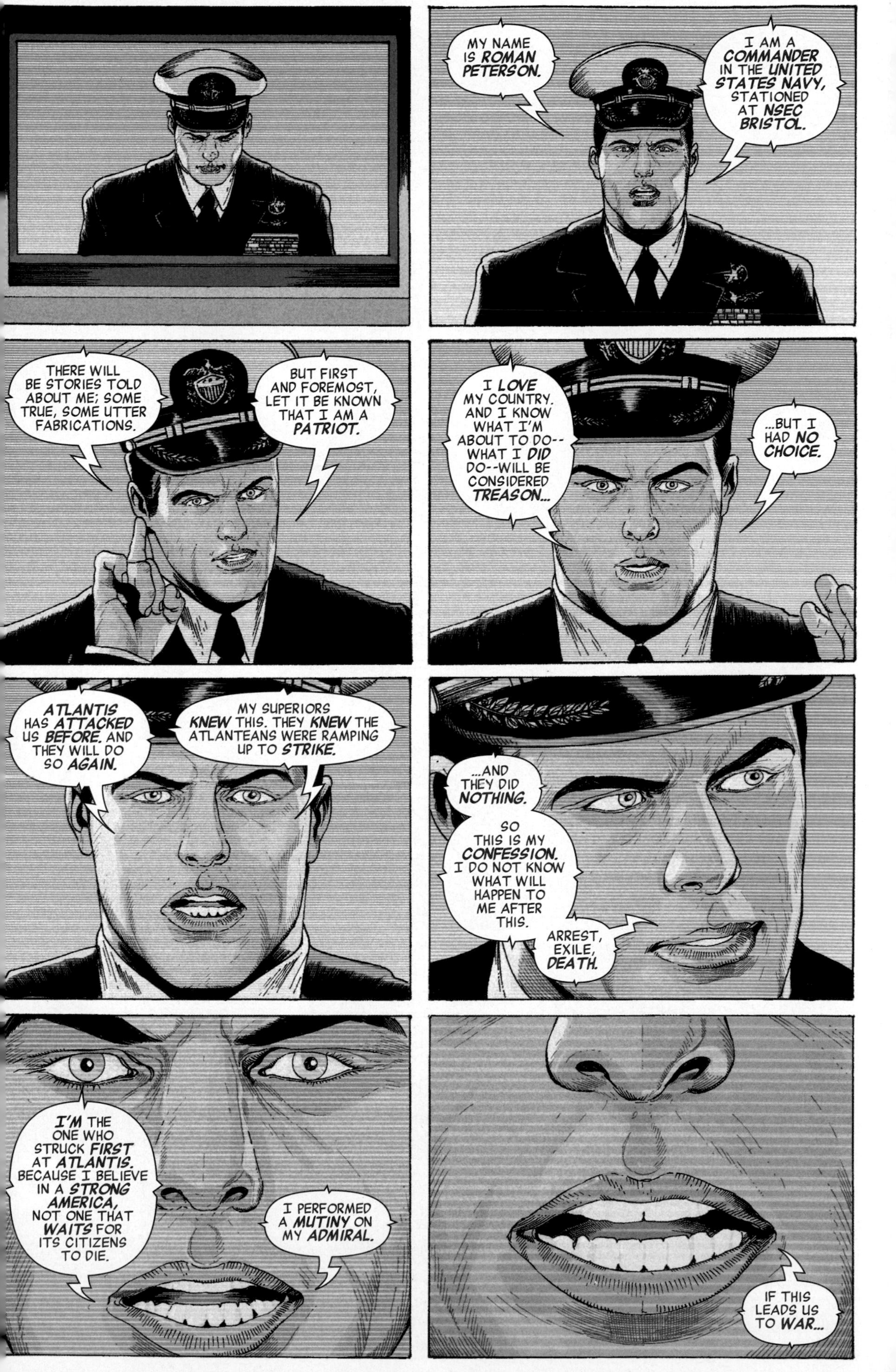

MY NAME IS ROMAN PETERSON.
I AM A COMMANDER IN THE UNITED STATES NAVY, STATIONED AT NSEC BRISTOL.
THERE WILL BE STORIES TOLD ABOUT ME; SOME TRUE, SOME UTTER FABRICATIONS.
BUT FIRST AND FOREMOST, LET IT BE KNOWN THAT I AM A PATRIOT.
I LOVE MY COUNTRY. AND I KNOW WHAT I'M ABOUT TO DO-- WHAT I DID DO--WILL BE CONSIDERED TREASON...
...BUT I HAD NO CHOICE.
ATLANTIS HAS ATTACKED US BEFORE. AND THEY WILL DO SO AGAIN.
MY SUPERIORS KNEW THIS. THEY KNEW THE ATLANTEANS WERE RAMPING UP TO STRIKE.
...AND THEY DID NOTHING.
SO THIS IS MY CONFESSION. I DO NOT KNOW WHAT WILL HAPPEN TO ME AFTER THIS.
ARREST, EXILE, DEATH.
I'M THE ONE WHO STRUCK FIRST AT ATLANTIS. BECAUSE I BELIEVE IN A STRONG AMERICA, NOT ONE THAT WAITS FOR ITS CITIZENS TO DIE.
I PERFORMED A MUTINY ON MY ADMIRAL.
IF THIS LEADS US TO WAR...

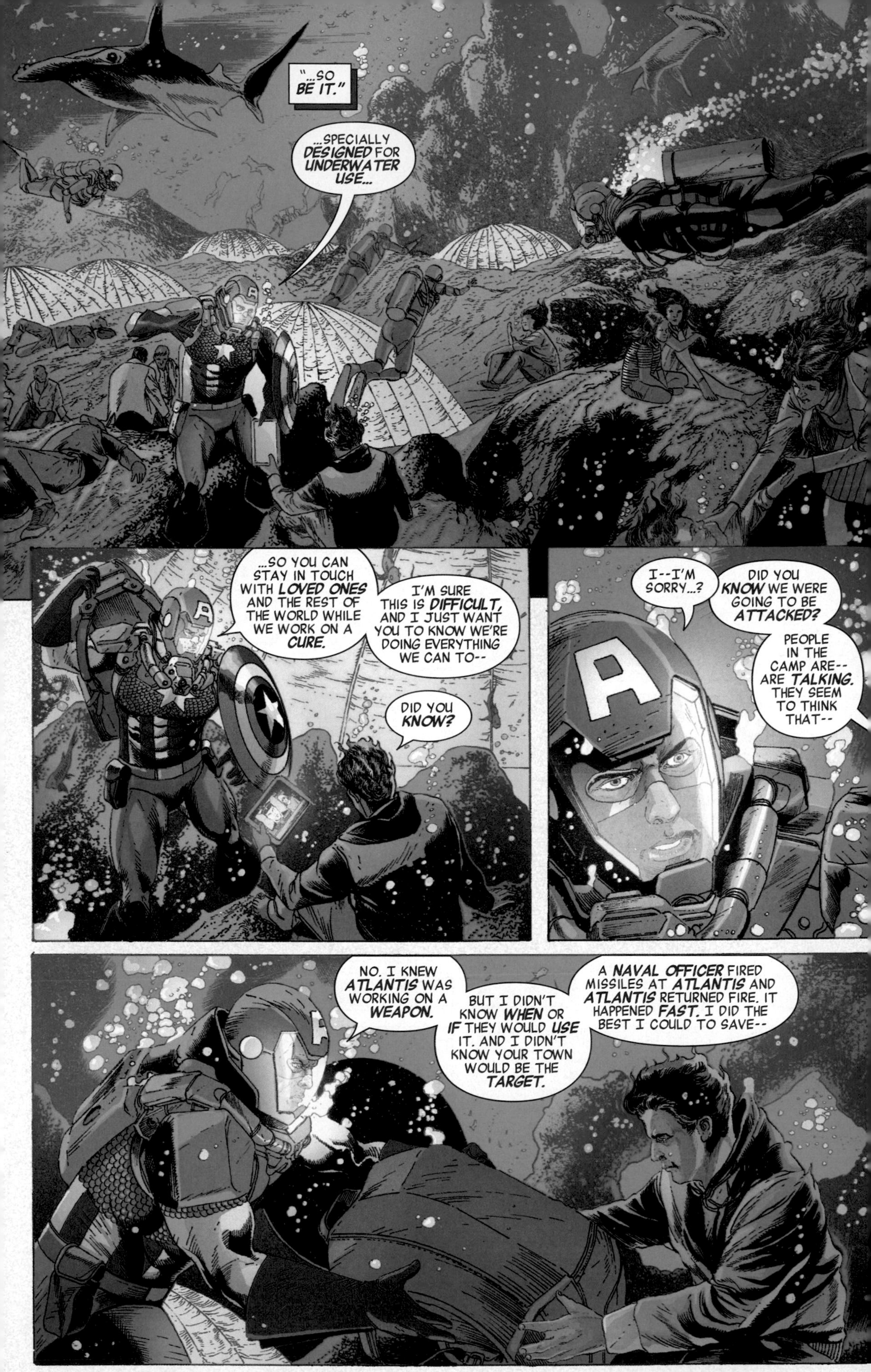
"...SO BE IT."
...SPECIALLY DESIGNED FOR UNDERWATER USE...
...SO YOU CAN STAY IN TOUCH WITH LOVED ONES AND THE REST OF THE WORLD WHILE WE WORK ON A CURE.
I'M SURE THIS IS DIFFICULT, AND I JUST WANT YOU TO KNOW WE'RE DOING EVERYTHING WE CAN TO--
DID YOU KNOW?
I--I'M SORRY...?
DID YOU KNOW WE WERE GOING TO BE ATTACKED?
PEOPLE IN THE CAMP ARE--ARE TALKING. THEY SEEM TO THINK THAT--
NO. I KNEW ATLANTIS WAS WORKING ON A WEAPON.
BUT I DIDN'T KNOW WHEN OR IF THEY WOULD USE IT. AND I DIDN'T KNOW YOUR TOWN WOULD BE THE TARGET.
A NAVAL OFFICER FIRED MISSILES AT ATLANTIS AND ATLANTIS RETURNED FIRE. IT HAPPENED FAST. I DID THE BEST I COULD TO SAVE--

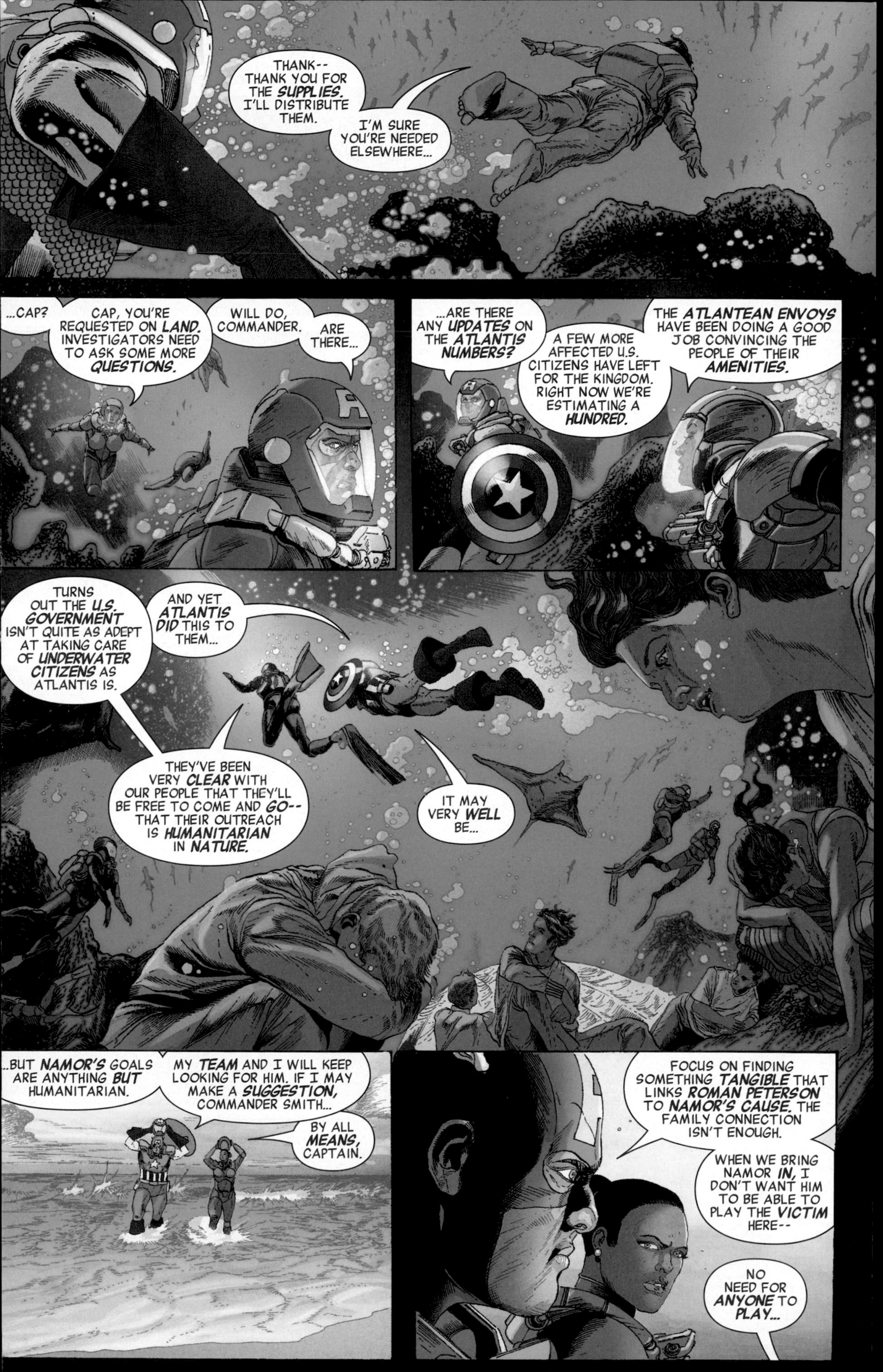
THANK-- THANK YOU FOR THE SUPPLIES. I'LL DISTRIBUTE THEM.
I'M SURE YOU'RE NEEDED ELSEWHERE...
...CAP?
CAP, YOU'RE REQUESTED ON LAND. INVESTIGATORS NEED TO ASK SOME MORE QUESTIONS.
WILL DO, COMMANDER.
ARE THERE...
...ARE THERE ANY UPDATES ON THE ATLANTIS NUMBERS?
A FEW MORE AFFECTED U.S. CITIZENS HAVE LEFT FOR THE KINGDOM. RIGHT NOW WE'RE ESTIMATING A HUNDRED.
THE ATLANTEAN ENVOYS HAVE BEEN DOING A GOOD JOB CONVINCING THE PEOPLE OF THEIR AMENITIES.
TURNS OUT THE U.S. GOVERNMENT ISN'T QUITE AS ADEPT AT TAKING CARE OF UNDERWATER CITIZENS AS ATLANTIS IS.
AND YET ATLANTIS DID THIS TO THEM...
THEY'VE BEEN VERY CLEAR WITH OUR PEOPLE THAT THEY'LL BE FREE TO COME AND GO-- THAT THEIR OUTREACH IS HUMANITARIAN IN NATURE.
IT MAY VERY WELL BE...
...BUT NAMOR'S GOALS ARE ANYTHING BUT HUMANITARIAN.
MY TEAM AND I WILL KEEP LOOKING FOR HIM. IF I MAY MAKE A SUGGESTION, COMMANDER SMITH...
BY ALL MEANS, CAPTAIN.
FOCUS ON FINDING SOMETHING TANGIBLE THAT LINKS ROMAN PETERSON TO NAMOR'S CAUSE. THE FAMILY CONNECTION ISN'T ENOUGH.
WHEN WE BRING NAMOR IN, I DON'T WANT HIM TO BE ABLE TO PLAY THE VICTIM HERE--
NO NEED FOR ANYONE TO PLAY...

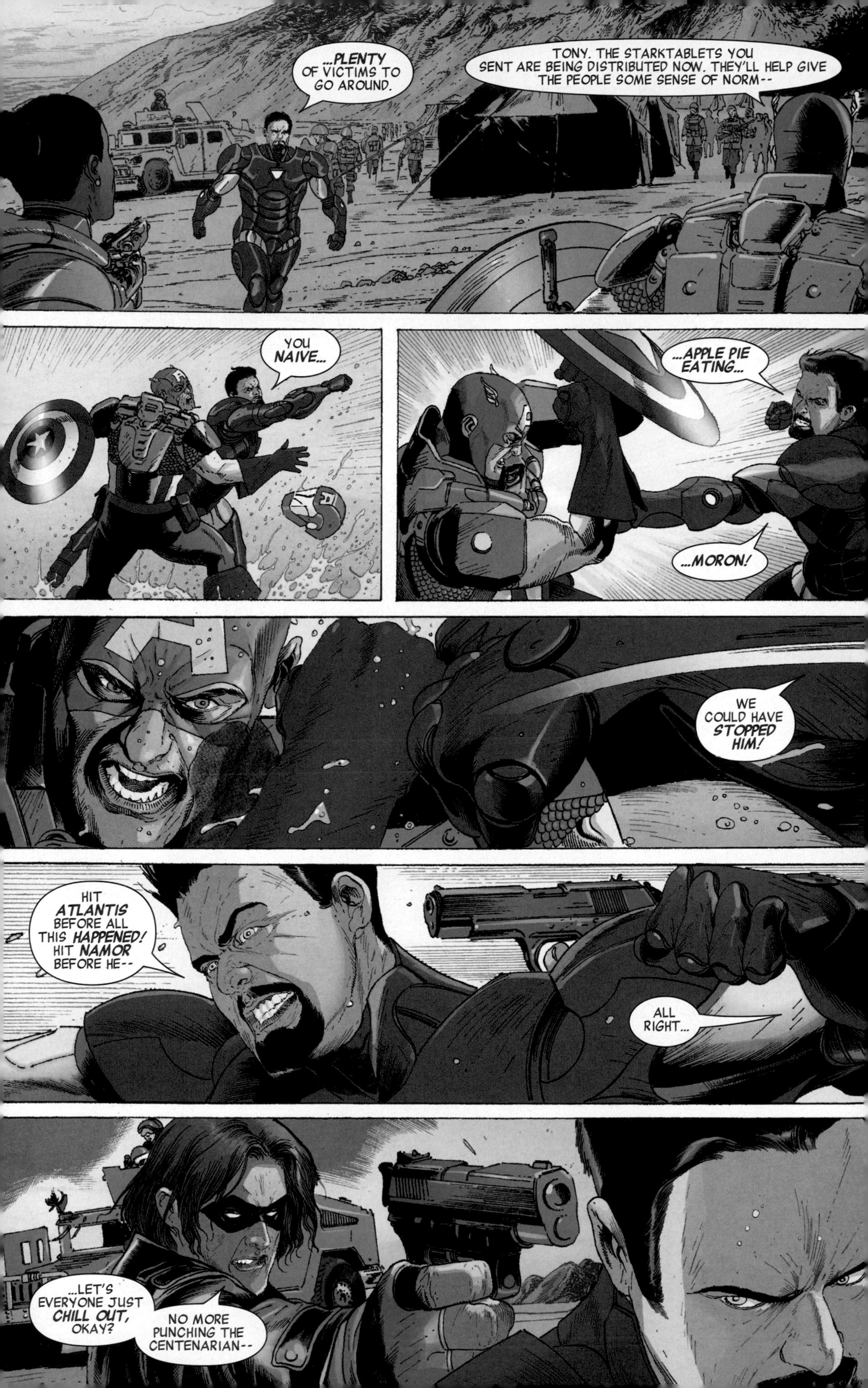
...PLENTY OF VICTIMS TO GO AROUND.
TONY. THE STARKTABLETS YOU SENT ARE BEING DISTRIBUTED NOW. THEY'LL HELP GIVE THE PEOPLE SOME SENSE OF NORM--
YOU NAIVE...
...APPLE PIE EATING...
...MORON!
WE COULD HAVE STOPPED HIM!
HIT ATLANTIS BEFORE ALL THIS HAPPENED! HIT NAMOR BEFORE HE--
ALL RIGHT...
...LET'S EVERYONE JUST CHILL OUT, OKAY?
NO MORE PUNCHING THE CENTENARIAN--

SHFWOOOSHH

HNH!

BACK **OFF,** CAP JUNIOR! THIS IS BETWEEN **ME** AND THE OLD **MAN!**

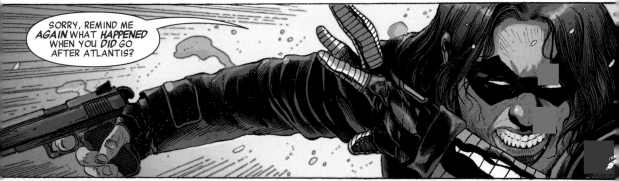

SORRY, REMIND ME **AGAIN** WHAT **HAPPENED** WHEN YOU **DID** GO AFTER ATLANTIS?

THAT'S NOT--

FORCE FIELDS? MISSILES NOT EVEN **THERE?**

AH! $#%@! THAT--

A LITTLE MORE **GIVE** WHERE IT **BENDS,** EH?

KBANG

KNEW YOU HAD TO HAVE A **WEAKNESS** OTHER THAN YOUR **MASSIVE** EGO.

NGH... YOU **BRAT.** WON'T...GET A SECOND SHOT--

ENOUGH.

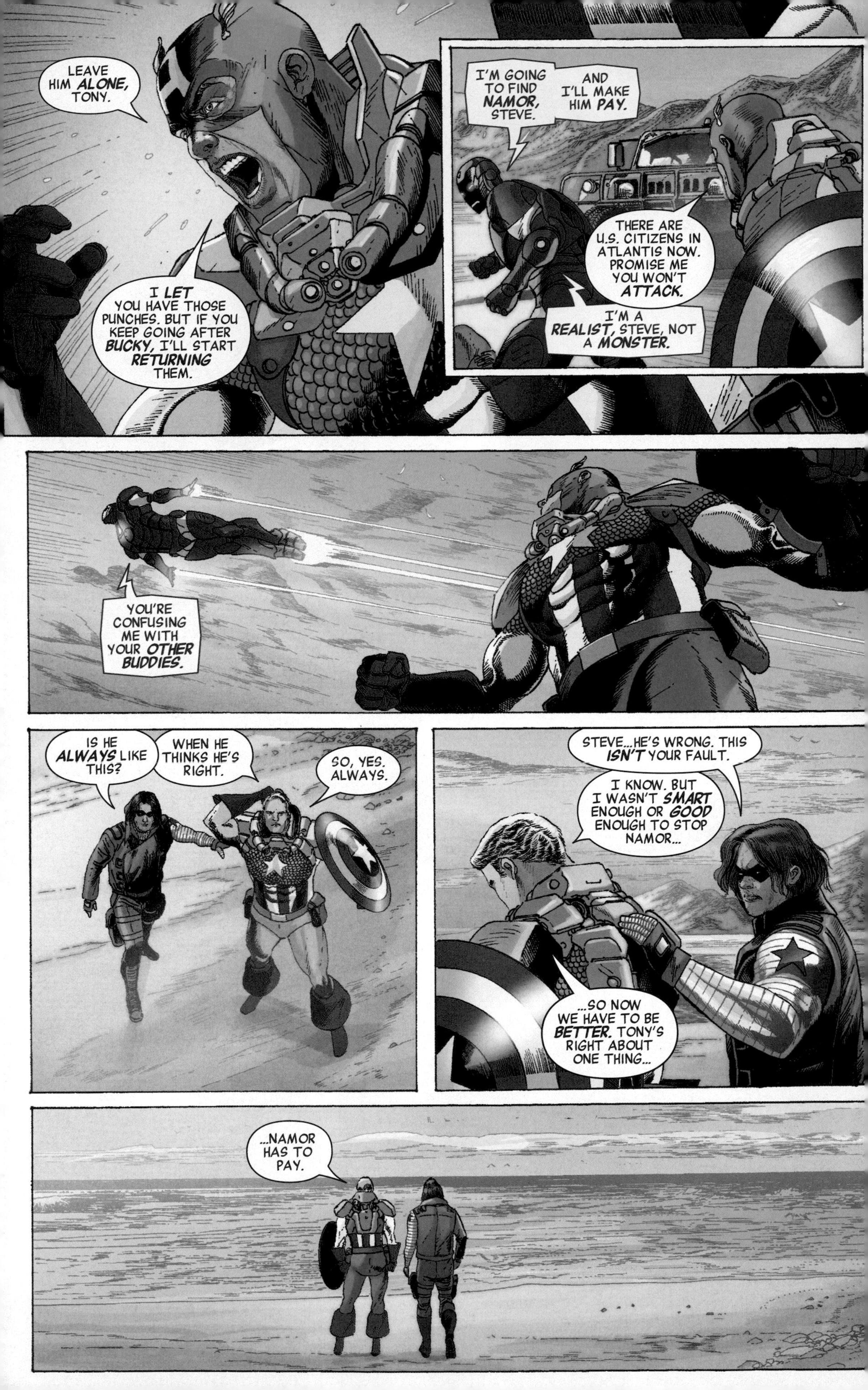
LEAVE HIM ALONE, TONY.
I LET YOU HAVE THOSE PUNCHES. BUT IF YOU KEEP GOING AFTER BUCKY, I'LL START RETURNING THEM.
I'M GOING TO FIND NAMOR, STEVE.
AND I'LL MAKE HIM PAY.
THERE ARE U.S. CITIZENS IN ATLANTIS NOW. PROMISE ME YOU WON'T ATTACK.
I'M A REALIST, STEVE, NOT A MONSTER.
YOU'RE CONFUSING ME WITH YOUR OTHER BUDDIES.
IS HE ALWAYS LIKE THIS?
WHEN HE THINKS HE'S RIGHT.
SO, YES. ALWAYS.
STEVE...HE'S WRONG. THIS ISN'T YOUR FAULT.
I KNOW. BUT I WASN'T SMART ENOUGH OR GOOD ENOUGH TO STOP NAMOR...
...SO NOW WE HAVE TO BE BETTER. TONY'S RIGHT ABOUT ONE THING...
...NAMOR HAS TO PAY.

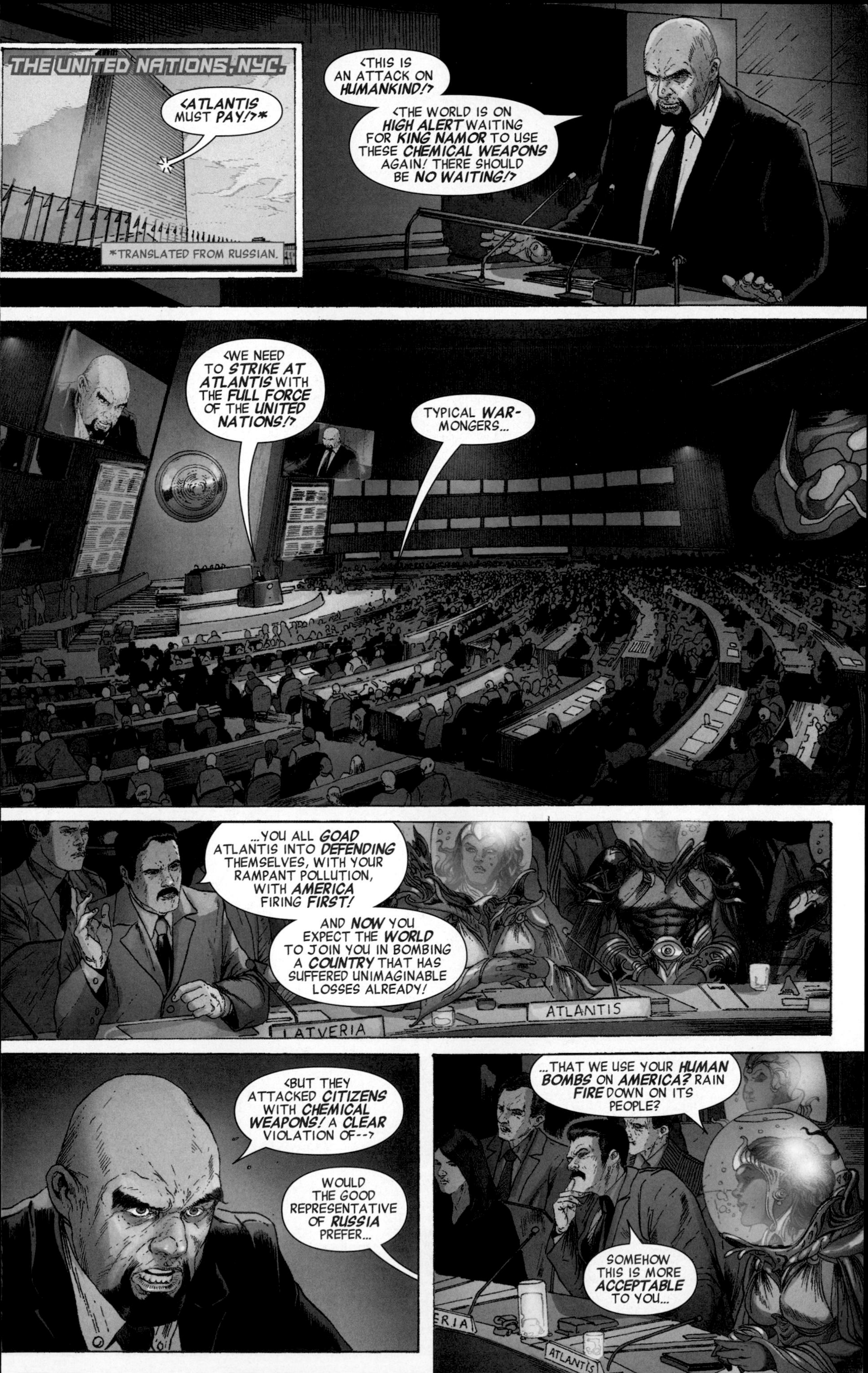
THE UNITED NATIONS, NYC.
<ATLANTIS MUST PAY!>*
*TRANSLATED FROM RUSSIAN.
<THIS IS AN ATTACK ON HUMANKIND!>
<THE WORLD IS ON HIGH ALERT WAITING FOR KING NAMOR TO USE THESE CHEMICAL WEAPONS AGAIN! THERE SHOULD BE NO WAITING!>
<WE NEED TO STRIKE AT ATLANTIS WITH THE FULL FORCE OF THE UNITED NATIONS!>
TYPICAL WAR-MONGERS...
...YOU ALL GOAD ATLANTIS INTO DEFENDING THEMSELVES, WITH YOUR RAMPANT POLLUTION, WITH AMERICA FIRING FIRST!
AND NOW YOU EXPECT THE WORLD TO JOIN YOU IN BOMBING A COUNTRY THAT HAS SUFFERED UNIMAGINABLE LOSSES ALREADY!
LATVERIA
ATLANTIS
<BUT THEY ATTACKED CITIZENS WITH CHEMICAL WEAPONS! A CLEAR VIOLATION OF-->
WOULD THE GOOD REPRESENTATIVE OF RUSSIA PREFER...
...THAT WE USE YOUR HUMAN BOMBS ON AMERICA? RAIN FIRE DOWN ON ITS PEOPLE?
SOMEHOW THIS IS MORE ACCEPTABLE TO YOU...
ATLANTIS

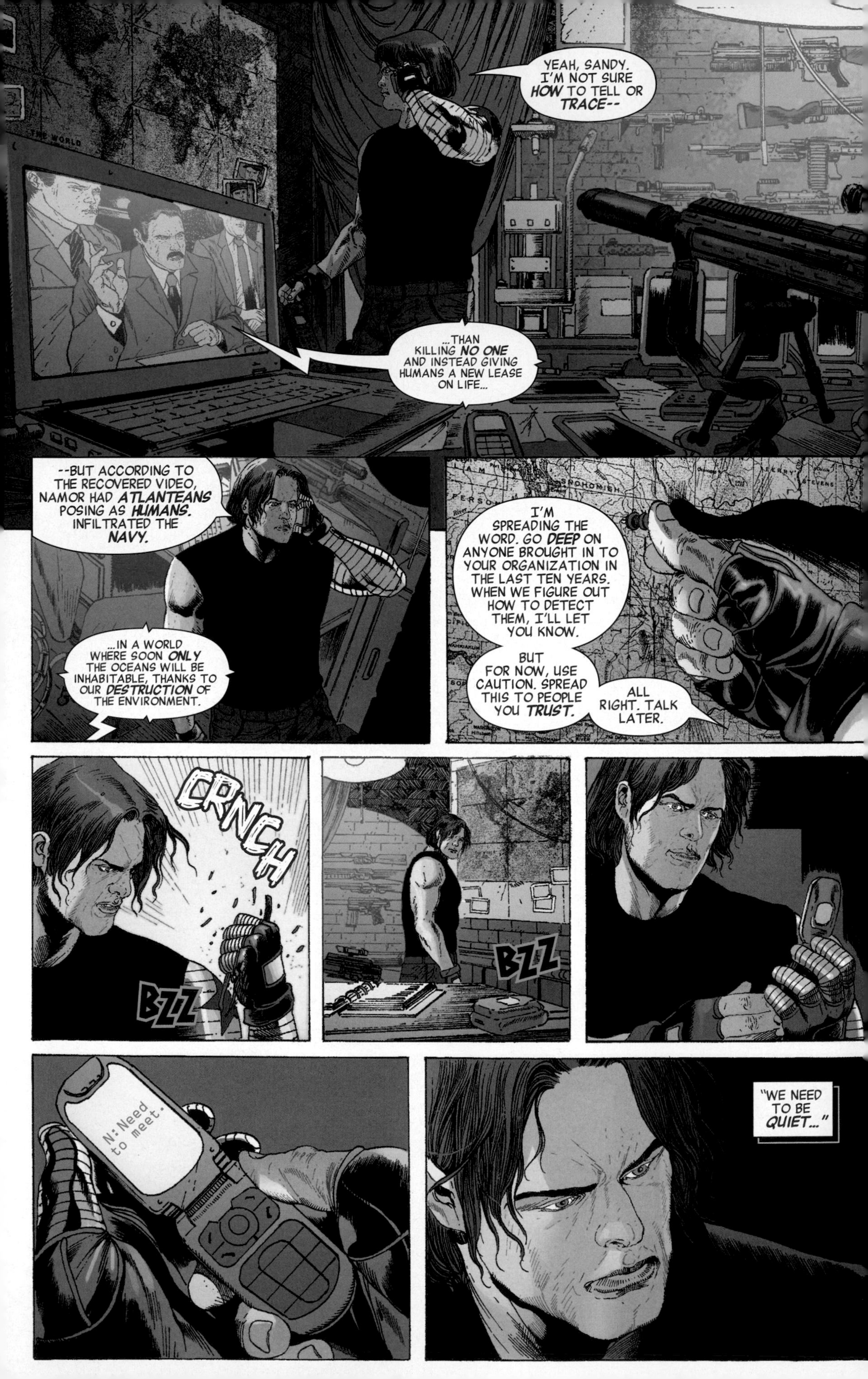
YEAH, SANDY. I'M NOT SURE HOW TO TELL OR TRACE--
...THAN KILLING NO ONE AND INSTEAD GIVING HUMANS A NEW LEASE ON LIFE...
--BUT ACCORDING TO THE RECOVERED VIDEO, NAMOR HAD ATLANTEANS POSING AS HUMANS. INFILTRATED THE NAVY.
...IN A WORLD WHERE SOON ONLY THE OCEANS WILL BE INHABITABLE, THANKS TO OUR DESTRUCTION OF THE ENVIRONMENT.
I'M SPREADING THE WORD. GO DEEP ON ANYONE BROUGHT IN TO YOUR ORGANIZATION IN THE LAST TEN YEARS. WHEN WE FIGURE OUT HOW TO DETECT THEM, I'LL LET YOU KNOW.
BUT FOR NOW, USE CAUTION. SPREAD THIS TO PEOPLE YOU TRUST.
ALL RIGHT. TALK LATER.
CRNCH
BZZ
BZZ
N: Need to meet.
"WE NEED TO BE QUIET..."

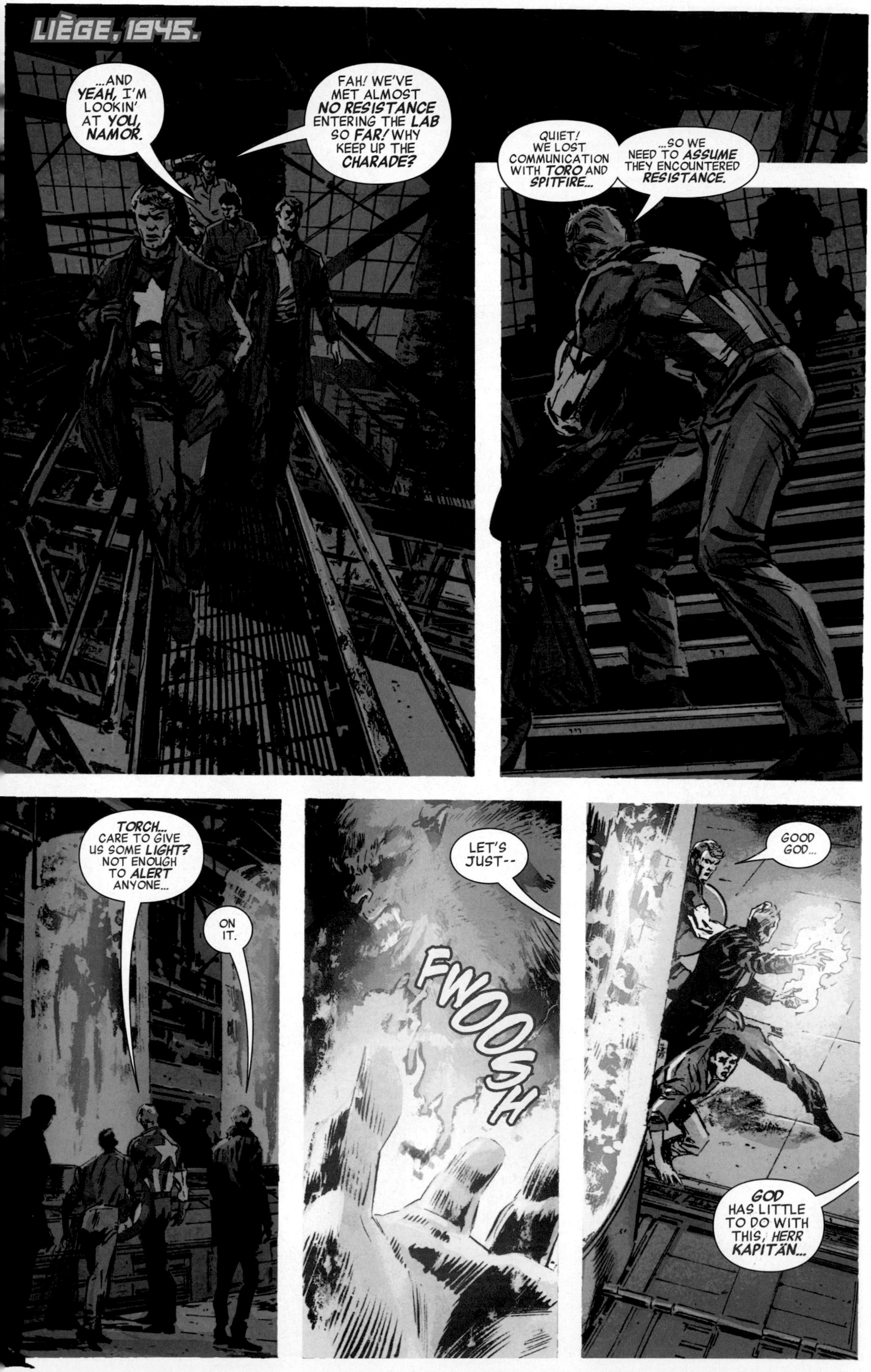
LIÈGE, 1945.
...AND YEAH, I'M LOOKIN' AT YOU, NAMOR.
FAH! WE'VE MET ALMOST NO RESISTANCE ENTERING THE LAB SO FAR! WHY KEEP UP THE CHARADE?
QUIET! WE LOST COMMUNICATION WITH TORO AND SPITFIRE...
...SO WE NEED TO ASSUME THEY ENCOUNTERED RESISTANCE.
TORCH... CARE TO GIVE US SOME LIGHT? NOT ENOUGH TO ALERT ANYONE...
ON IT.
LET'S JUST--
FWOOSH
GOOD GOD...
GOD HAS LITTLE TO DO WITH THIS, HERR KAPITÄN...

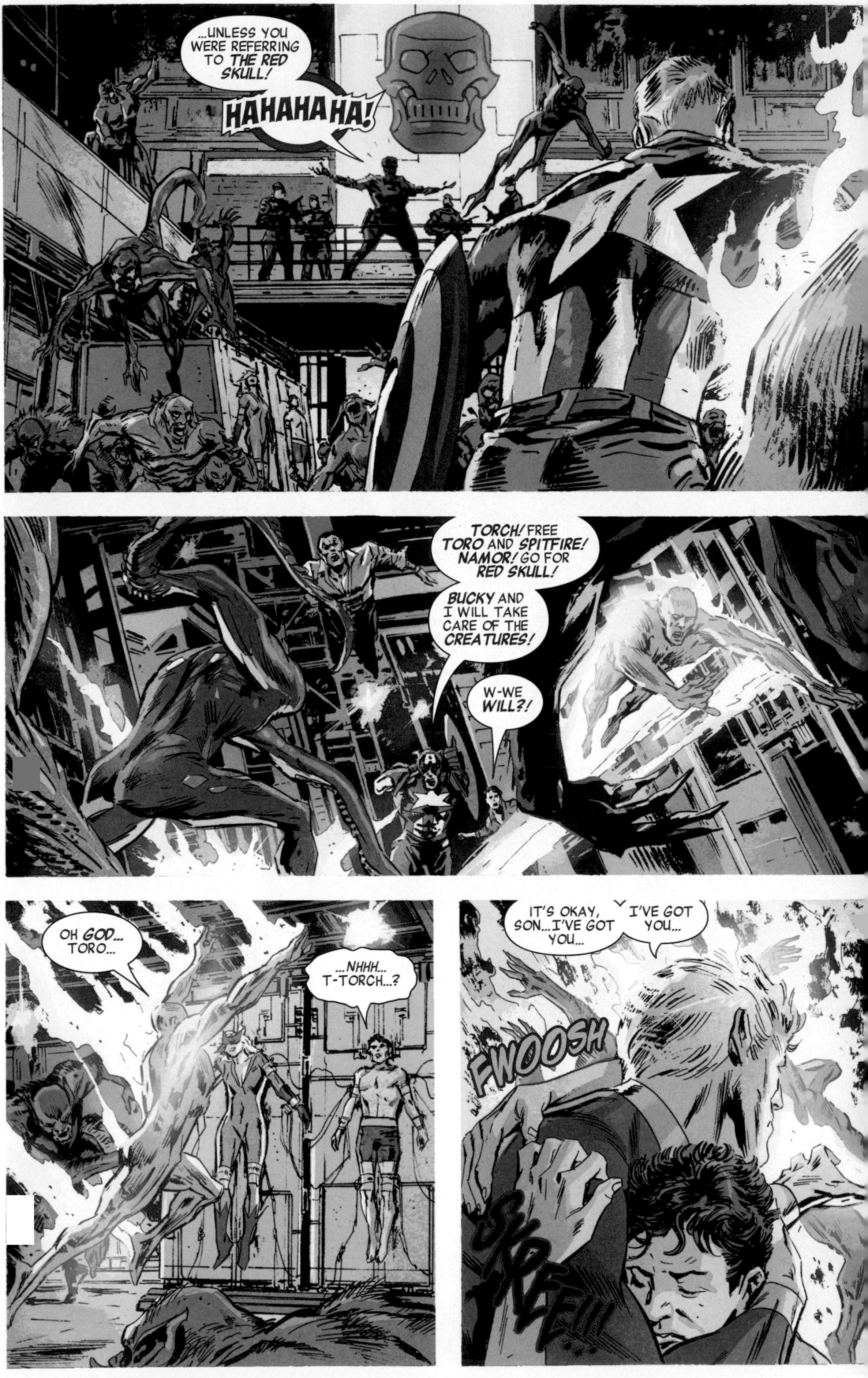
...UNLESS YOU WERE REFERRING TO THE RED SKULL!
HAHAHAHA!
TORCH! FREE TORO AND SPITFIRE! NAMOR! GO FOR RED SKULL!
BUCKY AND I WILL TAKE CARE OF THE CREATURES!
W-WE WILL?!
OH GOD... TORO...
...NHHH... T-TORCH...?
IT'S OKAY, SON...I'VE GOT YOU...
I'VE GOT YOU...
FWOOSH
SKREE!!

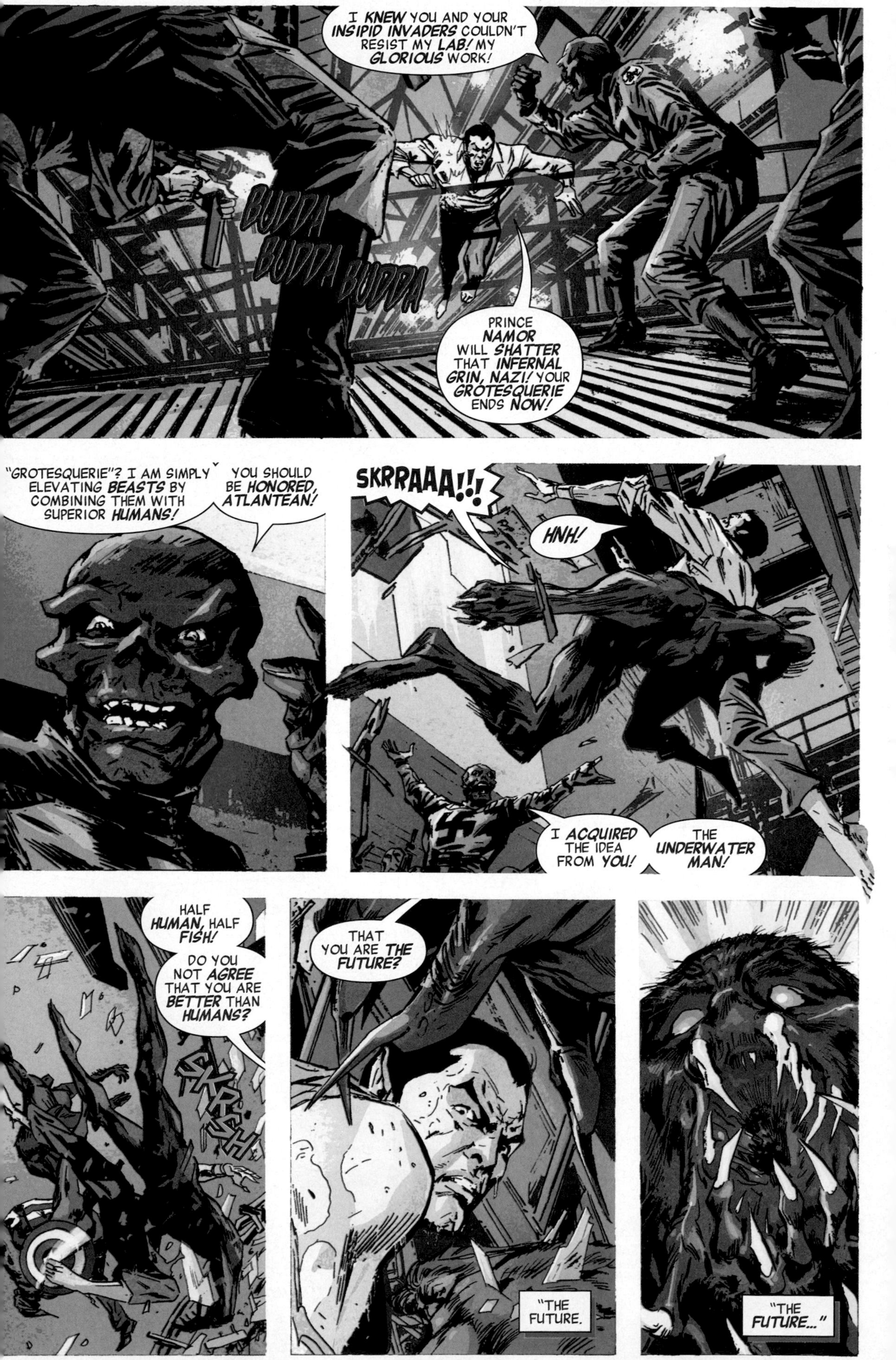
I KNEW YOU AND YOUR INSIPID INVADERS COULDN'T RESIST MY LAB! MY GLORIOUS WORK!
BUDDA BUDDA BUDDA BUDDA
PRINCE NAMOR WILL SHATTER THAT INFERNAL GRIN, NAZI! YOUR GROTESQUERIE ENDS NOW!
"GROTESQUERIE"? I AM SIMPLY ELEVATING BEASTS BY COMBINING THEM WITH SUPERIOR HUMANS!
YOU SHOULD BE HONORED, ATLANTEAN!
SKRRAAA!!!
HNH!
I ACQUIRED THE IDEA FROM YOU!
THE UNDERWATER MAN!
HALF HUMAN, HALF FISH!
DO YOU NOT AGREE THAT YOU ARE BETTER THAN HUMANS?
SKRSH
THAT YOU ARE THE FUTURE?
"THE FUTURE.
"THE FUTURE..."

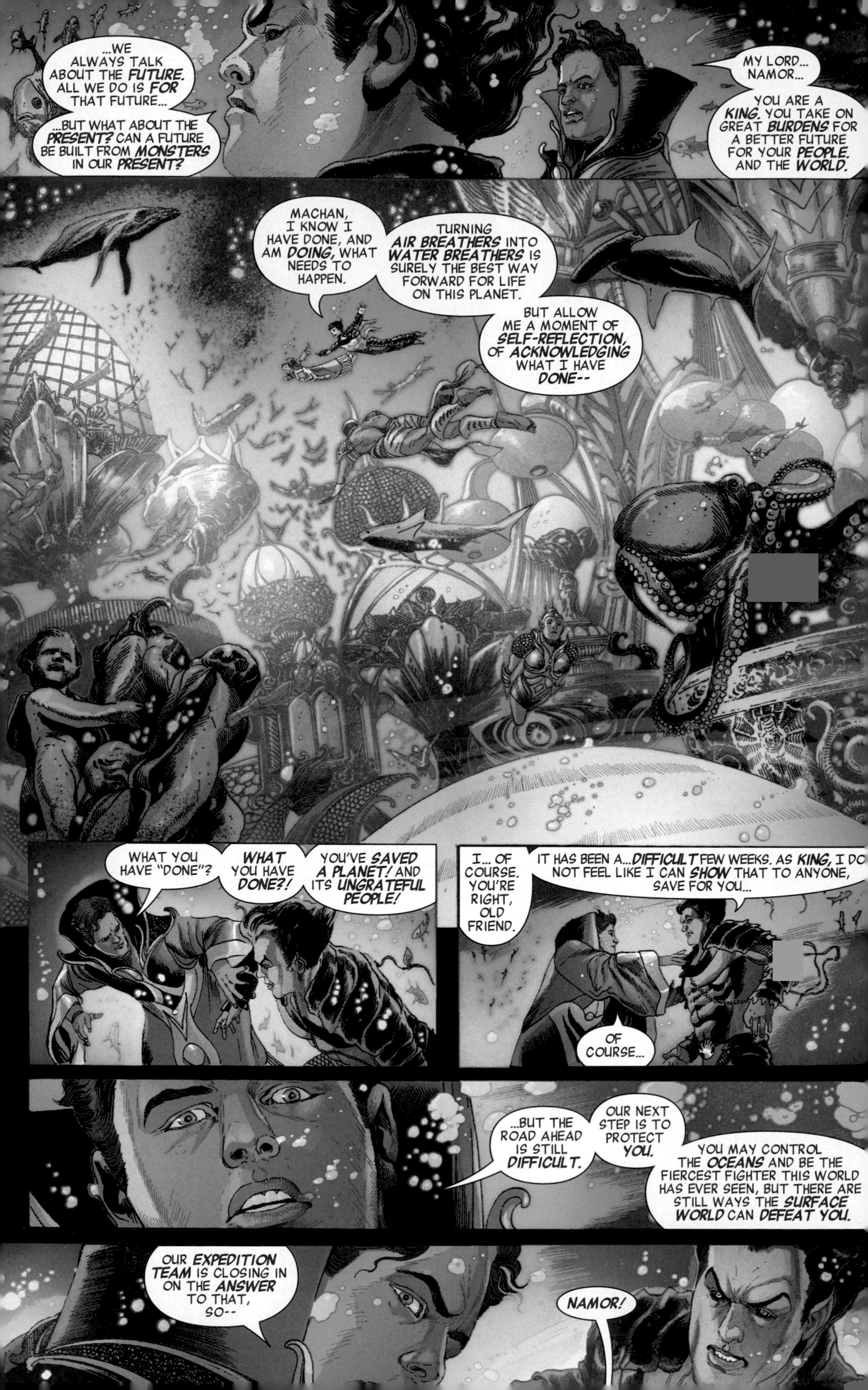
...WE ALWAYS TALK ABOUT THE FUTURE. ALL WE DO IS FOR THAT FUTURE...
...BUT WHAT ABOUT THE PRESENT? CAN A FUTURE BE BUILT FROM MONSTERS IN OUR PRESENT?
MY LORD... NAMOR...
YOU ARE A KING. YOU TAKE ON GREAT BURDENS FOR A BETTER FUTURE FOR YOUR PEOPLE. AND THE WORLD.
MACHAN, I KNOW I HAVE DONE, AND AM DOING, WHAT NEEDS TO HAPPEN.
TURNING AIR BREATHERS INTO WATER BREATHERS IS SURELY THE BEST WAY FORWARD FOR LIFE ON THIS PLANET.
BUT ALLOW ME A MOMENT OF SELF-REFLECTION, OF ACKNOWLEDGING WHAT I HAVE DONE--
WHAT YOU HAVE "DONE"?
WHAT YOU HAVE DONE?!
YOU'VE SAVED A PLANET! AND ITS UNGRATEFUL PEOPLE!
I... OF COURSE. YOU'RE RIGHT, OLD FRIEND.
IT HAS BEEN A...DIFFICULT FEW WEEKS. AS KING, I DO NOT FEEL LIKE I CAN SHOW THAT TO ANYONE, SAVE FOR YOU...
OF COURSE...
...BUT THE ROAD AHEAD IS STILL DIFFICULT.
OUR NEXT STEP IS TO PROTECT YOU.
YOU MAY CONTROL THE OCEANS AND BE THE FIERCEST FIGHTER THIS WORLD HAS EVER SEEN, BUT THERE ARE STILL WAYS THE SURFACE WORLD CAN DEFEAT YOU.
OUR EXPEDITION TEAM IS CLOSING IN ON THE ANSWER TO THAT, SO--
NAMOR!

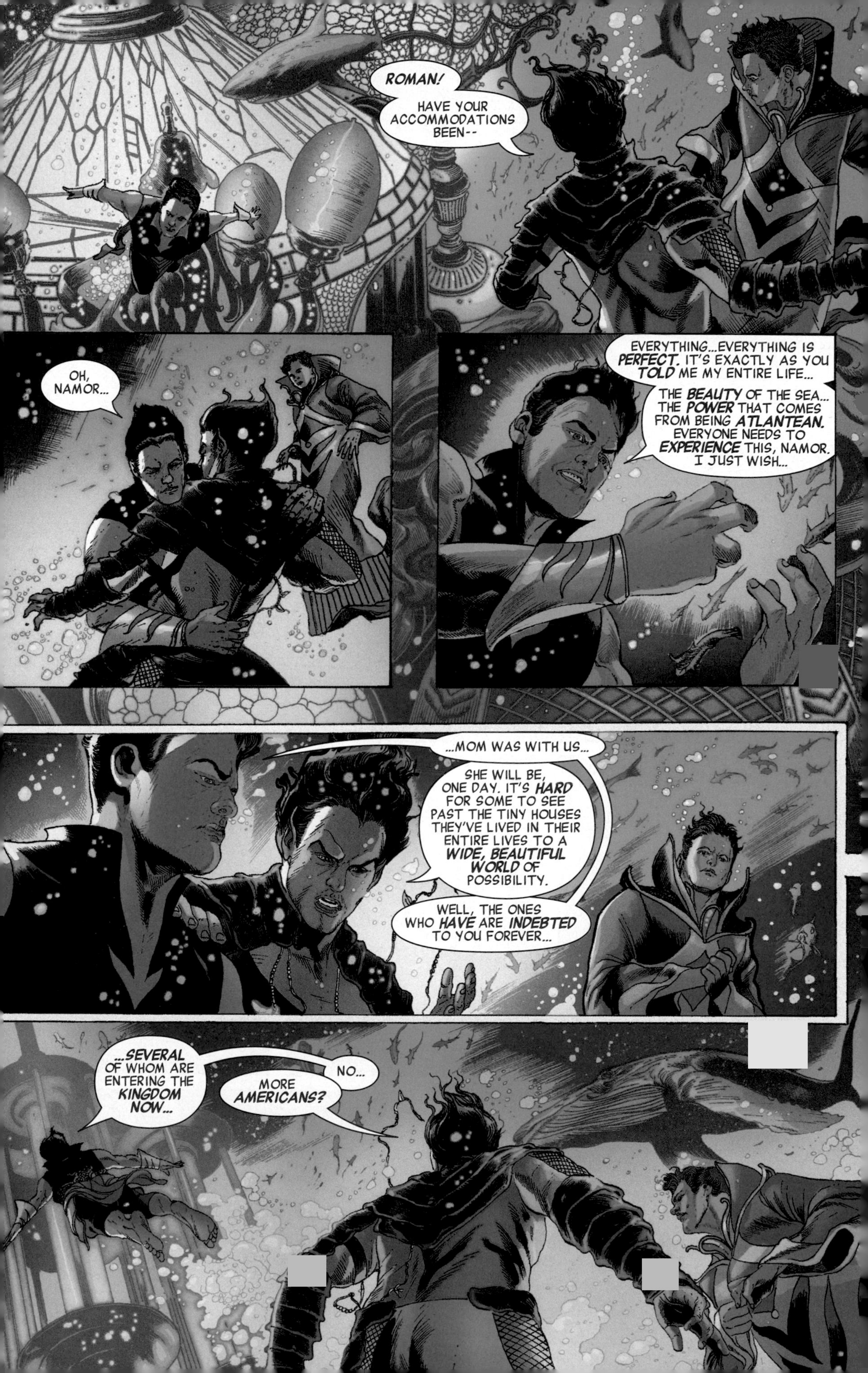
ROMAN!
HAVE YOUR ACCOMMODATIONS BEEN--
OH, NAMOR...
EVERYTHING...EVERYTHING IS PERFECT. IT'S EXACTLY AS YOU TOLD ME MY ENTIRE LIFE...
THE BEAUTY OF THE SEA... THE POWER THAT COMES FROM BEING ATLANTEAN. EVERYONE NEEDS TO EXPERIENCE THIS, NAMOR. I JUST WISH...
...MOM WAS WITH US...
SHE WILL BE, ONE DAY. IT'S HARD FOR SOME TO SEE PAST THE TINY HOUSES THEY'VE LIVED IN THEIR ENTIRE LIVES TO A WIDE, BEAUTIFUL WORLD OF POSSIBILITY.
WELL, THE ONES WHO HAVE ARE INDEBTED TO YOU FOREVER...
...SEVERAL OF WHOM ARE ENTERING THE KINGDOM NOW...
NO...
MORE AMERICANS?

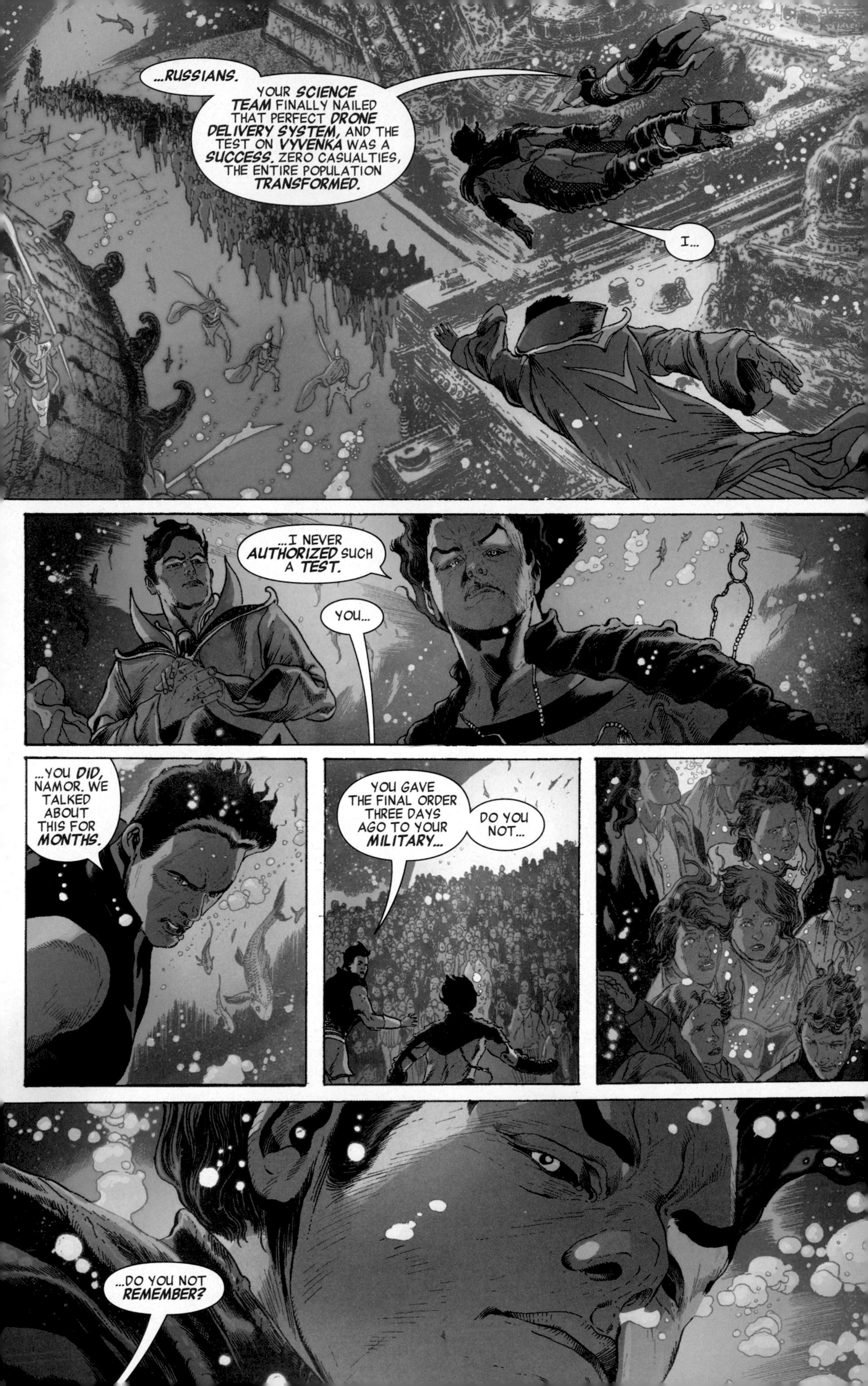
...RUSSIANS.
YOUR SCIENCE TEAM FINALLY NAILED THAT PERFECT DRONE DELIVERY SYSTEM, AND THE TEST ON VYVENKA WAS A SUCCESS. ZERO CASUALTIES, THE ENTIRE POPULATION TRANSFORMED.
I...
...I NEVER AUTHORIZED SUCH A TEST.
YOU...
...YOU DID, NAMOR. WE TALKED ABOUT THIS FOR MONTHS.
YOU GAVE THE FINAL ORDER THREE DAYS AGO TO YOUR MILITARY...
DO YOU NOT...
...DO YOU NOT REMEMBER?

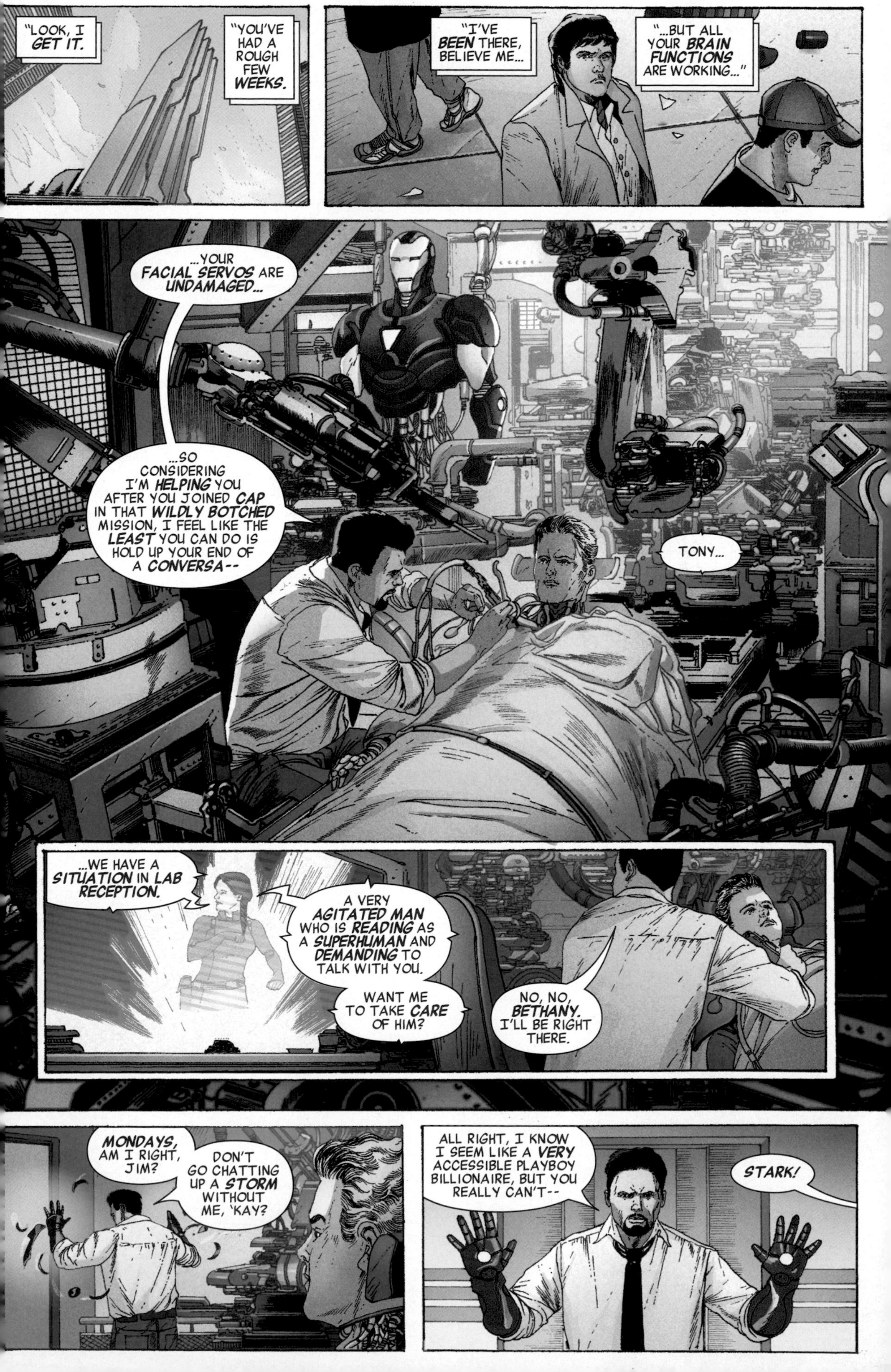
"LOOK, I GET IT.
"YOU'VE HAD A ROUGH FEW WEEKS.
"I'VE BEEN THERE, BELIEVE ME...
"...BUT ALL YOUR BRAIN FUNCTIONS ARE WORKING..."
...YOUR FACIAL SERVOS ARE UNDAMAGED...
...SO CONSIDERING I'M HELPING YOU AFTER YOU JOINED CAP IN THAT WILDLY BOTCHED MISSION, I FEEL LIKE THE LEAST YOU CAN DO IS HOLD UP YOUR END OF A CONVERSA--
TONY...
...WE HAVE A SITUATION IN LAB RECEPTION.
A VERY AGITATED MAN WHO IS READING AS A SUPERHUMAN AND DEMANDING TO TALK WITH YOU.
WANT ME TO TAKE CARE OF HIM?
NO, NO, BETHANY. I'LL BE RIGHT THERE.
MONDAYS, AM I RIGHT, JIM?
DON'T GO CHATTING UP A STORM WITHOUT ME, 'KAY?
ALL RIGHT, I KNOW I SEEM LIKE A VERY ACCESSIBLE PLAYBOY BILLIONAIRE, BUT YOU REALLY CAN'T--
STARK!

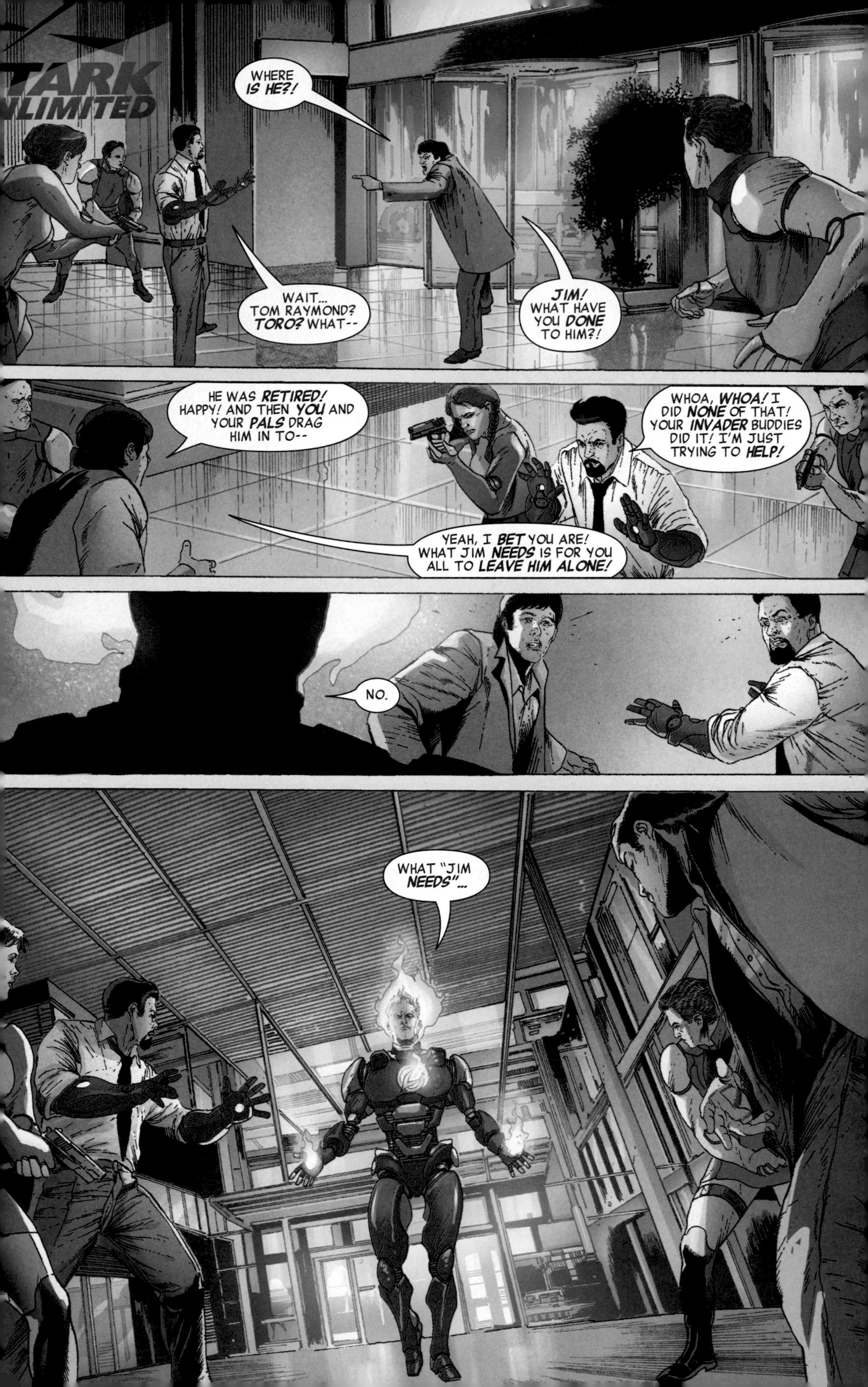
STARK UNLIMITED
WHERE IS HE?!
WAIT... TOM RAYMOND? TORO? WHAT--
JIM! WHAT HAVE YOU DONE TO HIM?!
HE WAS RETIRED! HAPPY! AND THEN YOU AND YOUR PALS DRAG HIM IN TO--
WHOA, WHOA! I DID NONE OF THAT! YOUR INVADER BUDDIES DID IT! I'M JUST TRYING TO HELP!
YEAH, I BET YOU ARE! WHAT JIM NEEDS IS FOR YOU ALL TO LEAVE HIM ALONE!
NO.
WHAT "JIM NEEDS"...

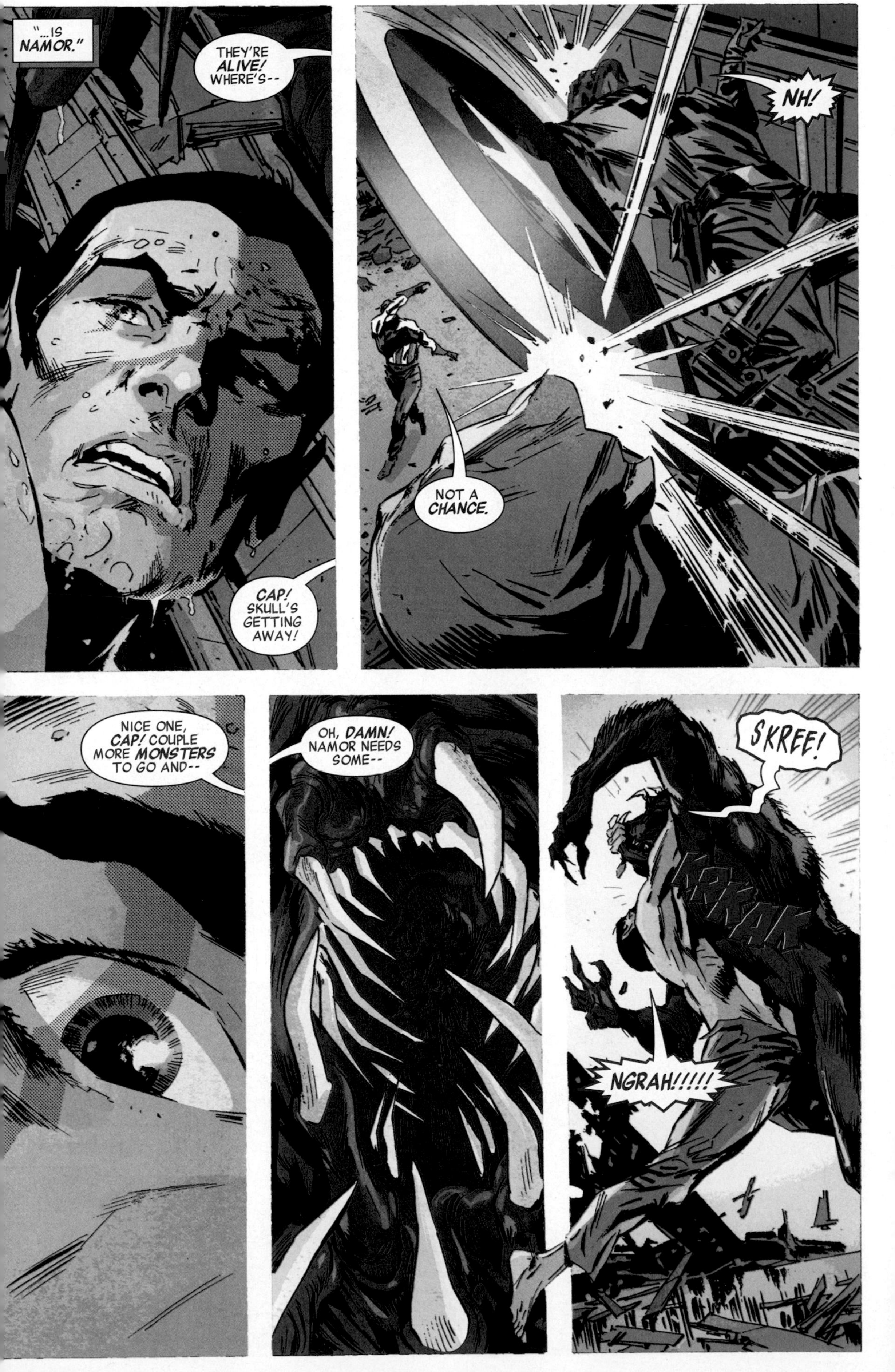
"...IS NAMOR."
THEY'RE ALIVE! WHERE'S--
CAP! SKULL'S GETTING AWAY!
NH!
NOT A CHANCE.
NICE ONE, CAP! COUPLE MORE MONSTERS TO GO AND--
OH, DAMN! NAMOR NEEDS SOME--
SKREE!
KRAK
NGRAH!!!!!

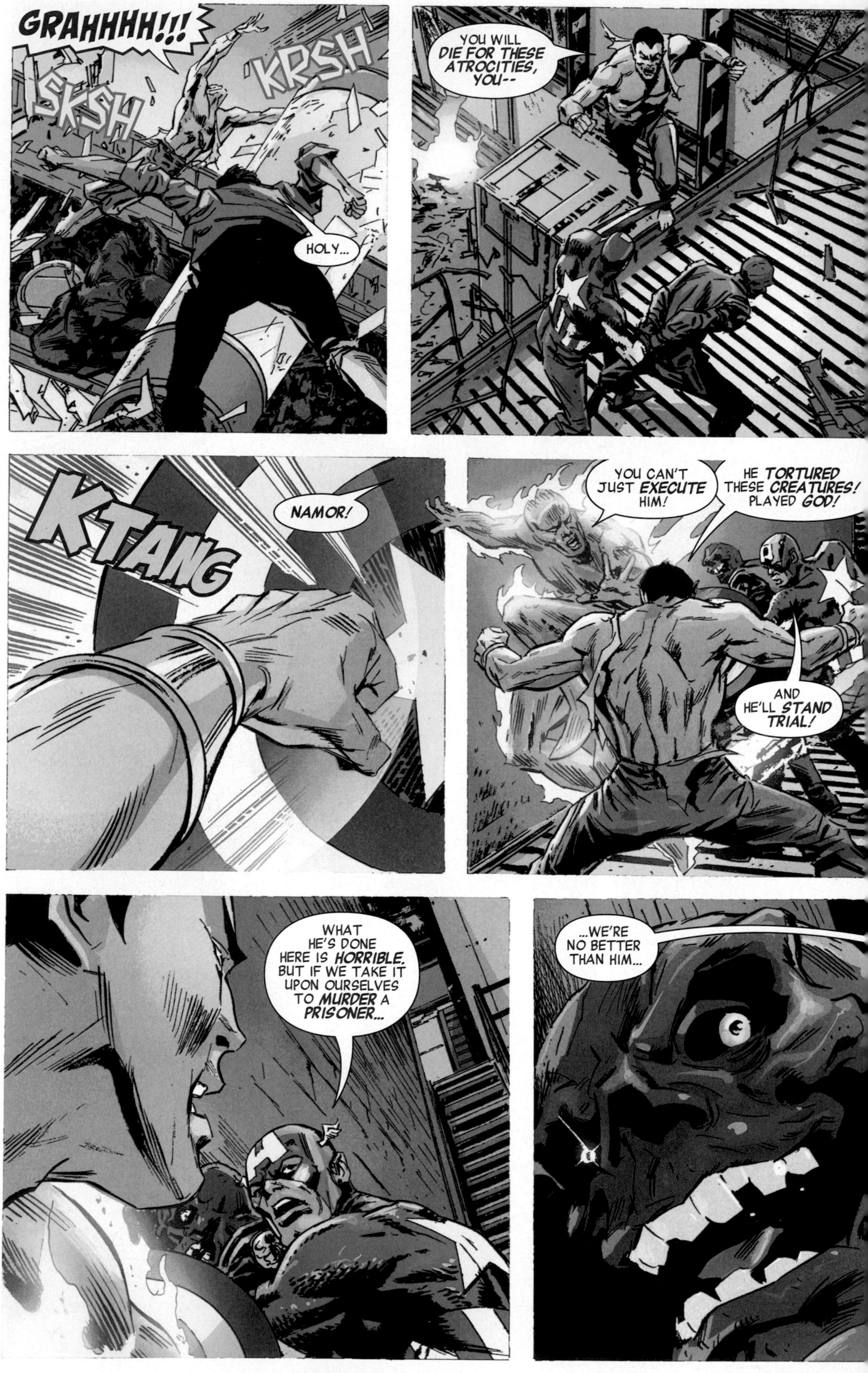
GRAHHHH!!!
SKSH
KRSH
HOLY...
YOU WILL DIE FOR THESE ATROCITIES, YOU--
KTANG
NAMOR!
YOU CAN'T JUST EXECUTE HIM!
HE TORTURED THESE CREATURES! PLAYED GOD!
AND HE'LL STAND TRIAL!
WHAT HE'S DONE HERE IS HORRIBLE. BUT IF WE TAKE IT UPON OURSELVES TO MURDER A PRISONER...
...WE'RE NO BETTER THAN HIM...

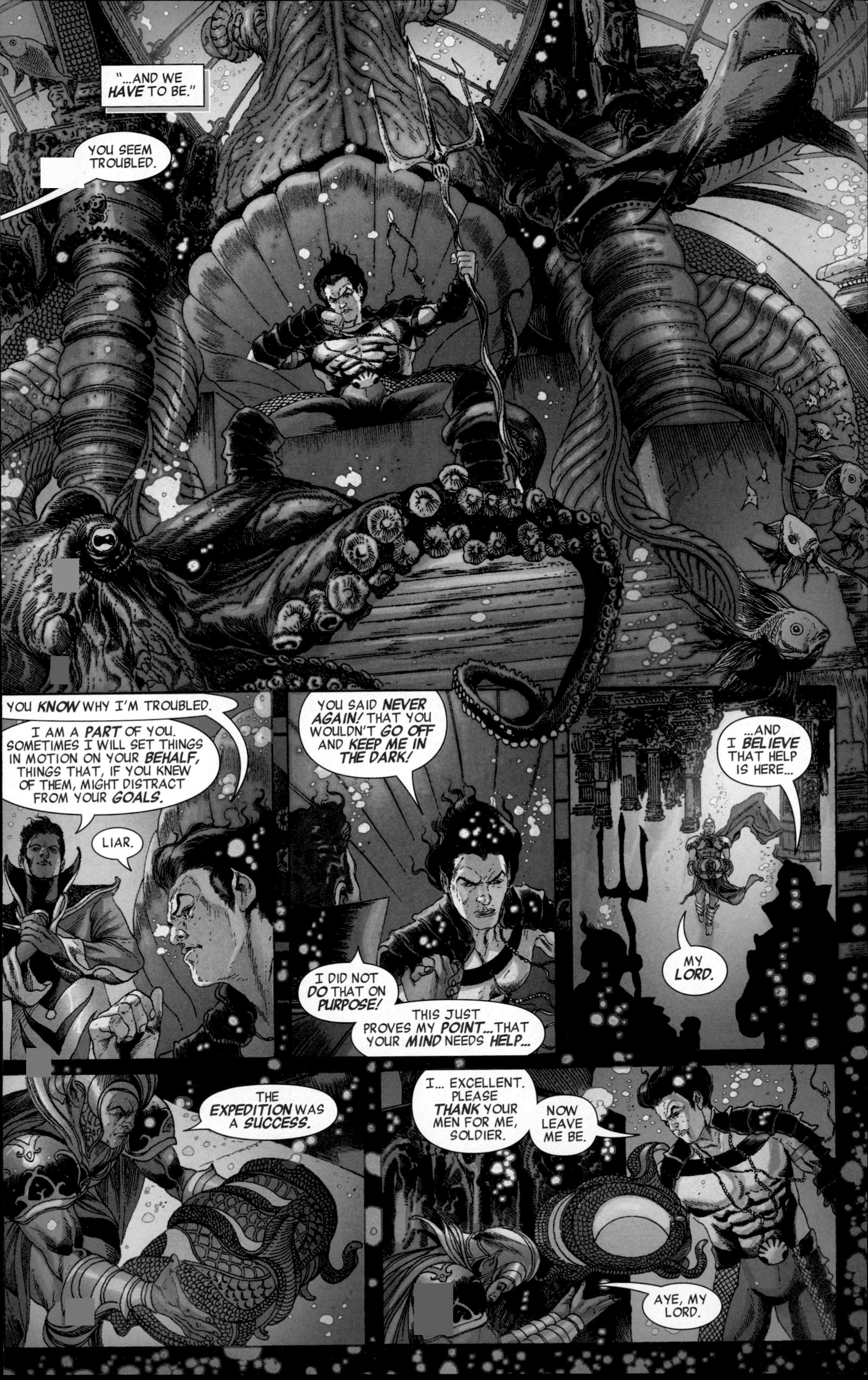
"...AND WE HAVE TO BE."
YOU SEEM TROUBLED.
YOU KNOW WHY I'M TROUBLED.
I AM A PART OF YOU. SOMETIMES I WILL SET THINGS IN MOTION ON YOUR BEHALF, THINGS THAT, IF YOU KNEW OF THEM, MIGHT DISTRACT FROM YOUR GOALS.
LIAR.
YOU SAID NEVER AGAIN! THAT YOU WOULDN'T GO OFF AND KEEP ME IN THE DARK!
I DID NOT DO THAT ON PURPOSE!
THIS JUST PROVES MY POINT... THAT YOUR MIND NEEDS HELP...
...AND I BELIEVE THAT HELP IS HERE...
MY LORD.
THE EXPEDITION WAS A SUCCESS.
I... EXCELLENT. PLEASE THANK YOUR MEN FOR ME, SOLDIER.
NOW LEAVE ME BE.
AYE, MY LORD.

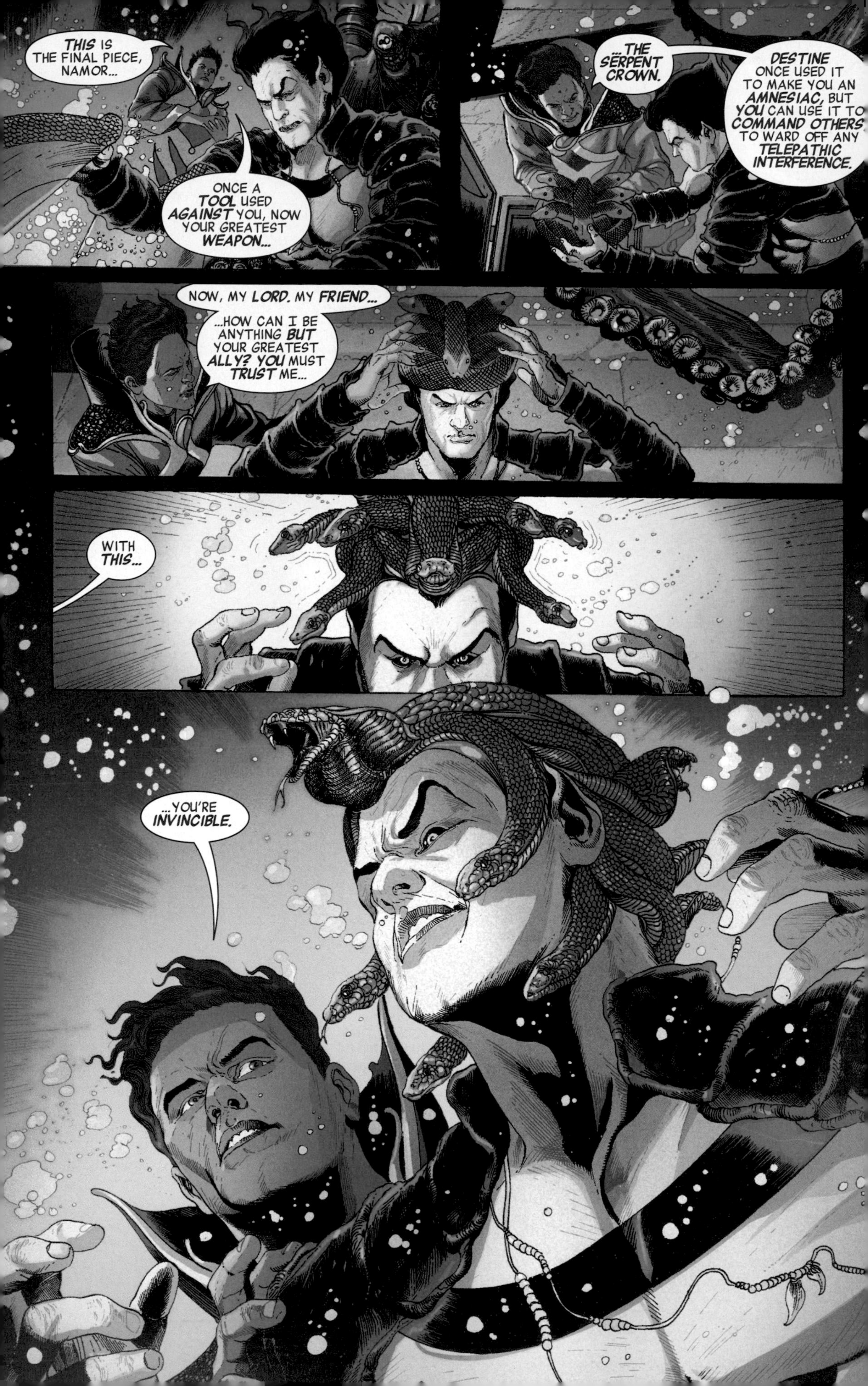
THIS IS THE FINAL PIECE, NAMOR...
ONCE A TOOL USED AGAINST YOU, NOW YOUR GREATEST WEAPON...
...THE SERPENT CROWN.
DESTINE ONCE USED IT TO MAKE YOU AN AMNESIAC, BUT YOU CAN USE IT TO COMMAND OTHERS TO WARD OFF ANY TELEPATHIC INTERFERENCE.
NOW, MY LORD. MY FRIEND...
...HOW CAN I BE ANYTHING BUT YOUR GREATEST ALLY? YOU MUST TRUST ME...
WITH THIS...
...YOU'RE INVINCIBLE.

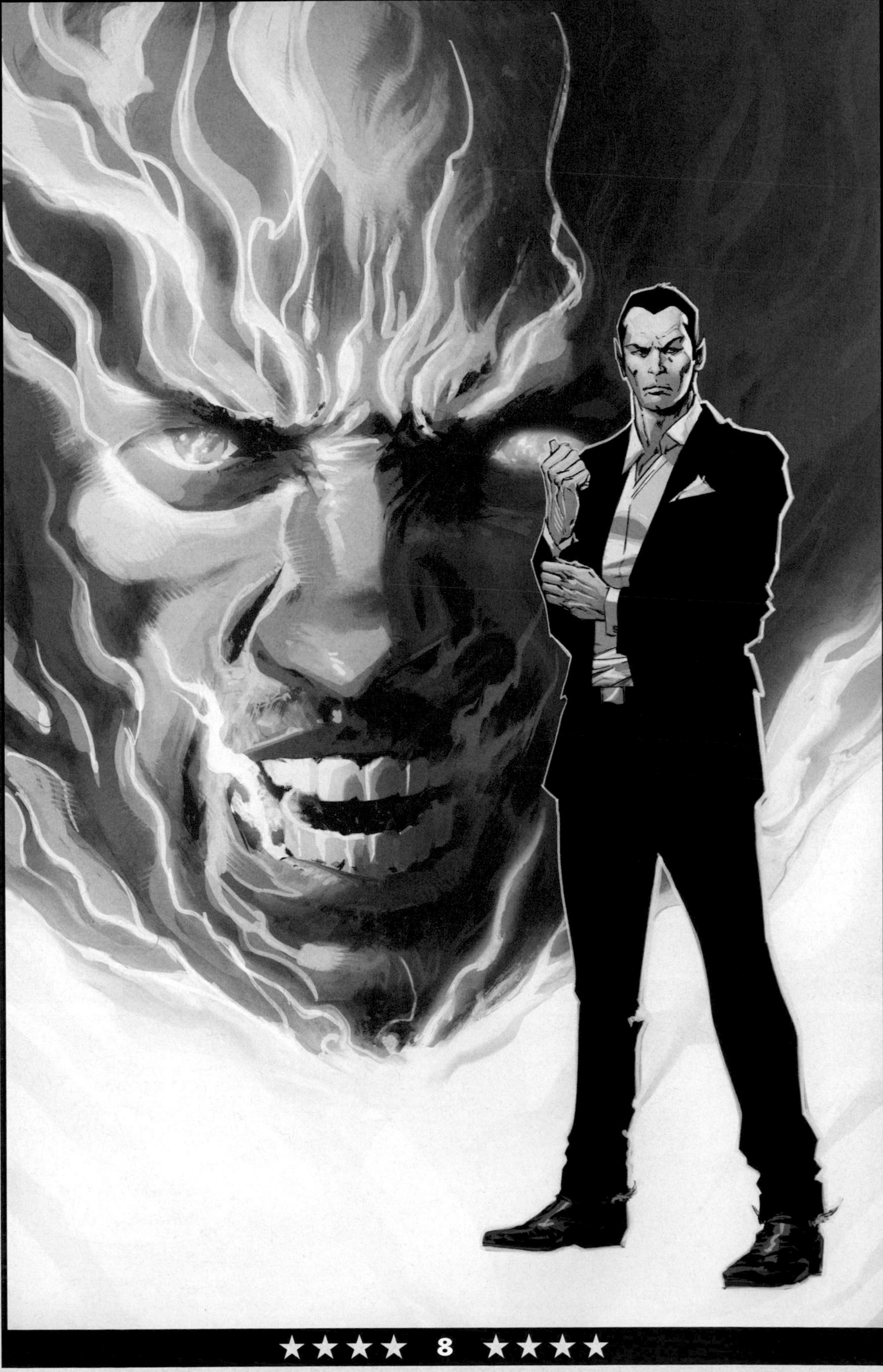

...COMPOUNDED BY THE FACT THAT *ATLANTIS* ISN'T TAKING RESPONSIBILITY FOR THE ATTACK.

MR. SECRETARY, DOES THIS *CHANGE* THE U.S.'S POSITION AT ALL?

WHILE I HAVE *EMPATHY* FOR THE ATLANTEAN PEOPLE, IT WAS THEIR *KING* WHO DID THIS. *NAMOR* IS THE LEADER OF ATLANTIS, *USED* ATLANTEAN RESOURCES TO BUILD THESE BOMBS...

...SO THIS IS AN ATTACK BY *ATLANTIS.* NOT SOME ROGUE LEADER. WE CAN'T AFFORD TO THINK ONE ISN'T THE OTHER.

THE U.S. IS WILLING TO WAIT FOR THE UNITED NATIONS INVESTIGATION TO FINISH, PROVIDED IT'S DONE IN A *TIMELY* MANNER.

BUT REST ASSURED, WE *WILL* STOP ATLANTIS, WITH OR WITHOUT THEIR BACKING, TO KEEP OUR CITIZENS *SAFE.*

SPEAKING OF *CITIZENS*...

...THE VICTIMS OF THE ATTACK, THE ONES PEOPLE ARE CALLING *"THE SUNKEN."* WHAT'S BEING DONE FOR *THEM?*

PAUL WRIGHT
SECRETARY OF HOMELAND SAFETY
THE PRESSURE ROOM
LIVE
CBN
8:12 AM PT

I BELIEVE I CAN ANSWER THAT, ANGIE.

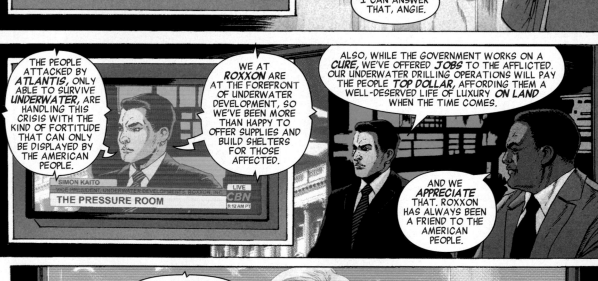

THE PEOPLE ATTACKED BY *ATLANTIS,* ONLY ABLE TO SURVIVE *UNDERWATER,* ARE HANDLING THIS CRISIS WITH THE KIND OF FORTITUDE THAT CAN ONLY BE DISPLAYED BY THE AMERICAN PEOPLE.

WE AT *ROXXON* ARE AT THE FOREFRONT OF UNDERWATER DEVELOPMENT, SO WE'VE BEEN MORE THAN HAPPY TO OFFER SUPPLIES AND BUILD SHELTERS FOR THOSE AFFECTED.

ALSO, WHILE THE GOVERNMENT WORKS ON A *CURE,* WE'VE OFFERED *JOBS* TO THE AFFLICTED. OUR UNDERWATER DRILLING OPERATIONS WILL PAY THE PEOPLE *TOP DOLLAR,* AFFORDING THEM A WELL-DESERVED LIFE OF LUXURY *ON LAND* WHEN THE TIME COMES.

SIMON KAITO
VICE PRESIDENT, UNDERWATER DEVELOPMENTS, ROXXON INC.
THE PRESSURE ROOM
LIVE
CBN
8:12 AM PT

AND WE *APPRECIATE* THAT. ROXXON HAS ALWAYS BEEN A FRIEND TO THE AMERICAN PEOPLE.

WELL, HOPEFULLY A CURE ISN'T TOO FAR OFF. THANK YOU, GENTLEMEN.

TUNE IN TONIGHT FOR *ERIC MASON'S* CLOSE LOOK AT THE U.N.'S INVESTIGATION INTO THE *ATLANTEAN INCIDENT,* ONLY ON CBN.

I'M *ANGIE WESTWORTH,* AND THIS HAS BEEN *THE PRESSURE ROOM.*

LIVE
CBN
8:18 AM PT

UP NEXT: SYMKARIA INCREASES RHETORIC

WHITE HOUSE SUPPORTS ROXXON AID TO "THE SUNKEN"

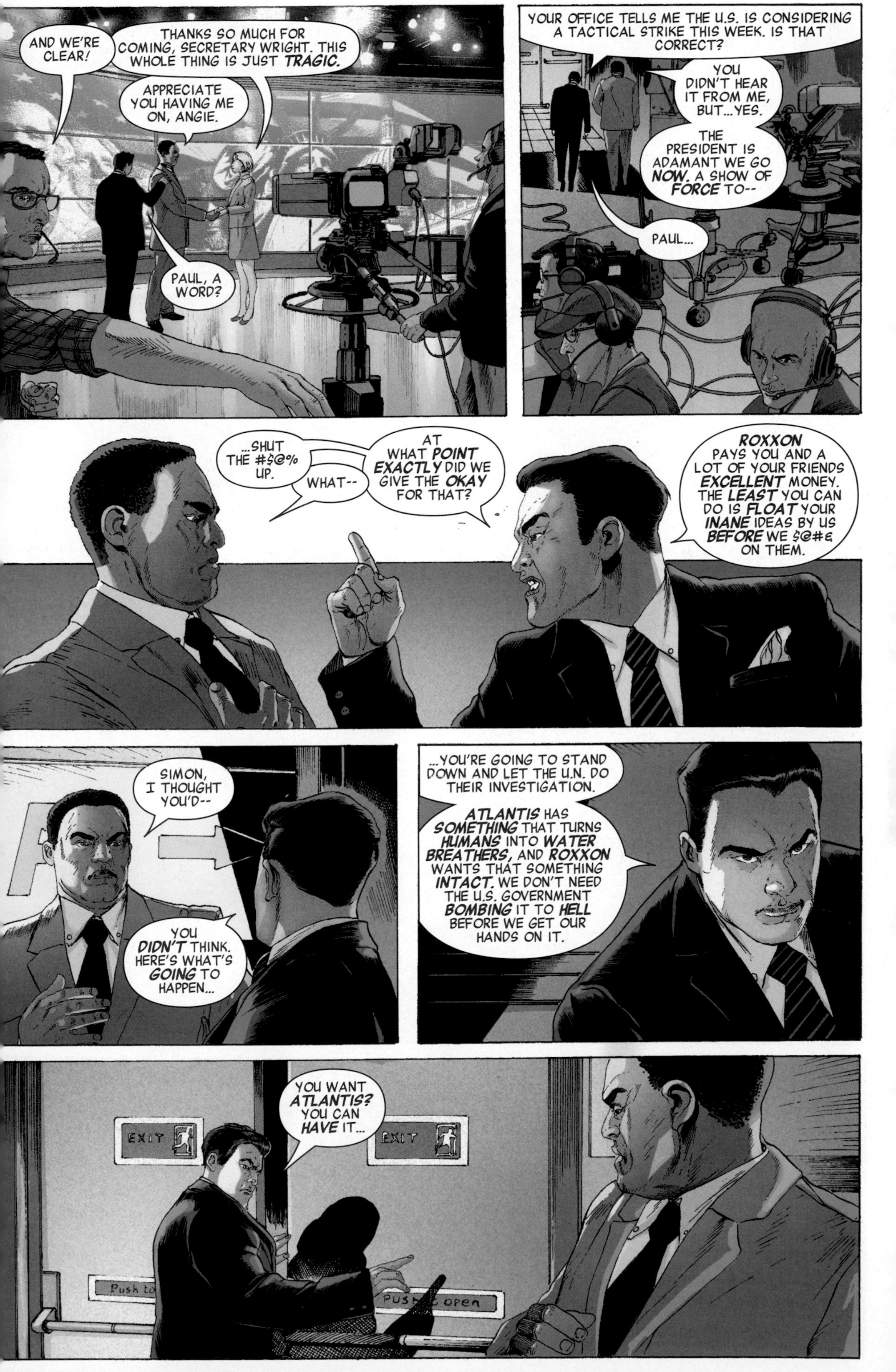
AND WE'RE CLEAR!
THANKS SO MUCH FOR COMING, SECRETARY WRIGHT. THIS WHOLE THING IS JUST TRAGIC.
APPRECIATE YOU HAVING ME ON, ANGIE.
PAUL, A WORD?
YOUR OFFICE TELLS ME THE U.S. IS CONSIDERING A TACTICAL STRIKE THIS WEEK. IS THAT CORRECT?
YOU DIDN'T HEAR IT FROM ME, BUT...YES.
THE PRESIDENT IS ADAMANT WE GO NOW. A SHOW OF FORCE TO--
PAUL...
AT WHAT POINT EXACTLY DID WE GIVE THE OKAY FOR THAT?
WHAT--
...SHUT THE #$@% UP.
ROXXON PAYS YOU AND A LOT OF YOUR FRIENDS EXCELLENT MONEY. THE LEAST YOU CAN DO IS FLOAT YOUR INANE IDEAS BY US BEFORE WE $@#& ON THEM.
SIMON, I THOUGHT YOU'D--
YOU DIDN'T THINK. HERE'S WHAT'S GOING TO HAPPEN...
...YOU'RE GOING TO STAND DOWN AND LET THE U.N. DO THEIR INVESTIGATION.
ATLANTIS HAS SOMETHING THAT TURNS HUMANS INTO WATER BREATHERS, AND ROXXON WANTS THAT SOMETHING INTACT. WE DON'T NEED THE U.S. GOVERNMENT BOMBING IT TO HELL BEFORE WE GET OUR HANDS ON IT.
EXIT
EXIT
YOU WANT ATLANTIS? YOU CAN HAVE IT...

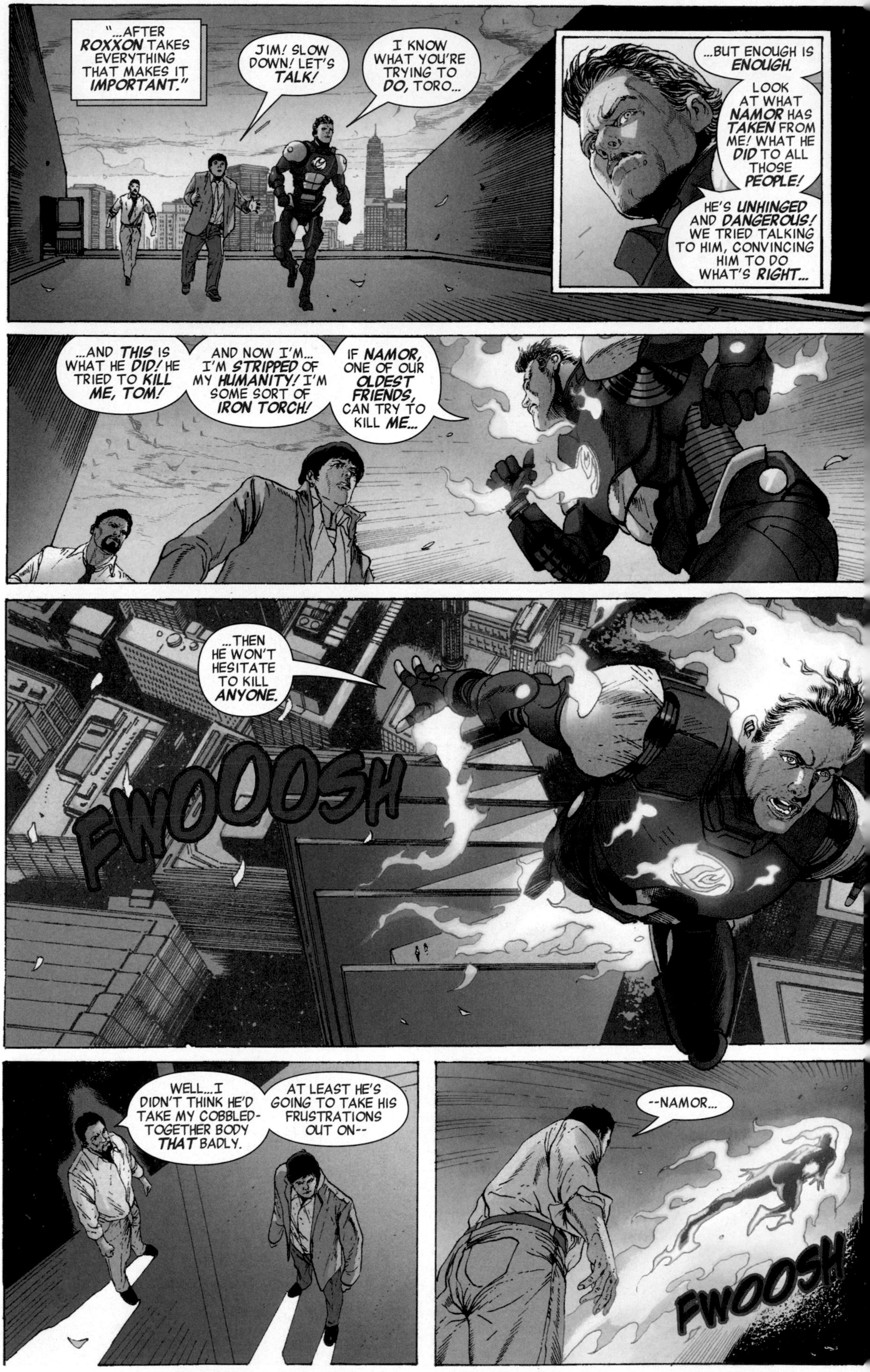
"...AFTER ROXXON TAKES EVERYTHING THAT MAKES IT IMPORTANT."
JIM! SLOW DOWN! LET'S TALK!
I KNOW WHAT YOU'RE TRYING TO DO, TORO...
...BUT ENOUGH IS ENOUGH.
LOOK AT WHAT NAMOR HAS TAKEN FROM ME! WHAT HE DID TO ALL THOSE PEOPLE!
HE'S UNHINGED AND DANGEROUS! WE TRIED TALKING TO HIM, CONVINCING HIM TO DO WHAT'S RIGHT...
...AND THIS IS WHAT HE DID! HE TRIED TO KILL ME, TOM!
AND NOW I'M... I'M STRIPPED OF MY HUMANITY! I'M SOME SORT OF IRON TORCH!
IF NAMOR, ONE OF OUR OLDEST FRIENDS, CAN TRY TO KILL ME...
...THEN HE WON'T HESITATE TO KILL ANYONE.
FWOOOSH
WELL...I DIDN'T THINK HE'D TAKE MY COBBLED-TOGETHER BODY THAT BADLY.
AT LEAST HE'S GOING TO TAKE HIS FRUSTRATIONS OUT ON--
--NAMOR...
FWOOSH

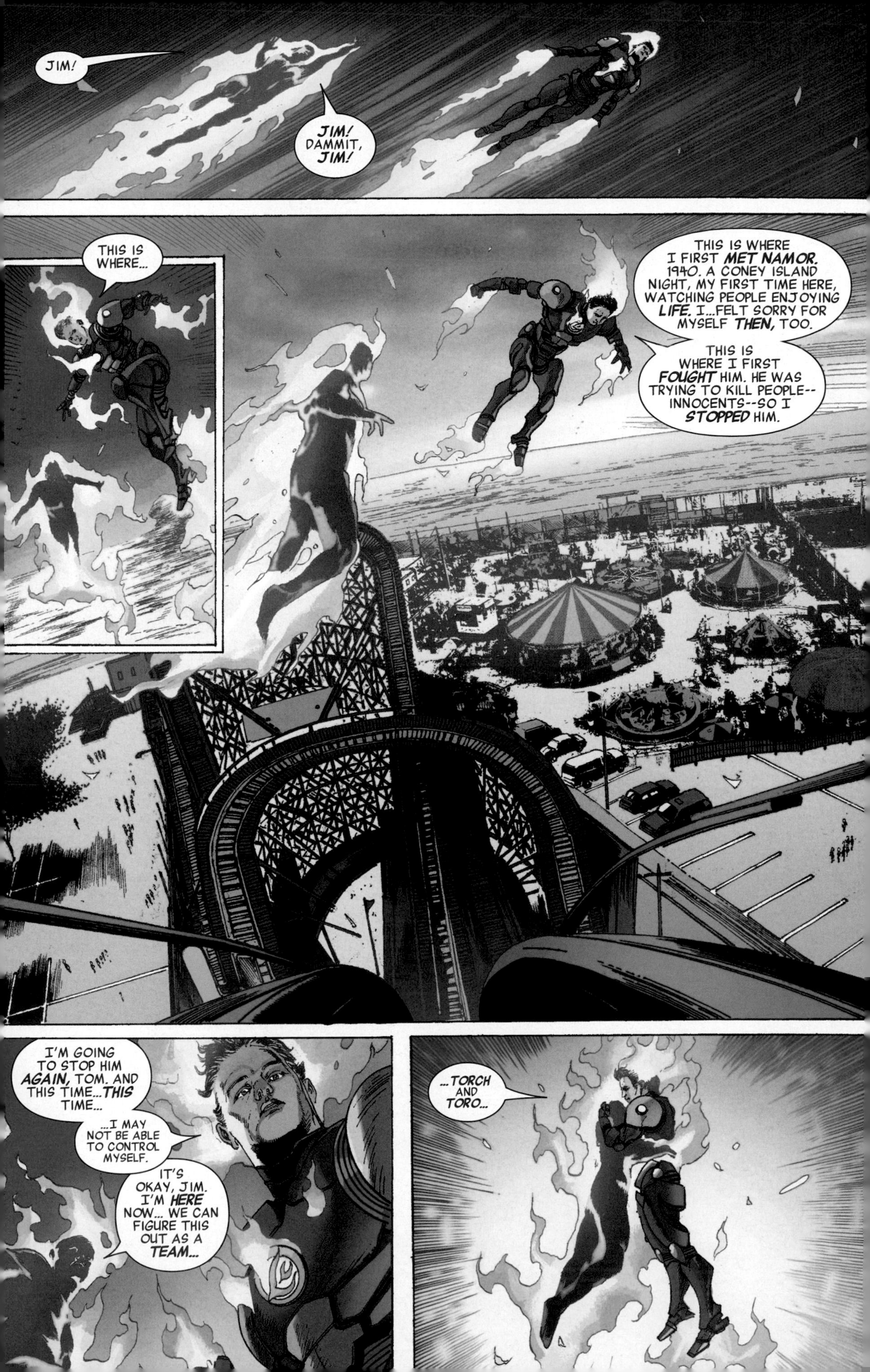
JIM!
JIM! DAMMIT, JIM!
THIS IS WHERE...
THIS IS WHERE I FIRST MET NAMOR. 1940. A CONEY ISLAND NIGHT, MY FIRST TIME HERE, WATCHING PEOPLE ENJOYING LIFE. I...FELT SORRY FOR MYSELF THEN, TOO.
THIS IS WHERE I FIRST FOUGHT HIM. HE WAS TRYING TO KILL PEOPLE-- INNOCENTS--SO I STOPPED HIM.
I'M GOING TO STOP HIM AGAIN, TOM. AND THIS TIME...THIS TIME...
...I MAY NOT BE ABLE TO CONTROL MYSELF.
IT'S OKAY, JIM. I'M HERE NOW... WE CAN FIGURE THIS OUT AS A TEAM...
...TORCH AND TORO...

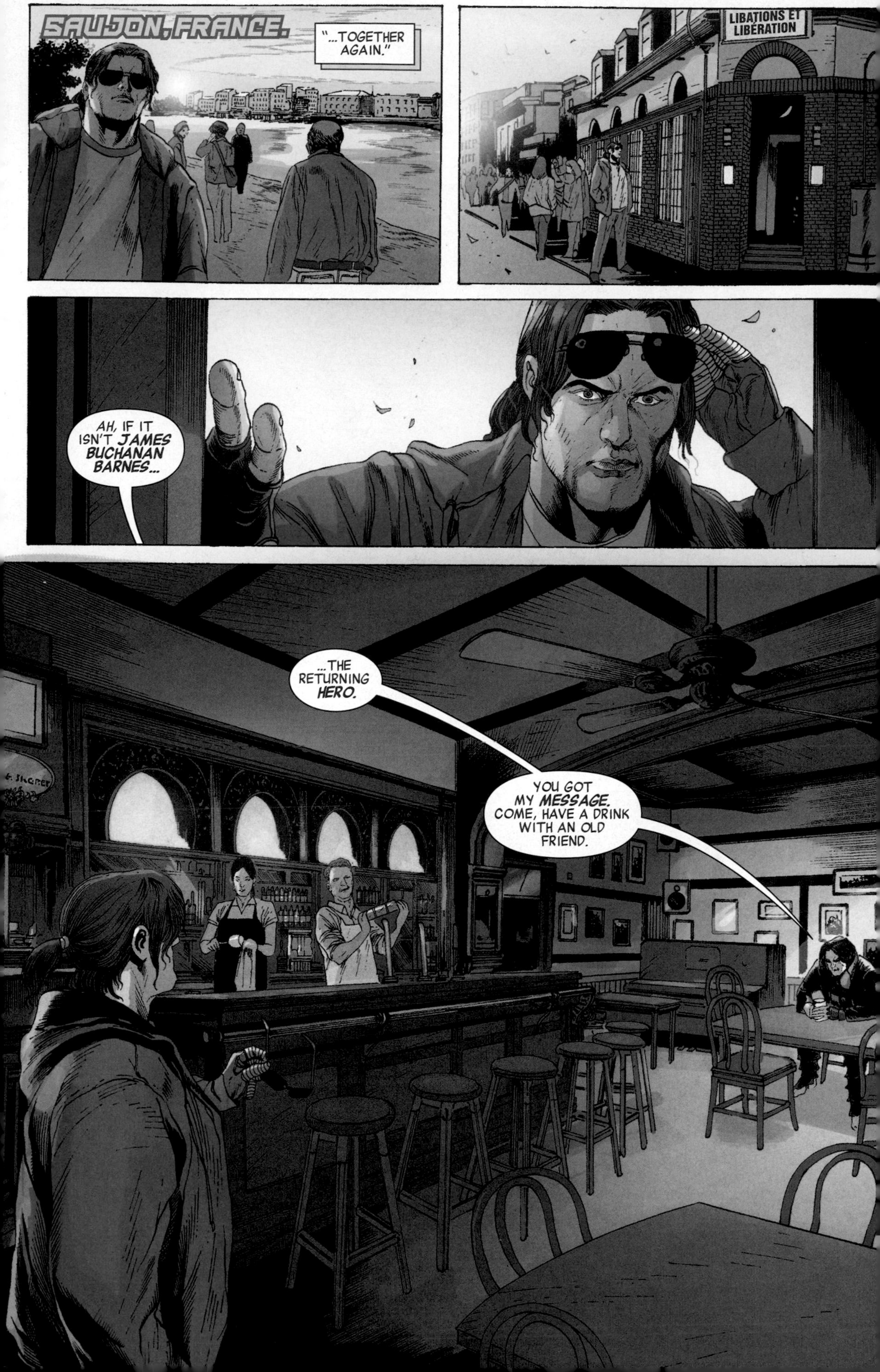
SAUJON, FRANCE.
"...TOGETHER AGAIN."
LIBATIONS ET LIBÉRATION
AH, IF IT ISN'T JAMES BUCHANAN BARNES...
...THE RETURNING HERO.
YOU GOT MY MESSAGE. COME, HAVE A DRINK WITH AN OLD FRIEND.

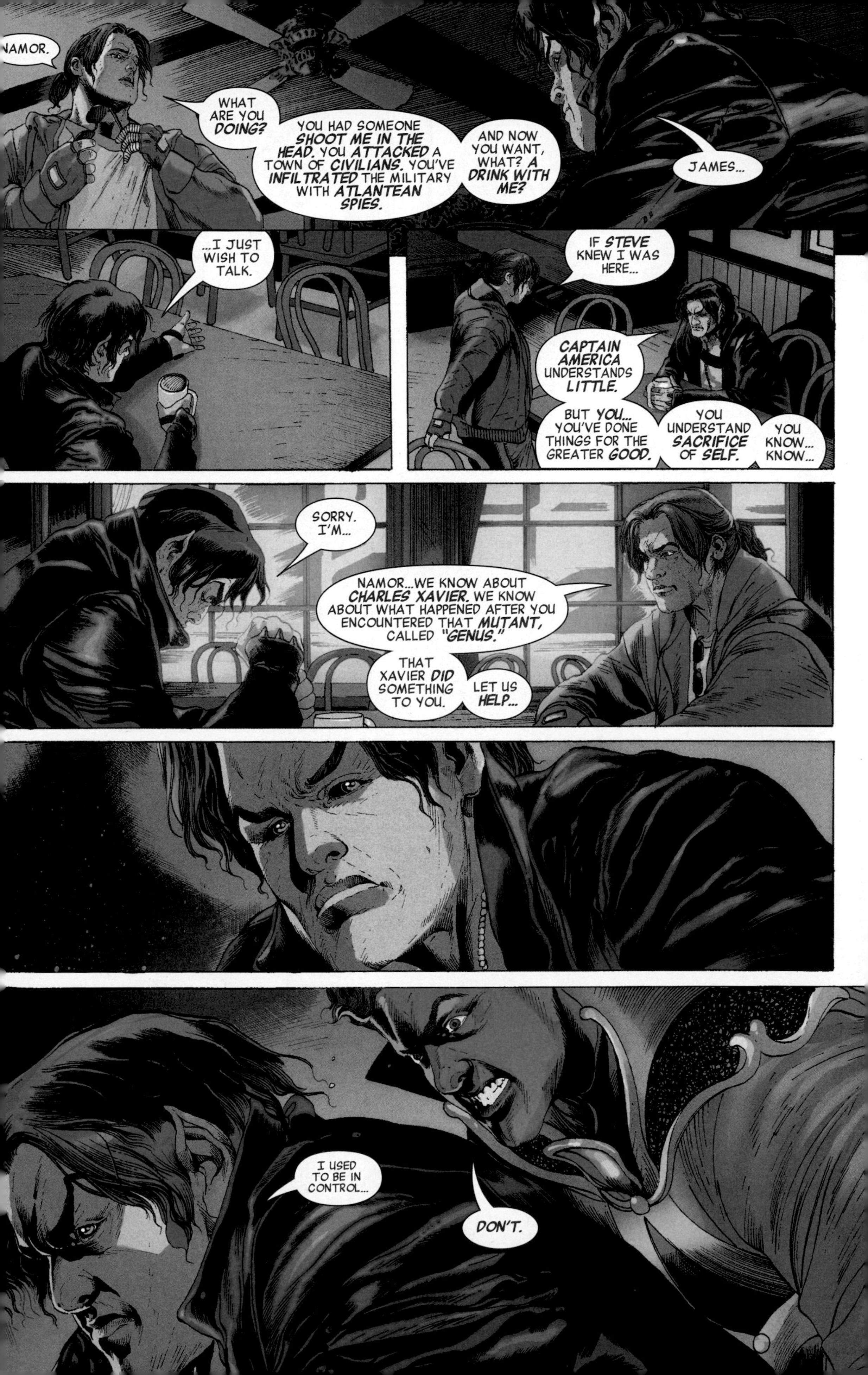
NAMOR.
WHAT ARE YOU DOING?
YOU HAD SOMEONE SHOOT ME IN THE HEAD. YOU ATTACKED A TOWN OF CIVILIANS. YOU'VE INFILTRATED THE MILITARY WITH ATLANTEAN SPIES.
AND NOW YOU WANT, WHAT? A DRINK WITH ME?
JAMES...
...I JUST WISH TO TALK.
IF STEVE KNEW I WAS HERE...
CAPTAIN AMERICA UNDERSTANDS LITTLE.
BUT YOU... YOU'VE DONE THINGS FOR THE GREATER GOOD.
YOU UNDERSTAND SACRIFICE OF SELF.
YOU KNOW... KNOW...
SORRY. I'M...
NAMOR...WE KNOW ABOUT CHARLES XAVIER. WE KNOW ABOUT WHAT HAPPENED AFTER YOU ENCOUNTERED THAT MUTANT, CALLED "GENUS."
THAT XAVIER DID SOMETHING TO YOU.
LET US HELP...
I USED TO BE IN CONTROL...
DON'T.

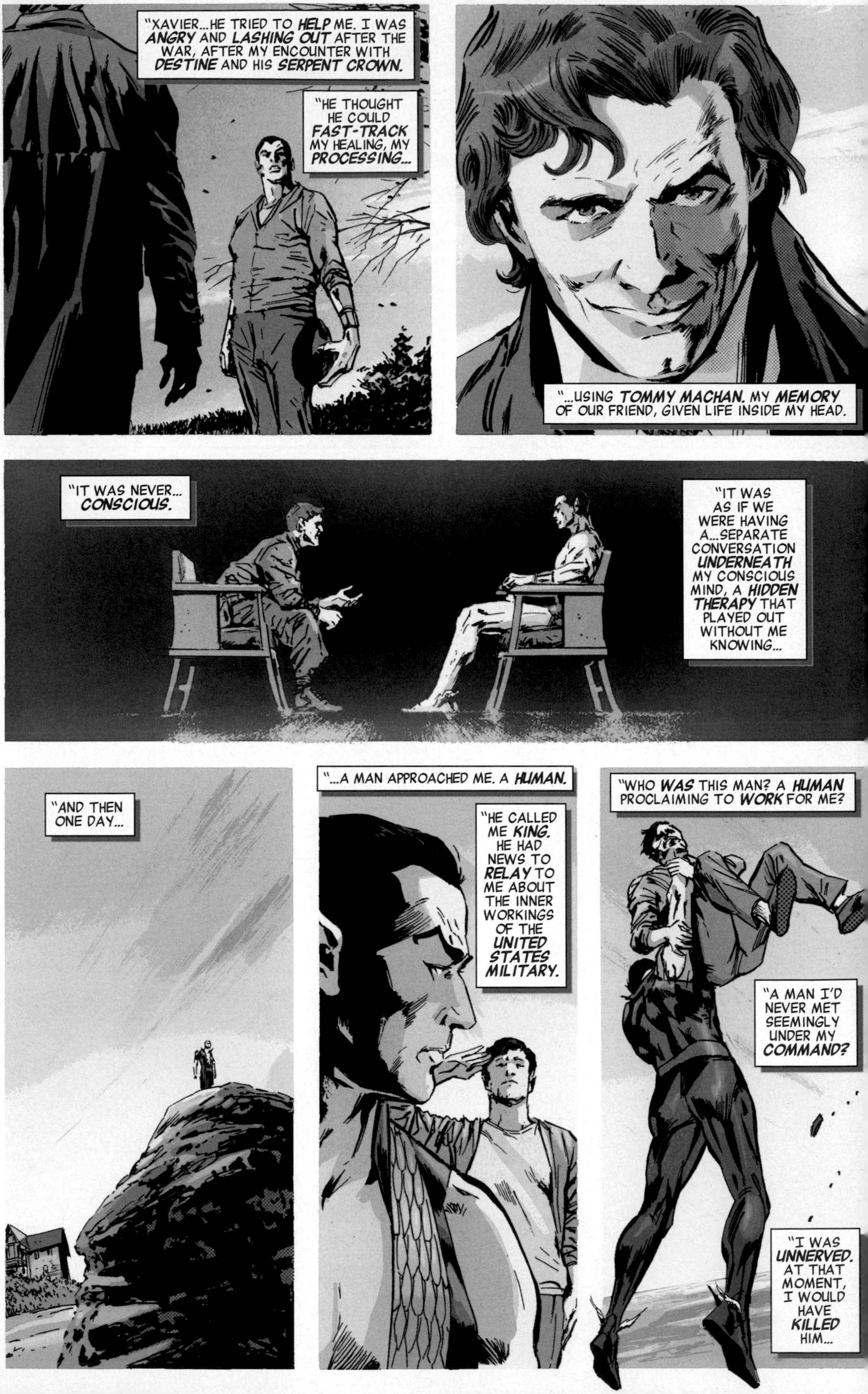
"XAVIER...HE TRIED TO HELP ME. I WAS ANGRY AND LASHING OUT AFTER THE WAR, AFTER MY ENCOUNTER WITH DESTINE AND HIS SERPENT CROWN.
"HE THOUGHT HE COULD FAST-TRACK MY HEALING, MY PROCESSING...
"...USING TOMMY MACHAN. MY MEMORY OF OUR FRIEND, GIVEN LIFE INSIDE MY HEAD.
"IT WAS NEVER... CONSCIOUS.
"IT WAS AS IF WE WERE HAVING A...SEPARATE CONVERSATION UNDERNEATH MY CONSCIOUS MIND, A HIDDEN THERAPY THAT PLAYED OUT WITHOUT ME KNOWING...
"AND THEN ONE DAY...
"...A MAN APPROACHED ME. A HUMAN.
"HE CALLED ME KING. HE HAD NEWS TO RELAY TO ME ABOUT THE INNER WORKINGS OF THE UNITED STATES MILITARY.
"WHO WAS THIS MAN? A HUMAN PROCLAIMING TO WORK FOR ME?
"A MAN I'D NEVER MET SEEMINGLY UNDER MY COMMAND?
"I WAS UNNERVED. AT THAT MOMENT, I WOULD HAVE KILLED HIM...

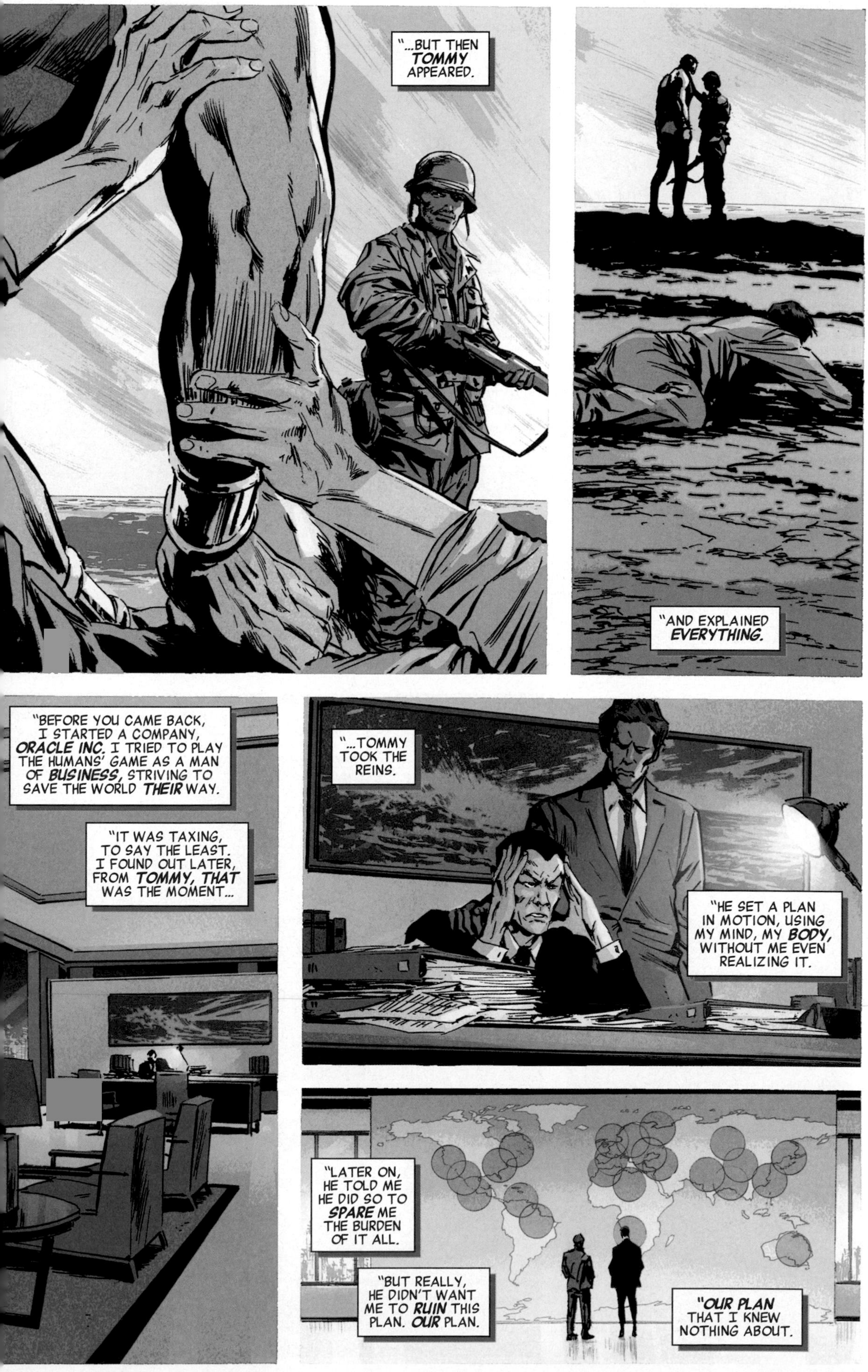
"...BUT THEN TOMMY APPEARED.
"AND EXPLAINED EVERYTHING.
"BEFORE YOU CAME BACK, I STARTED A COMPANY, ORACLE INC. I TRIED TO PLAY THE HUMANS' GAME AS A MAN OF BUSINESS, STRIVING TO SAVE THE WORLD THEIR WAY.
"IT WAS TAXING, TO SAY THE LEAST. I FOUND OUT LATER, FROM TOMMY, THAT WAS THE MOMENT...
"...TOMMY TOOK THE REINS.
"HE SET A PLAN IN MOTION, USING MY MIND, MY BODY, WITHOUT ME EVEN REALIZING IT.
"LATER ON, HE TOLD ME HE DID SO TO SPARE ME THE BURDEN OF IT ALL.
"BUT REALLY, HE DIDN'T WANT ME TO RUIN THIS PLAN. OUR PLAN.
"OUR PLAN THAT I KNEW NOTHING ABOUT.

"WE DUG UP *GENUS' BODY*. HAD MY SCIENTISTS EXTRACT WHAT THEY COULD IN ORDER TO DUPLICATE HIS ABILITY TO CHANGE THE *SPECIES* OF OTHERS.

"*ATLANTEAN SOLDIERS* VOLUNTEERED TO HAVE IT TESTED ON THEM. TO BE TURNED INTO HUMANS *FOREVER*.

"THE BRAVEST MEN AND WOMEN OF THE KINGDOM.

"SACRIFICING EVERYTHING TO LIVE A *WEAKENED* LIFE...

"...IN ORDER TO *SERVE ATLANTIS*. TO INFILTRATE HUMAN MILITARIES, *GOVERNMENTS*, AS *SPIES*.

"AND I DIDN'T EVEN *KNOW* IT.

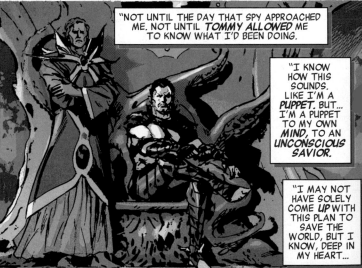

"NOT UNTIL THE DAY THAT SPY APPROACHED ME. NOT UNTIL *TOMMY ALLOWED* ME TO KNOW WHAT I'D BEEN DOING.

"I KNOW HOW THIS SOUNDS. LIKE I'M A *PUPPET*. BUT... I'M A PUPPET TO MY OWN *MIND*, TO AN *UNCONSCIOUS SAVIOR*.

"I MAY NOT HAVE SOLELY COME *UP* WITH THIS PLAN TO SAVE THE WORLD, BUT I KNOW, DEEP IN MY HEART...

"...IT'S A *GOOD PLAN*."

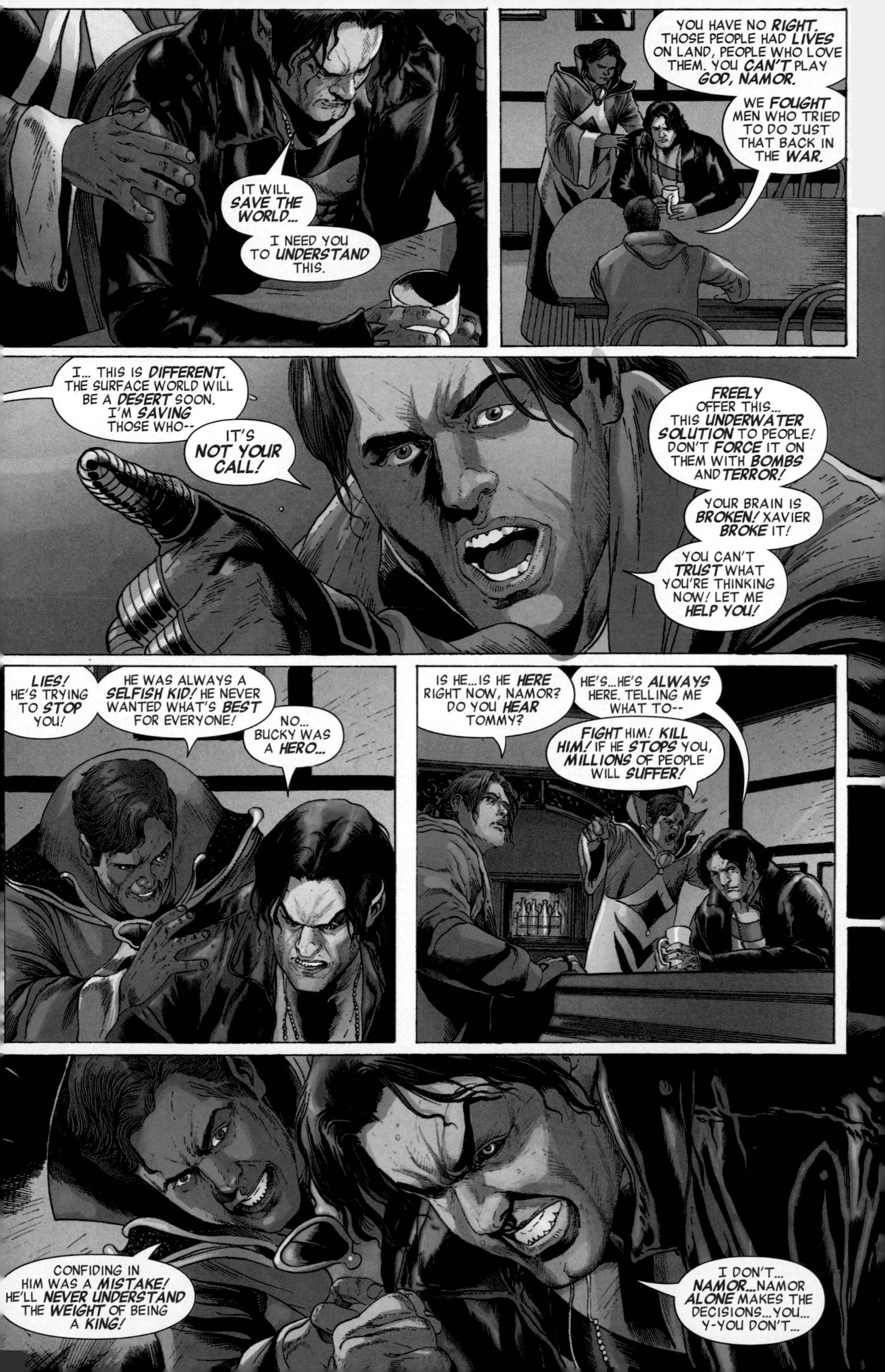
IT WILL SAVE THE WORLD...
I NEED YOU TO UNDERSTAND THIS.
YOU HAVE NO RIGHT. THOSE PEOPLE HAD LIVES ON LAND, PEOPLE WHO LOVE THEM. YOU CAN'T PLAY GOD, NAMOR.
WE FOUGHT MEN WHO TRIED TO DO JUST THAT BACK IN THE WAR.
I... THIS IS DIFFERENT. THE SURFACE WORLD WILL BE A DESERT SOON. I'M SAVING THOSE WHO--
IT'S NOT YOUR CALL!
FREELY OFFER THIS... THIS UNDERWATER SOLUTION TO PEOPLE! DON'T FORCE IT ON THEM WITH BOMBS AND TERROR!
YOUR BRAIN IS BROKEN! XAVIER BROKE IT!
YOU CAN'T TRUST WHAT YOU'RE THINKING NOW! LET ME HELP YOU!
LIES! HE'S TRYING TO STOP YOU!
HE WAS ALWAYS A SELFISH KID! HE NEVER WANTED WHAT'S BEST FOR EVERYONE!
NO... BUCKY WAS A HERO...
IS HE...IS HE HERE RIGHT NOW, NAMOR? DO YOU HEAR TOMMY?
HE'S...HE'S ALWAYS HERE. TELLING ME WHAT TO--
FIGHT HIM! KILL HIM! IF HE STOPS YOU, MILLIONS OF PEOPLE WILL SUFFER!
CONFIDING IN HIM WAS A MISTAKE! HE'LL NEVER UNDERSTAND THE WEIGHT OF BEING A KING!
I DON'T... NAMOR...NAMOR ALONE MAKES THE DECISIONS...YOU... Y-YOU DON'T...

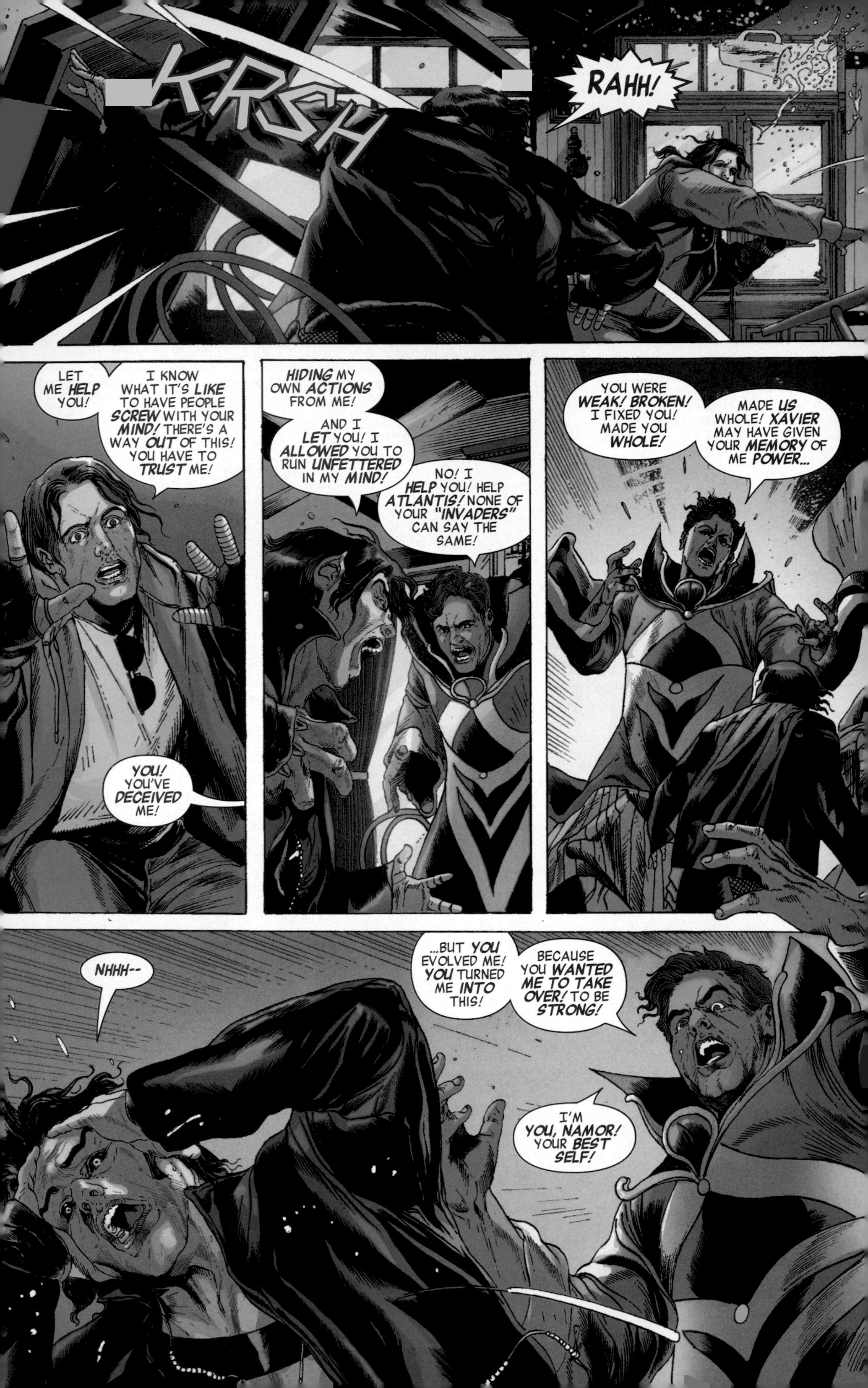
KRSH
RAHH!
LET ME HELP YOU!
I KNOW WHAT IT'S LIKE TO HAVE PEOPLE SCREW WITH YOUR MIND! THERE'S A WAY OUT OF THIS! YOU HAVE TO TRUST ME!
YOU! YOU'VE DECEIVED ME!
HIDING MY OWN ACTIONS FROM ME!
AND I LET YOU! I ALLOWED YOU TO RUN UNFETTERED IN MY MIND!
NO! I HELP YOU! HELP ATLANTIS! NONE OF YOUR "INVADERS" CAN SAY THE SAME!
YOU WERE WEAK! BROKEN! I FIXED YOU! MADE YOU WHOLE!
MADE US WHOLE! XAVIER MAY HAVE GIVEN YOUR MEMORY OF ME POWER...
NHHH--
...BUT YOU EVOLVED ME! YOU TURNED ME INTO THIS!
BECAUSE YOU WANTED ME TO TAKE OVER! TO BE STRONG!
I'M YOU, NAMOR! YOUR BEST SELF!

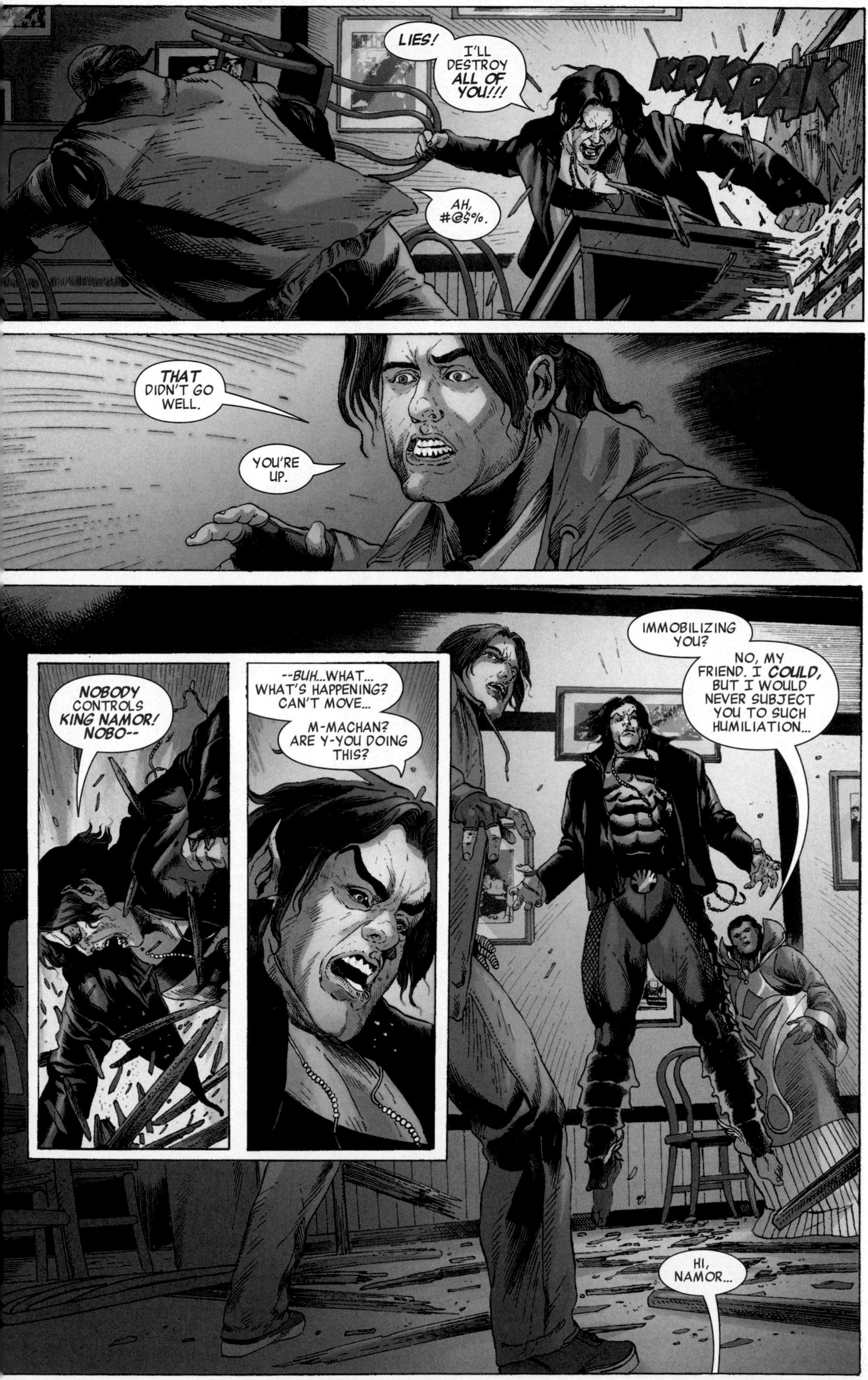
LIES!
I'LL DESTROY ALL OF YOU!!!
KRKRAK
AH, #@$%.
THAT DIDN'T GO WELL.
YOU'RE UP.
NOBODY CONTROLS KING NAMOR! NOBO--
--BUH...WHAT... WHAT'S HAPPENING? CAN'T MOVE...
M-MACHAN? ARE Y-YOU DOING THIS?
IMMOBILIZING YOU?
NO, MY FRIEND. I COULD, BUT I WOULD NEVER SUBJECT YOU TO SUCH HUMILIATION...
HI, NAMOR...

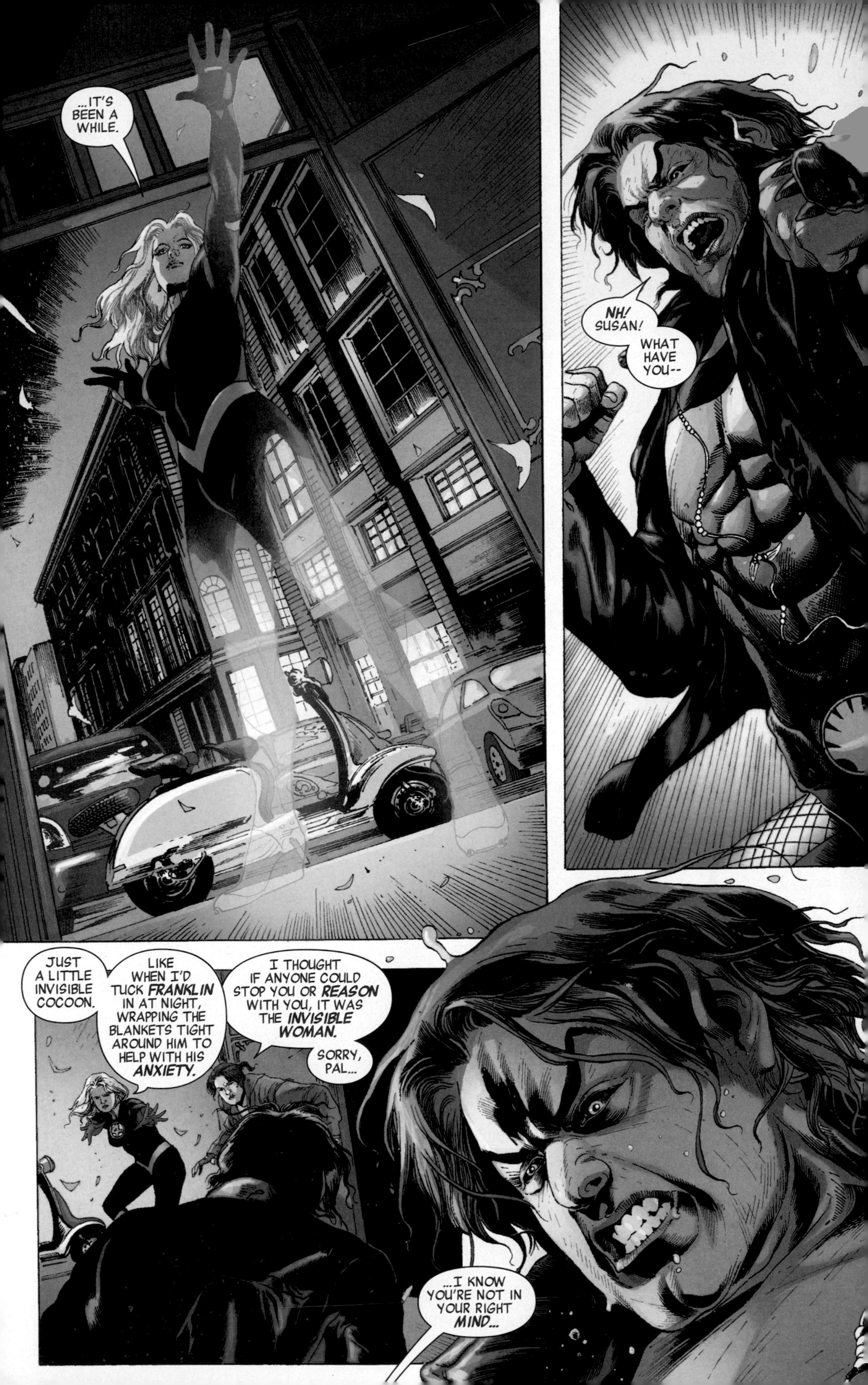
...IT'S BEEN A WHILE.
NH! SUSAN!
WHAT HAVE YOU--
JUST A LITTLE INVISIBLE COCOON.
LIKE WHEN I'D TUCK FRANKLIN IN AT NIGHT, WRAPPING THE BLANKETS TIGHT AROUND HIM TO HELP WITH HIS ANXIETY.
I THOUGHT IF ANYONE COULD STOP YOU OR REASON WITH YOU, IT WAS THE INVISIBLE WOMAN.
SORRY, PAL...
...I KNOW YOU'RE NOT IN YOUR RIGHT MIND...

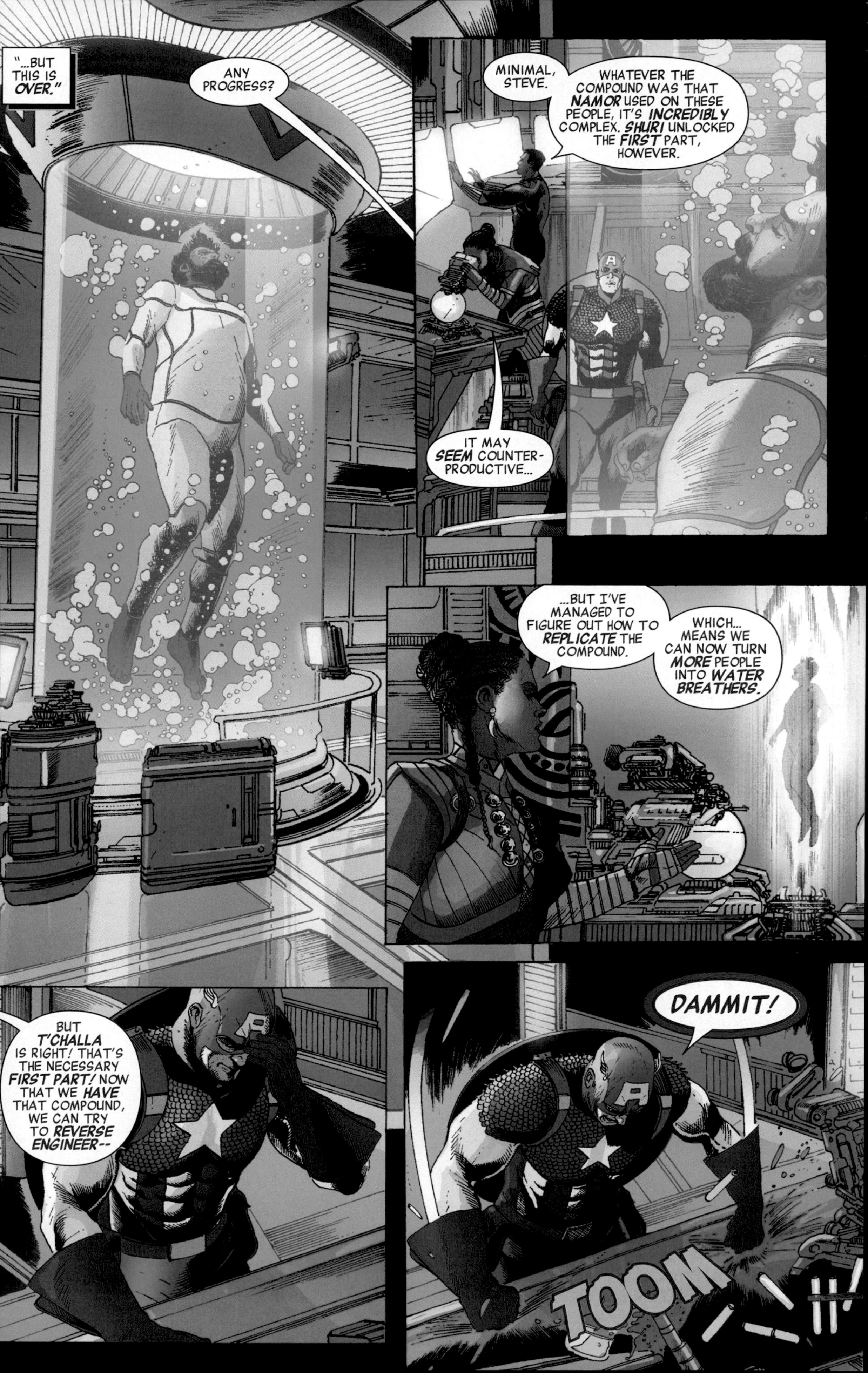
"...BUT THIS IS OVER."
ANY PROGRESS?
MINIMAL, STEVE.
WHATEVER THE COMPOUND WAS THAT NAMOR USED ON THESE PEOPLE, IT'S INCREDIBLY COMPLEX. SHURI UNLOCKED THE FIRST PART, HOWEVER.
IT MAY SEEM COUNTER-PRODUCTIVE...
...BUT I'VE MANAGED TO FIGURE OUT HOW TO REPLICATE THE COMPOUND.
WHICH... MEANS WE CAN NOW TURN MORE PEOPLE INTO WATER BREATHERS.
BUT T'CHALLA IS RIGHT! THAT'S THE NECESSARY FIRST PART! NOW THAT WE HAVE THAT COMPOUND, WE CAN TRY TO REVERSE ENGINEER--
DAMMIT!
TOOM

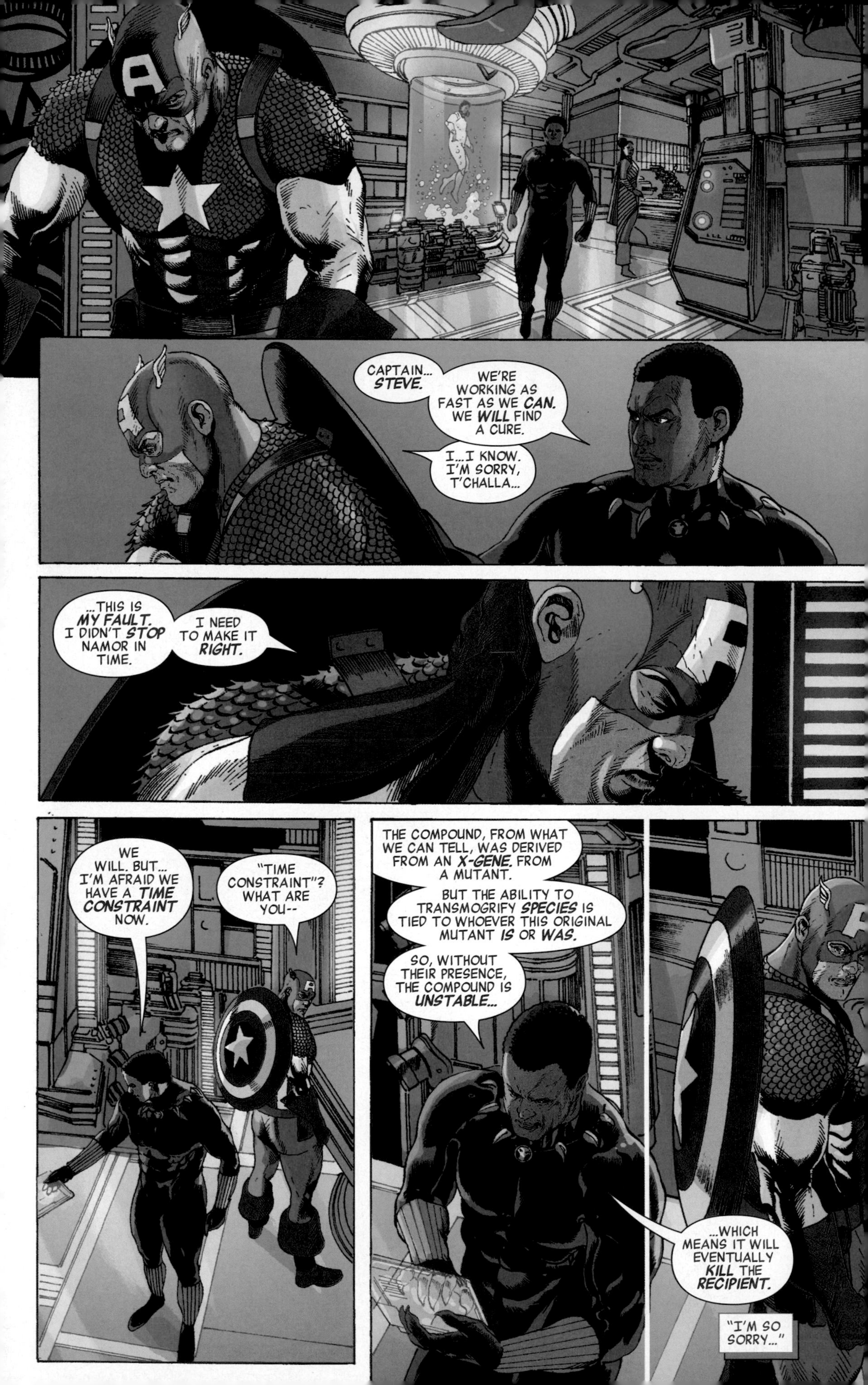
CAPTAIN... STEVE.
WE'RE WORKING AS FAST AS WE CAN. WE WILL FIND A CURE.
I...I KNOW. I'M SORRY, T'CHALLA...
...THIS IS MY FAULT. I DIDN'T STOP NAMOR IN TIME.
I NEED TO MAKE IT RIGHT.
WE WILL. BUT... I'M AFRAID WE HAVE A TIME CONSTRAINT NOW.
"TIME CONSTRAINT"? WHAT ARE YOU--
THE COMPOUND, FROM WHAT WE CAN TELL, WAS DERIVED FROM AN X-GENE. FROM A MUTANT.
BUT THE ABILITY TO TRANSMOGRIFY SPECIES IS TIED TO WHOEVER THIS ORIGINAL MUTANT IS OR WAS.
SO, WITHOUT THEIR PRESENCE, THE COMPOUND IS UNSTABLE...
...WHICH MEANS IT WILL EVENTUALLY KILL THE RECIPIENT.
"I'M SO SORRY..."

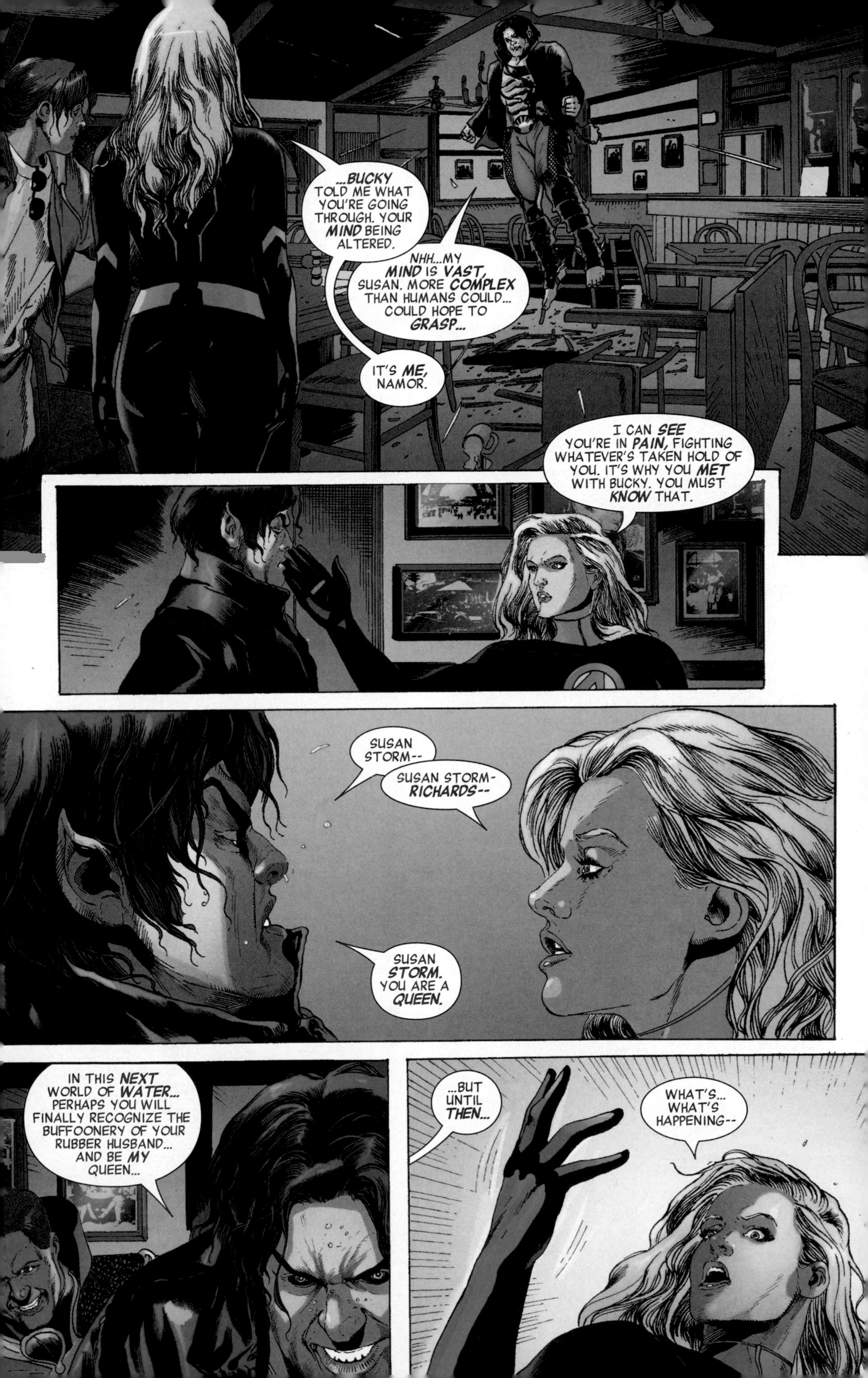
...BUCKY TOLD ME WHAT YOU'RE GOING THROUGH. YOUR MIND BEING ALTERED.
NHH...MY MIND IS VAST, SUSAN. MORE COMPLEX THAN HUMANS COULD... COULD HOPE TO GRASP...
IT'S ME, NAMOR.
I CAN SEE YOU'RE IN PAIN, FIGHTING WHATEVER'S TAKEN HOLD OF YOU. IT'S WHY YOU MET WITH BUCKY. YOU MUST KNOW THAT.
SUSAN STORM--
SUSAN STORM-RICHARDS--
SUSAN STORM. YOU ARE A QUEEN.
IN THIS NEXT WORLD OF WATER... PERHAPS YOU WILL FINALLY RECOGNIZE THE BUFFOONERY OF YOUR RUBBER HUSBAND... AND BE MY QUEEN...
...BUT UNTIL THEN...
WHAT'S... WHAT'S HAPPENING--

I CAN'T...THINK STRAIGHT, I...

NAMOR! WHAT ARE YOU--

OH, SUSAN...THERE'S MORE THAN ONE WAY...

...TO MAKE SOMETHING INVISIBLE.

NH! CAN'T...WHAT ARE YOU DOING, NAMOR? WHAT'S THAT--

OH, THIS?

IT'S THE SERPENT CROWN. ONCE UPON A TIME USED AGAINST ME, TURNING ME INTO A HOPELESS AMNESIAC.

BUT NOW IT'S THE FINAL PIECE OF MY PUZZLE. PROTECTION OF MY MIND. THE ABILITY TO CONTROL THE MINDS OF OTHERS.

DO YOU SEE HOW THEY WILL ALWAYS BETRAY AND ATTACK YOU?

I ONLY EVER DID WHAT I DID BECAUSE YOUR SENTIMENTALITY FOR THESE HUMANS WILL BE YOUR UNDOING.

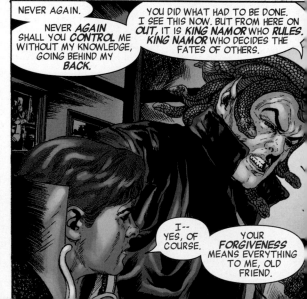

NEVER AGAIN.

NEVER AGAIN SHALL YOU CONTROL ME WITHOUT MY KNOWLEDGE, GOING BEHIND MY BACK.

YOU DID WHAT HAD TO BE DONE. I SEE THIS NOW. BUT FROM HERE ON OUT, IT IS KING NAMOR WHO RULES. KING NAMOR WHO DECIDES THE FATES OF OTHERS.

I-- YES, OF COURSE.

YOUR FORGIVENESS MEANS EVERYTHING TO ME, OLD FRIEND.

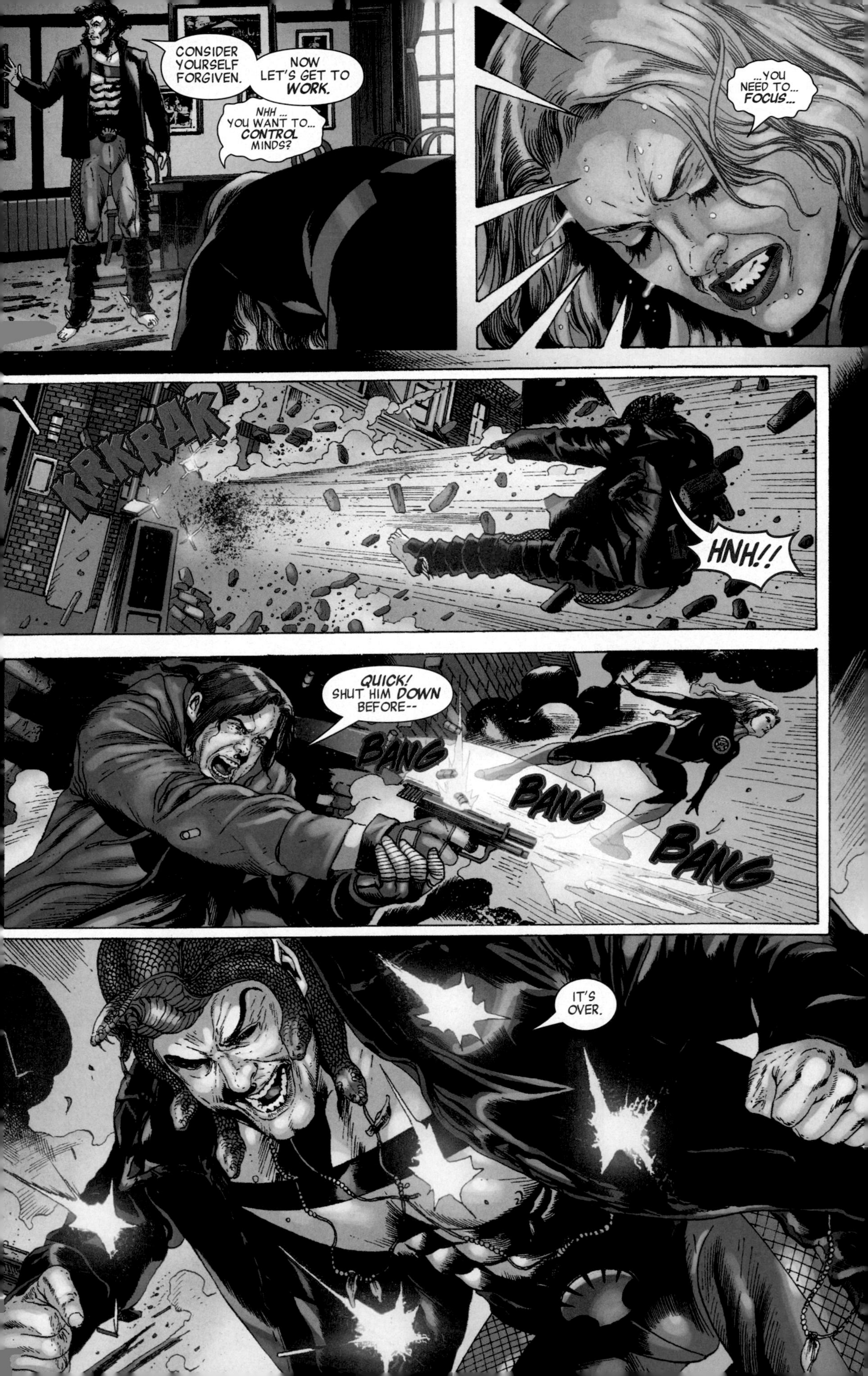
CONSIDER YOURSELF FORGIVEN.
NOW LET'S GET TO WORK.
NHH ... YOU WANT TO... CONTROL MINDS?
...YOU NEED TO... FOCUS...
KRKRAK
HNH!!
QUICK! SHUT HIM DOWN BEFORE--
BANG
BANG
BANG
IT'S OVER.

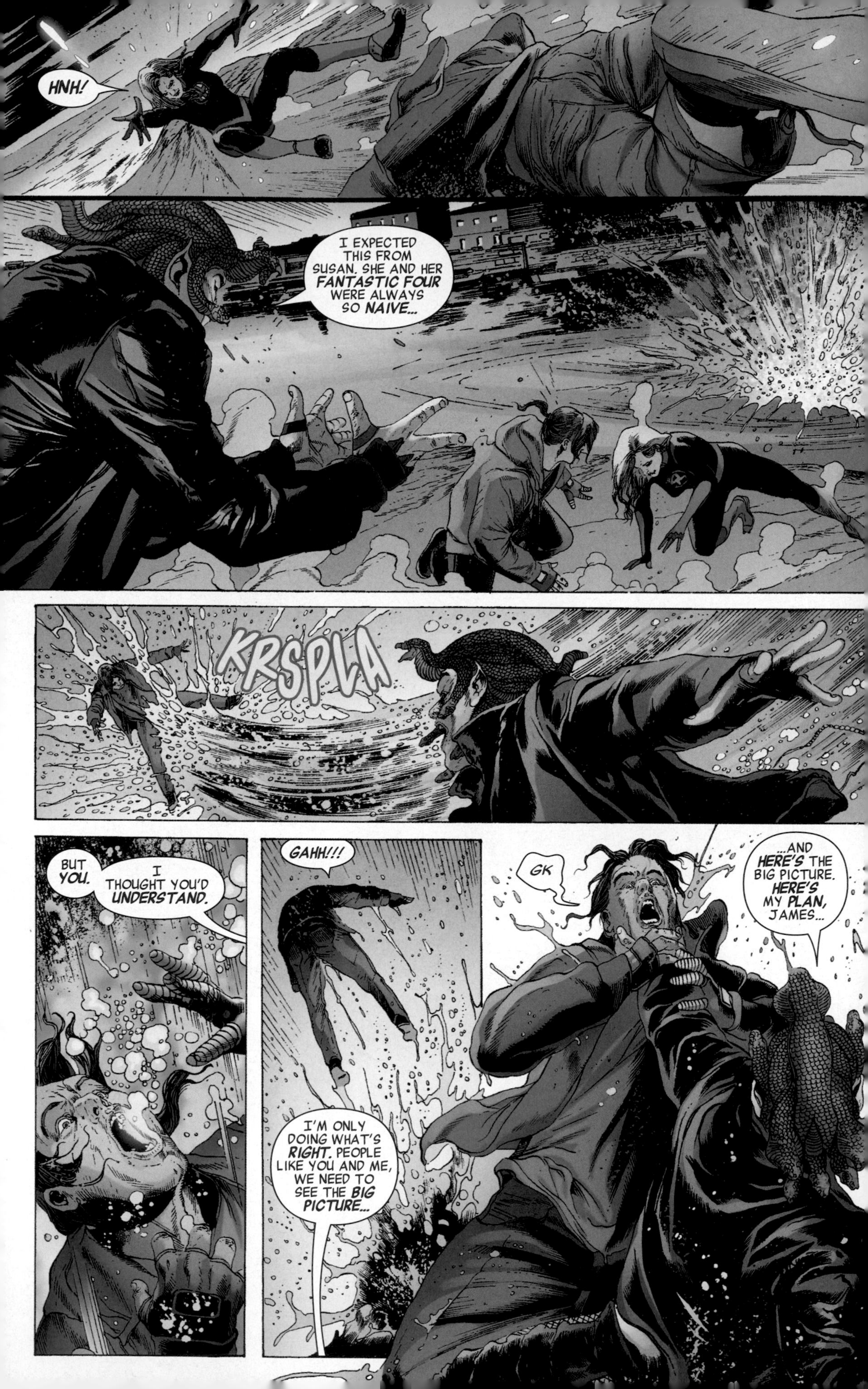
HNH!
I EXPECTED THIS FROM SUSAN. SHE AND HER FANTASTIC FOUR WERE ALWAYS SO NAIVE...
KRSPLA
BUT YOU.
I THOUGHT YOU'D UNDERSTAND.
GAHH!!!
I'M ONLY DOING WHAT'S RIGHT. PEOPLE LIKE YOU AND ME, WE NEED TO SEE THE BIG PICTURE...
GK
...AND HERE'S THE BIG PICTURE. HERE'S MY PLAN, JAMES...

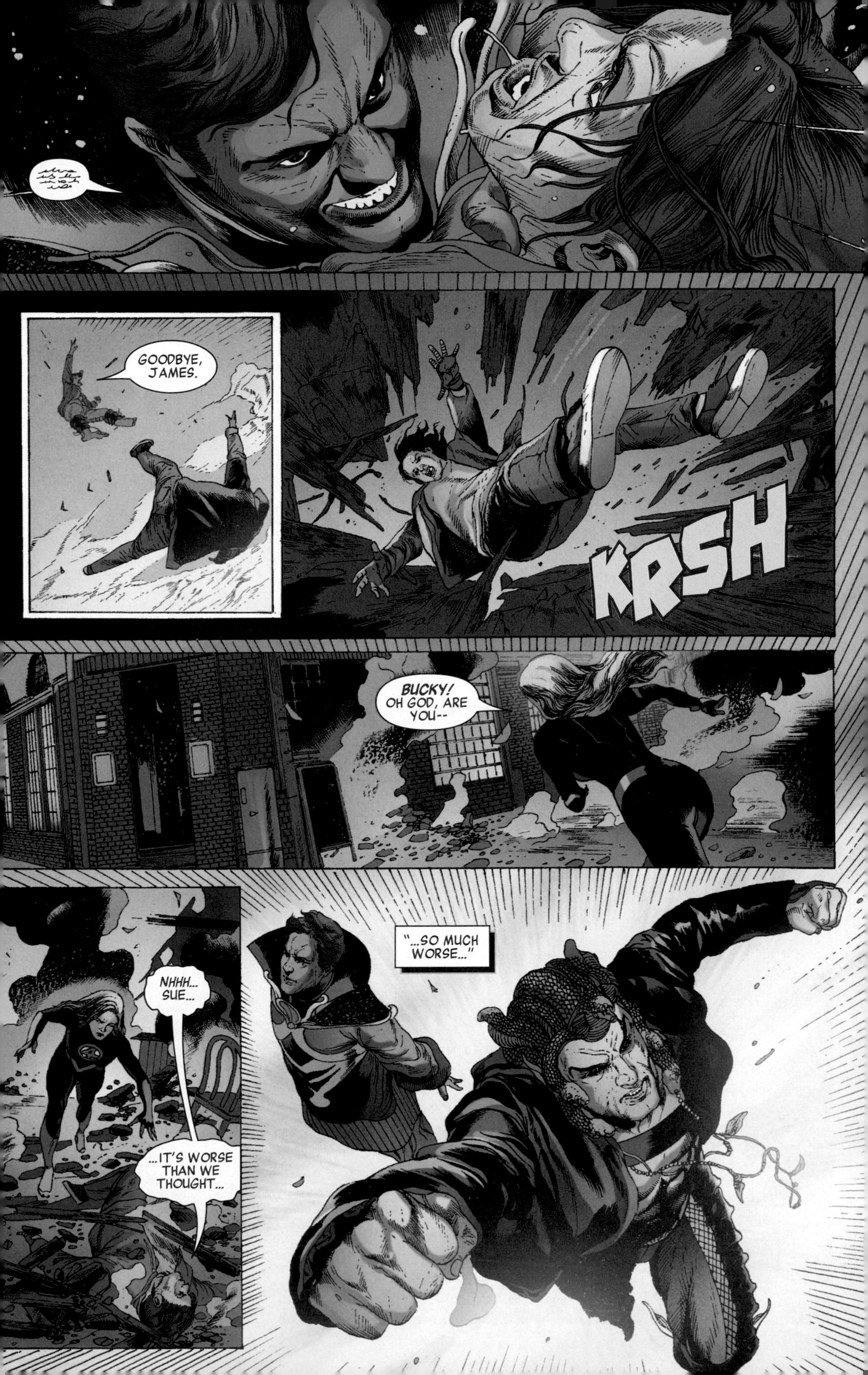
GOODBYE, JAMES.
KRSH
BUCKY! OH GOD, ARE YOU--
NHHH... SUE...
...IT'S WORSE THAN WE THOUGHT...
"...SO MUCH WORSE..."

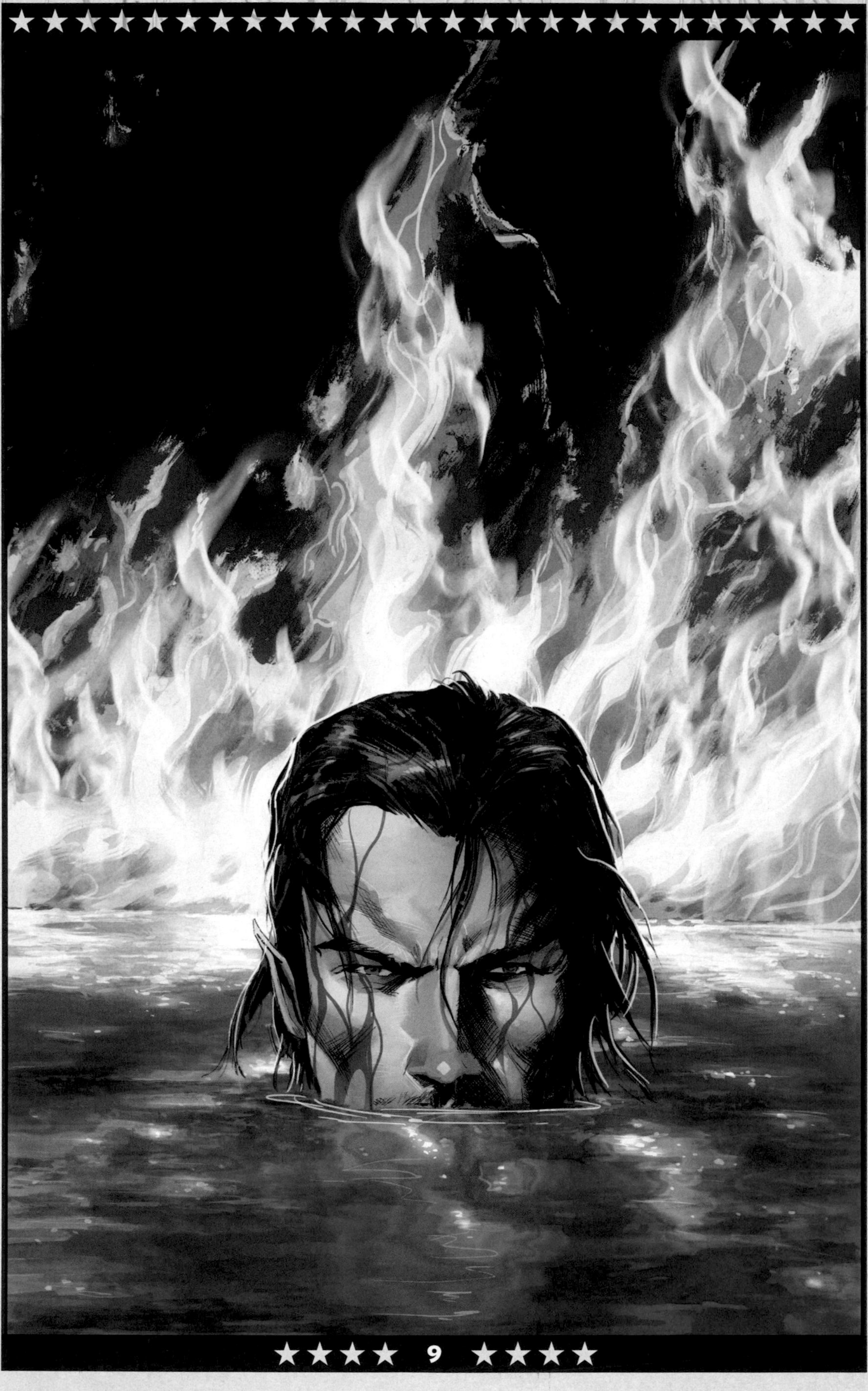

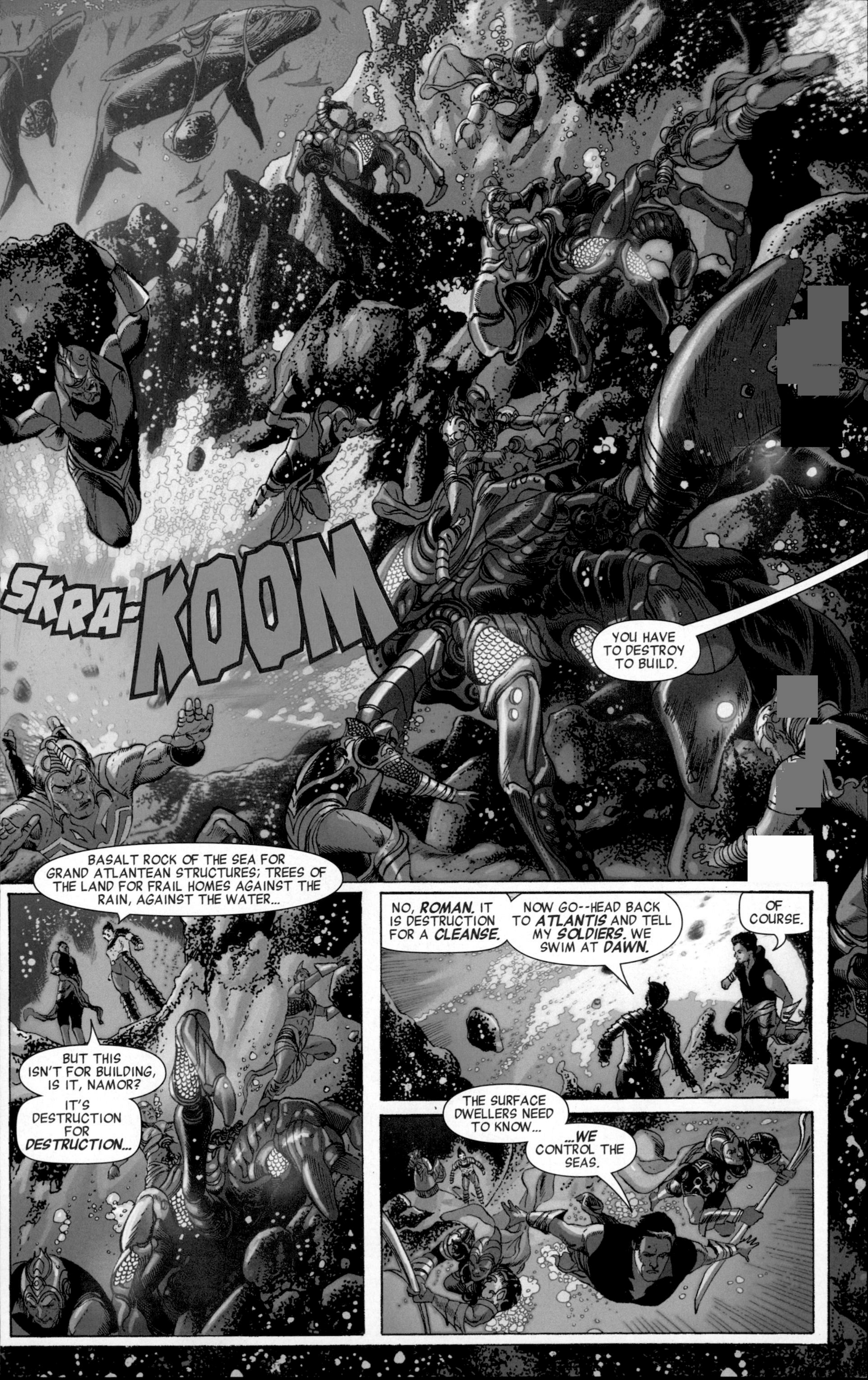
SKRA-KOOM
YOU HAVE TO DESTROY TO BUILD.
BASALT ROCK OF THE SEA FOR GRAND ATLANTEAN STRUCTURES; TREES OF THE LAND FOR FRAIL HOMES AGAINST THE RAIN, AGAINST THE WATER...
BUT THIS ISN'T FOR BUILDING, IS IT, NAMOR?
IT'S DESTRUCTION FOR DESTRUCTION...
NO, ROMAN. IT IS DESTRUCTION FOR A CLEANSE.
NOW GO--HEAD BACK TO ATLANTIS AND TELL MY SOLDIERS. WE SWIM AT DAWN.
OF COURSE.
THE SURFACE DWELLERS NEED TO KNOW...
...WE CONTROL THE SEAS.

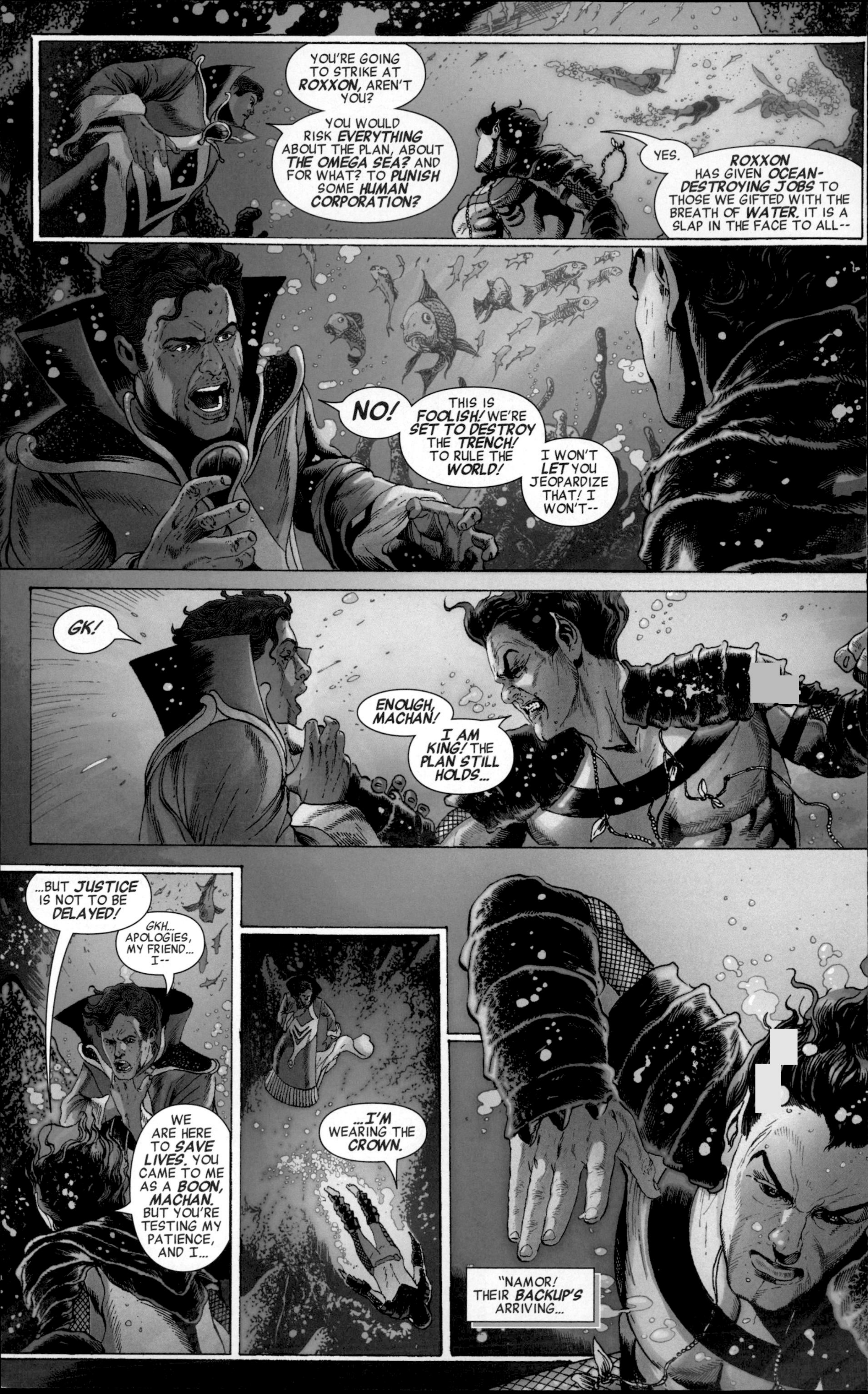

YOU'RE GOING TO STRIKE AT ROXXON, AREN'T YOU?
YOU WOULD RISK EVERYTHING ABOUT THE PLAN, ABOUT THE OMEGA SEA? AND FOR WHAT? TO PUNISH SOME HUMAN CORPORATION?
YES.
ROXXON HAS GIVEN OCEAN-DESTROYING JOBS TO THOSE WE GIFTED WITH THE BREATH OF WATER. IT IS A SLAP IN THE FACE TO ALL--
NO!
THIS IS FOOLISH! WE'RE SET TO DESTROY THE TRENCH! TO RULE THE WORLD!
I WON'T LET YOU JEOPARDIZE THAT! I WON'T--
GK!
ENOUGH, MACHAN!
I AM KING! THE PLAN STILL HOLDS...
...BUT JUSTICE IS NOT TO BE DELAYED!
GKH... APOLOGIES, MY FRIEND... I--
WE ARE HERE TO SAVE LIVES. YOU CAME TO ME AS A BOON, MACHAN. BUT YOU'RE TESTING MY PATIENCE, AND I...
...I'M WEARING THE CROWN.
"NAMOR! THEIR BACKUP'S ARRIVING...

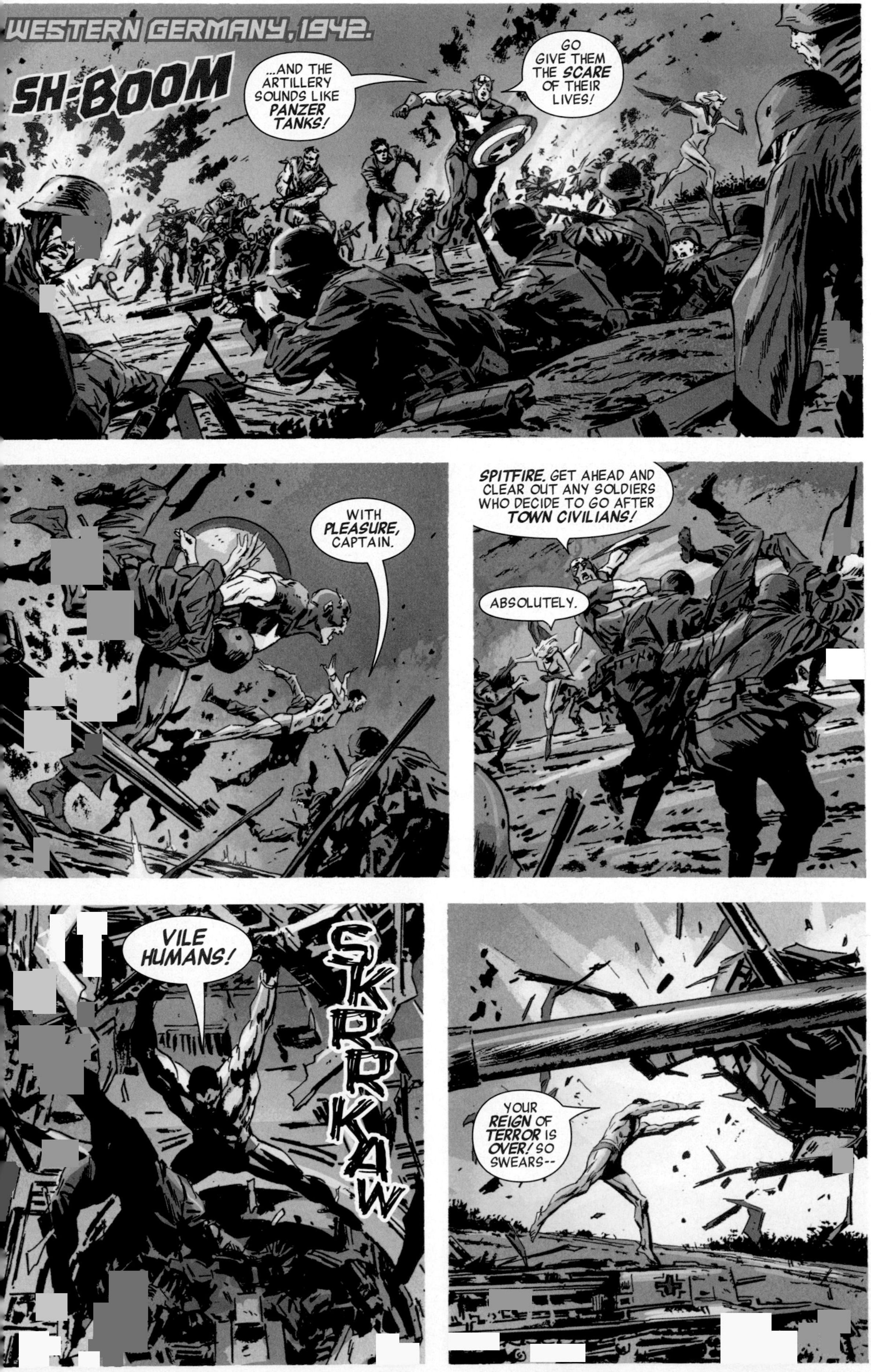
WESTERN GERMANY, 1942.
SH-BOOM
...AND THE ARTILLERY SOUNDS LIKE PANZER TANKS!
GO GIVE THEM THE SCARE OF THEIR LIVES!
WITH PLEASURE, CAPTAIN.
SPITFIRE. GET AHEAD AND CLEAR OUT ANY SOLDIERS WHO DECIDE TO GO AFTER TOWN CIVILIANS!
ABSOLUTELY.
VILE HUMANS!
SKRRKAW
YOUR REIGN OF TERROR IS OVER! SO SWEARS--

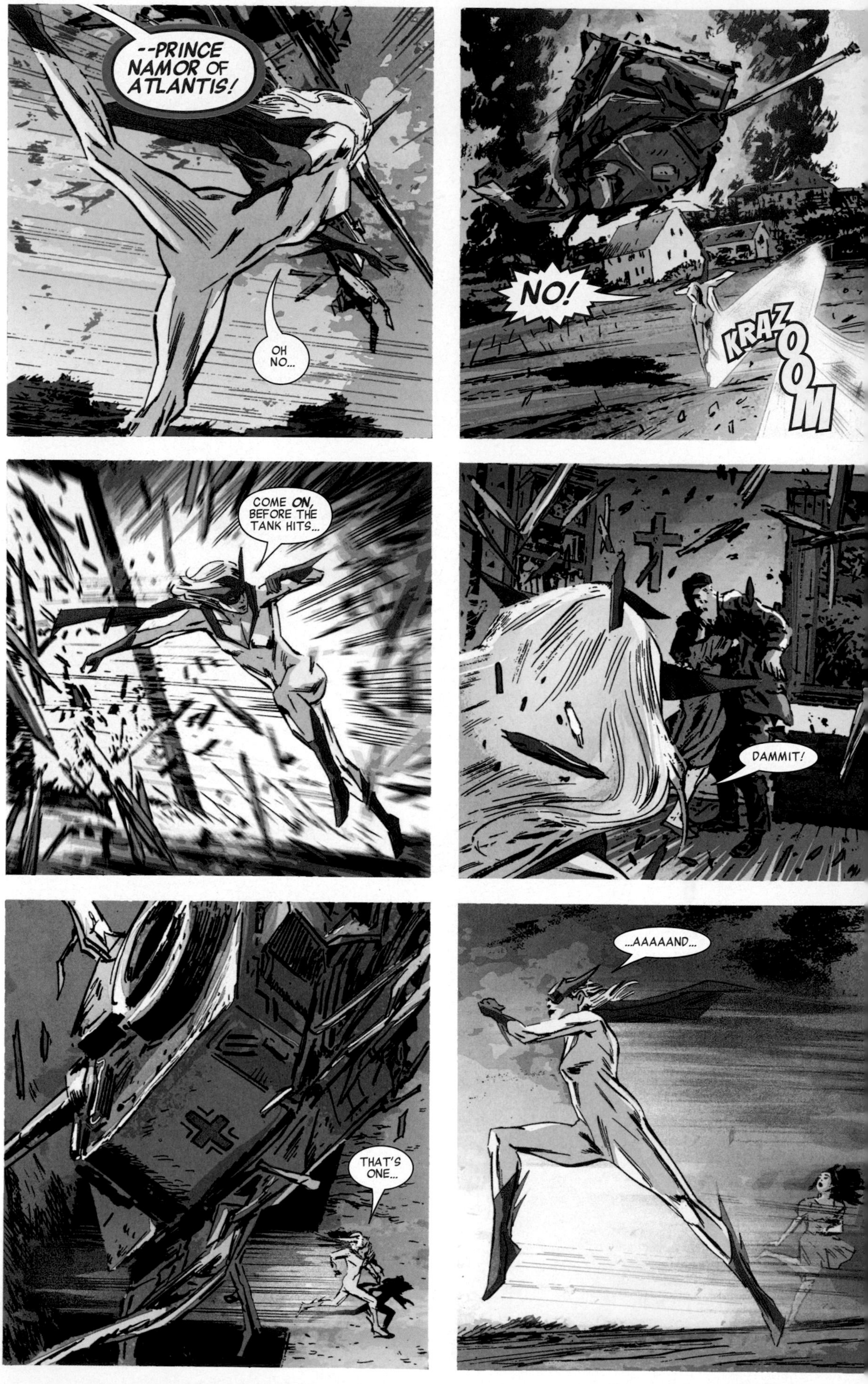
--PRINCE NAMOR OF ATLANTIS!
OH NO...
NO!
KRAZOOM
COME ON, BEFORE THE TANK HITS...
DAMMIT!
THAT'S ONE...
...AAAAAND...

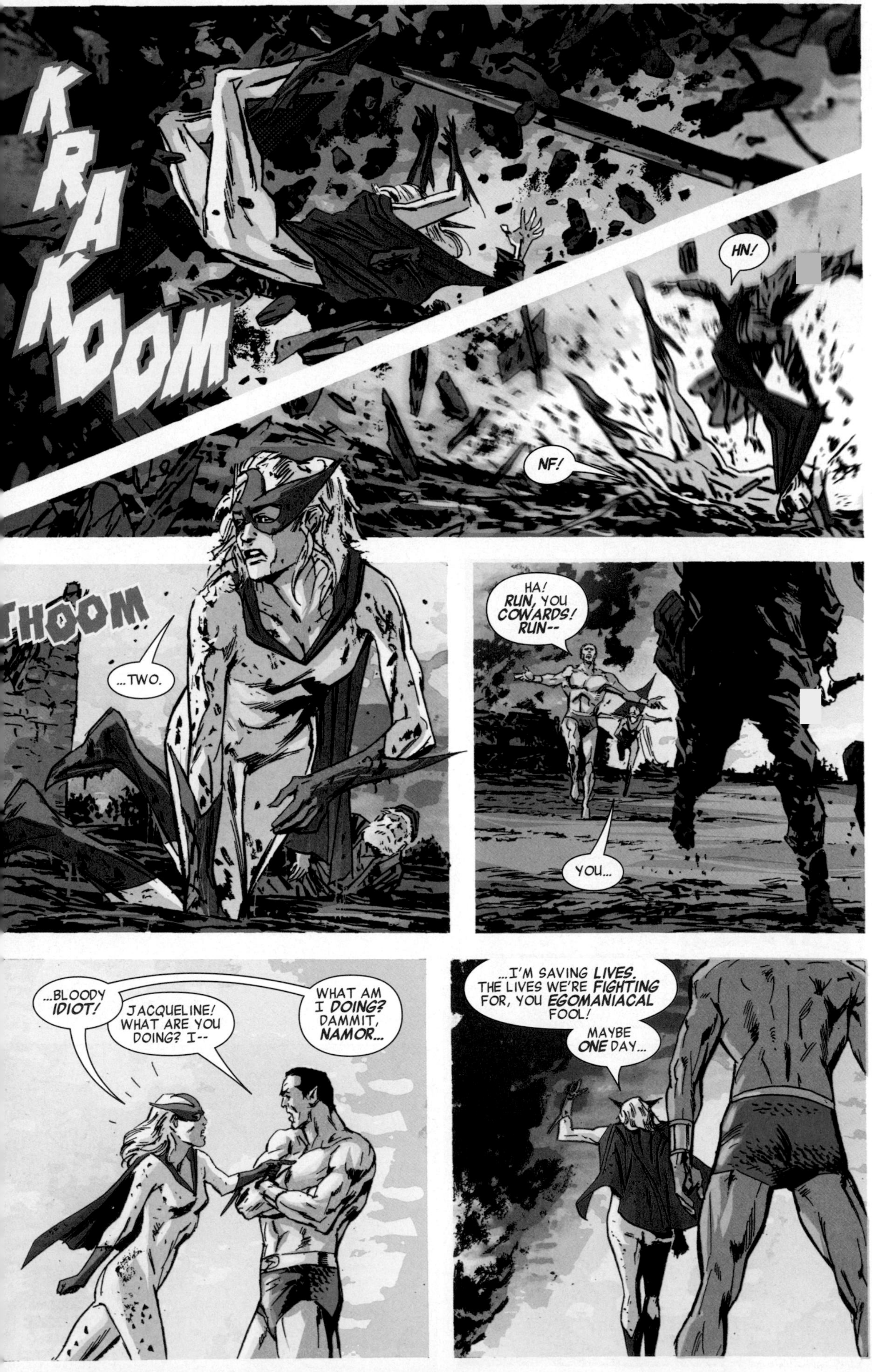
KRAKOOM
HN!
NF!
THOOM
...TWO.
HA! RUN, YOU COWARDS! RUN--
YOU...
...BLOODY IDIOT!
JACQUELINE! WHAT ARE YOU DOING? I--
WHAT AM I DOING? DAMMIT, NAMOR...
...I'M SAVING LIVES. THE LIVES WE'RE FIGHTING FOR, YOU EGOMANIACAL FOOL!
MAYBE ONE DAY...

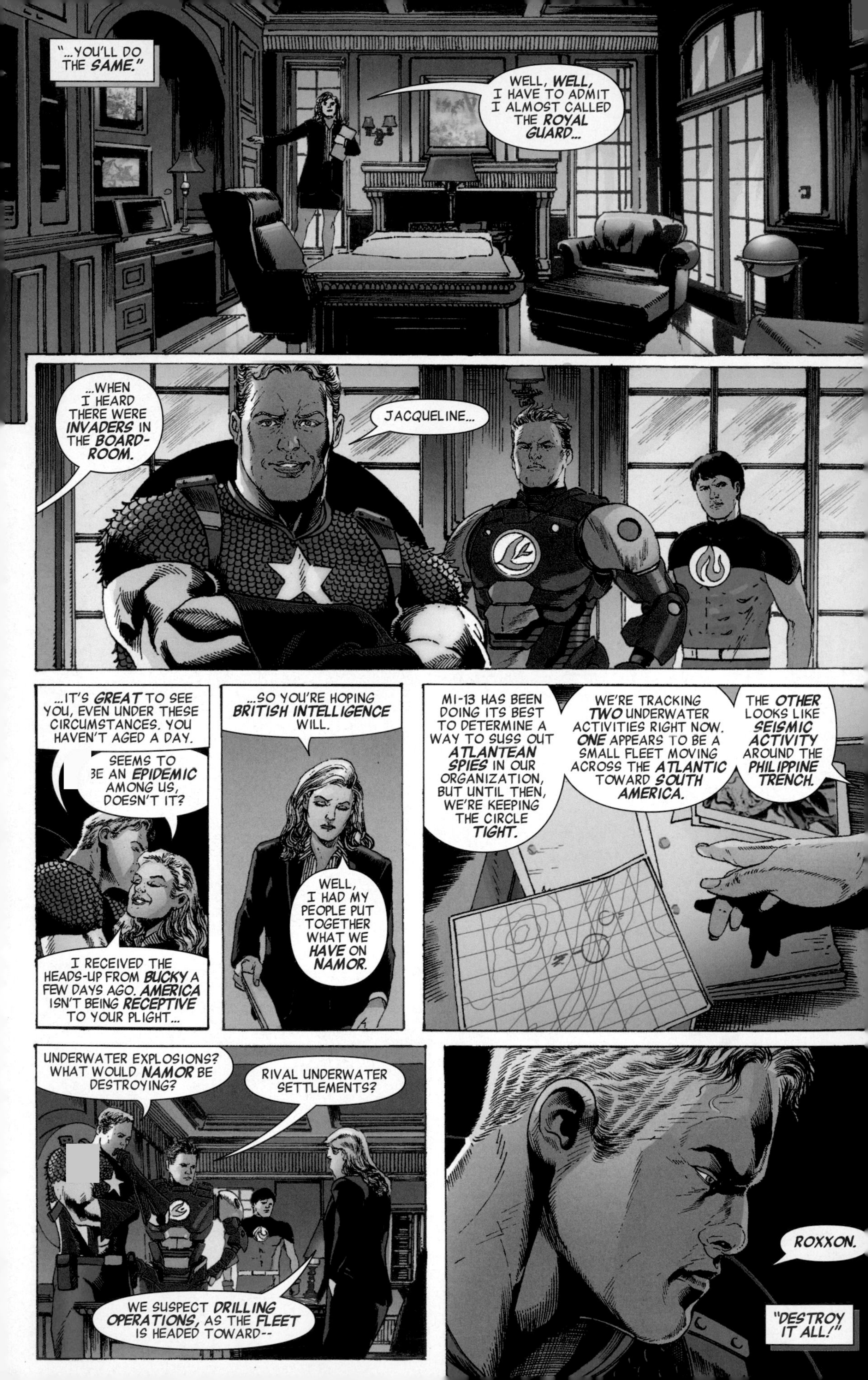

"...YOU'LL DO THE SAME."
WELL, WELL, I HAVE TO ADMIT I ALMOST CALLED THE ROYAL GUARD...
...WHEN I HEARD THERE WERE INVADERS IN THE BOARD-ROOM.
JACQUELINE...
...IT'S GREAT TO SEE YOU, EVEN UNDER THESE CIRCUMSTANCES. YOU HAVEN'T AGED A DAY.
SEEMS TO BE AN EPIDEMIC AMONG US, DOESN'T IT?
I RECEIVED THE HEADS-UP FROM BUCKY A FEW DAYS AGO. AMERICA ISN'T BEING RECEPTIVE TO YOUR PLIGHT...
...SO YOU'RE HOPING BRITISH INTELLIGENCE WILL.
WELL, I HAD MY PEOPLE PUT TOGETHER WHAT WE HAVE ON NAMOR.
MI-13 HAS BEEN DOING ITS BEST TO DETERMINE A WAY TO SUSS OUT ATLANTEAN SPIES IN OUR ORGANIZATION, BUT UNTIL THEN, WE'RE KEEPING THE CIRCLE TIGHT.
WE'RE TRACKING TWO UNDERWATER ACTIVITIES RIGHT NOW. ONE APPEARS TO BE A SMALL FLEET MOVING ACROSS THE ATLANTIC TOWARD SOUTH AMERICA.
THE OTHER LOOKS LIKE SEISMIC ACTIVITY AROUND THE PHILIPPINE TRENCH.
UNDERWATER EXPLOSIONS? WHAT WOULD NAMOR BE DESTROYING?
RIVAL UNDERWATER SETTLEMENTS?
WE SUSPECT DRILLING OPERATIONS, AS THE FLEET IS HEADED TOWARD--
ROXXON.
"DESTROY IT ALL!"

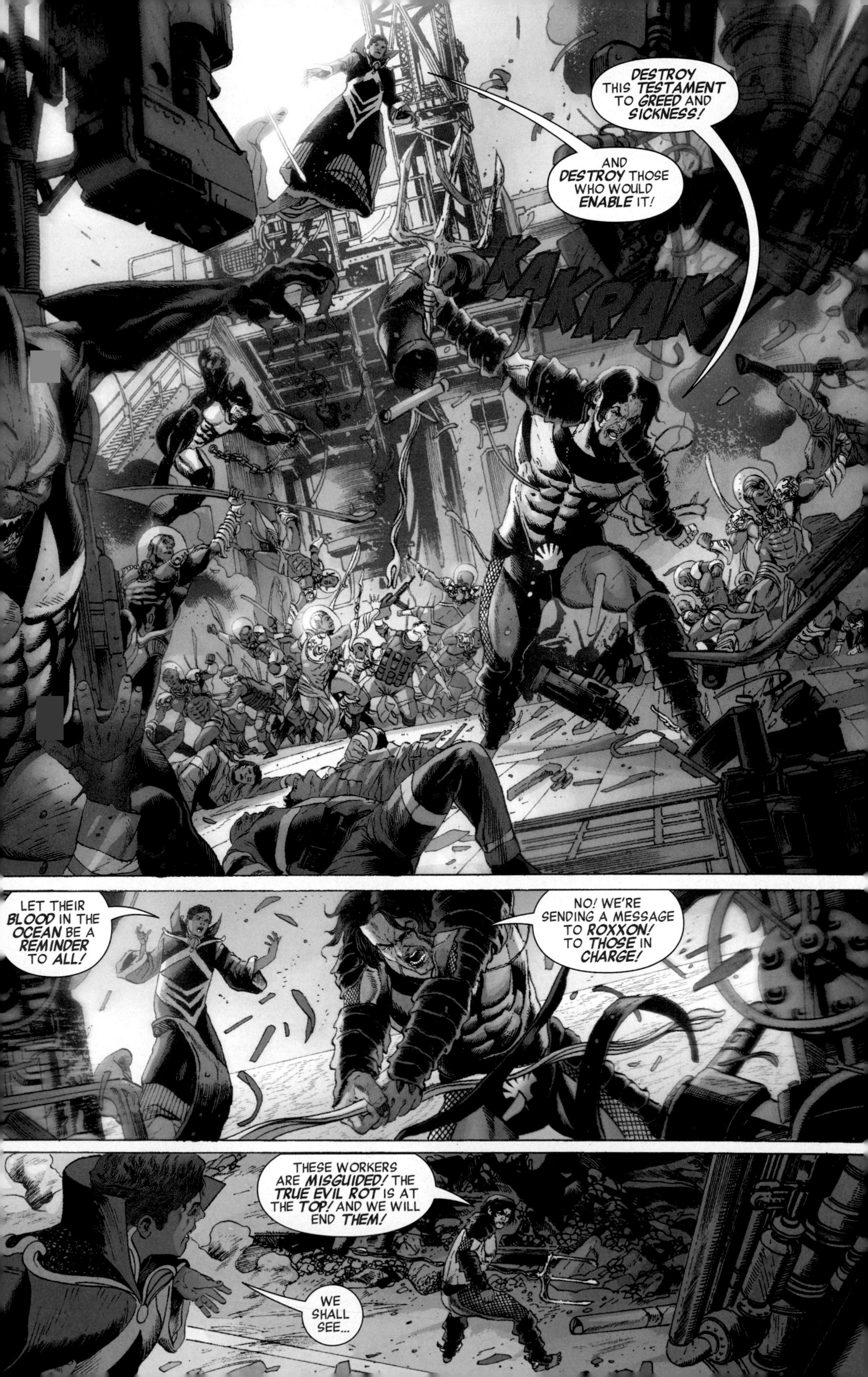
DESTROY THIS TESTAMENT TO GREED AND SICKNESS!
AND DESTROY THOSE WHO WOULD ENABLE IT!
KAKRAK
LET THEIR BLOOD IN THE OCEAN BE A REMINDER TO ALL!
NO! WE'RE SENDING A MESSAGE TO ROXXON! TO THOSE IN CHARGE!
THESE WORKERS ARE MISGUIDED! THE TRUE EVIL ROT IS AT THE TOP! AND WE WILL END THEM!
WE SHALL SEE...

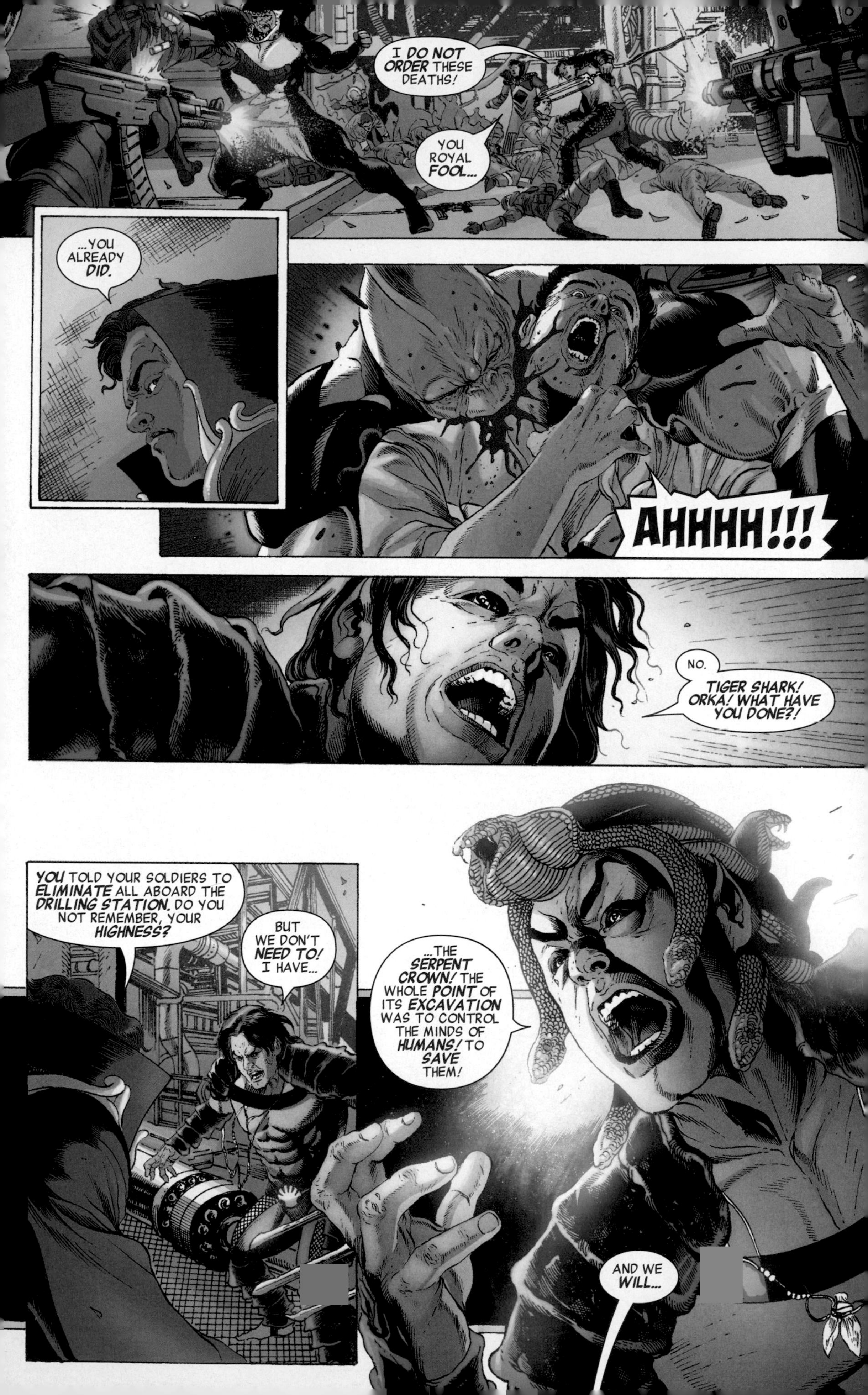
I DO NOT ORDER THESE DEATHS!
YOU ROYAL FOOL...
...YOU ALREADY DID.
AHHHH!!!
NO.
TIGER SHARK! ORKA! WHAT HAVE YOU DONE?!
YOU TOLD YOUR SOLDIERS TO ELIMINATE ALL ABOARD THE DRILLING STATION. DO YOU NOT REMEMBER, YOUR HIGHNESS?
BUT WE DON'T NEED TO! I HAVE...
...THE SERPENT CROWN! THE WHOLE POINT OF ITS EXCAVATION WAS TO CONTROL THE MINDS OF HUMANS! TO SAVE THEM!
AND WE WILL...

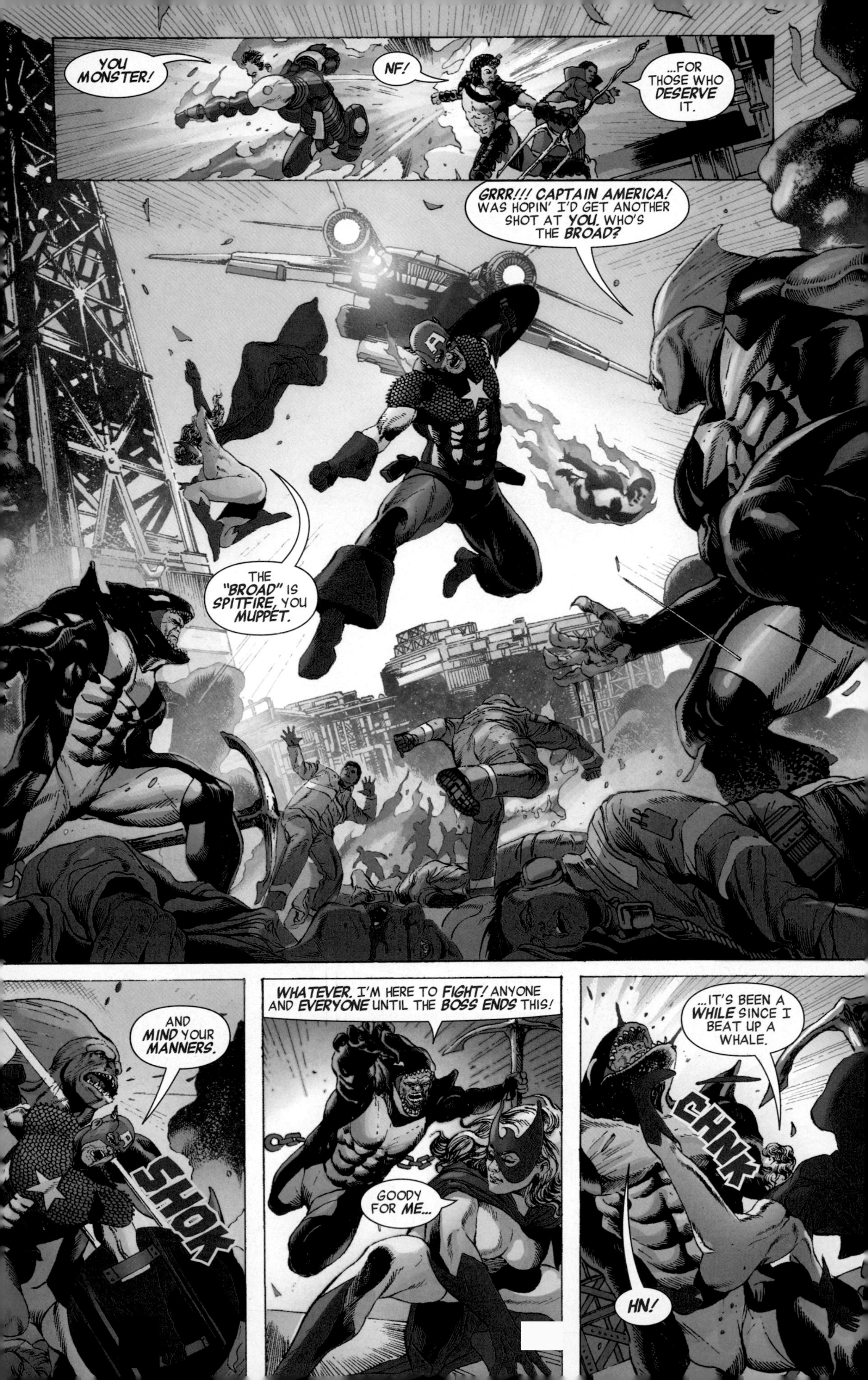
YOU MONSTER!
NF!
...FOR THOSE WHO DESERVE IT.
GRRR!!! CAPTAIN AMERICA! WAS HOPIN' I'D GET ANOTHER SHOT AT YOU. WHO'S THE BROAD?
THE "BROAD" IS SPITFIRE, YOU MUPPET.
AND MIND YOUR MANNERS.
SHOK
WHATEVER. I'M HERE TO FIGHT! ANYONE AND EVERYONE UNTIL THE BOSS ENDS THIS!
GOODY FOR ME...
...IT'S BEEN A WHILE SINCE I BEAT UP A WHALE.
CHNK
HN!

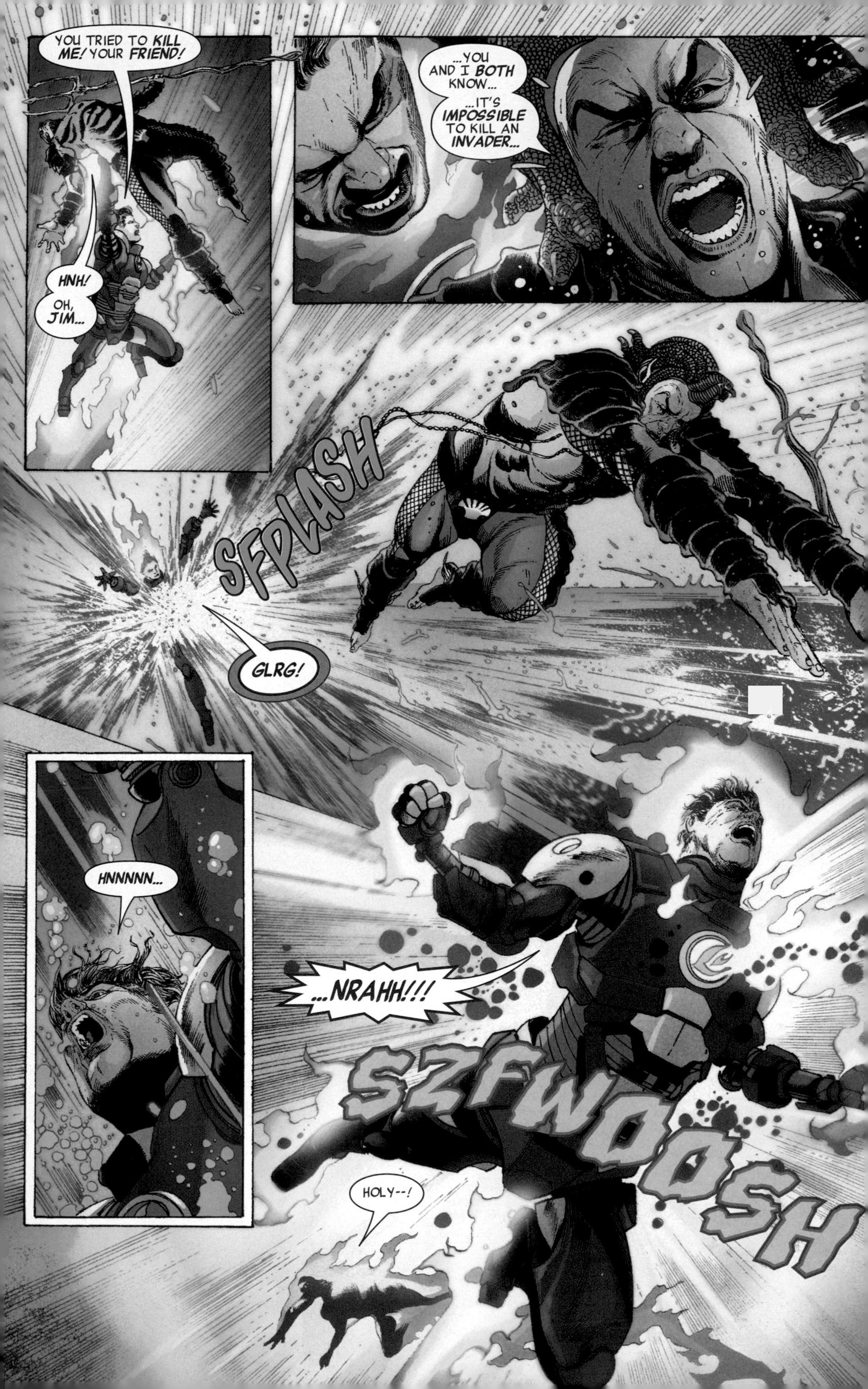
YOU TRIED TO KILL ME! YOUR FRIEND!
HNH!
OH, JIM...
...YOU AND I BOTH KNOW...
...IT'S IMPOSSIBLE TO KILL AN INVADER...
SFPLASH
GLRG!
HNNNNN...
...NRAHH!!!
SZFWOOSH
HOLY--!

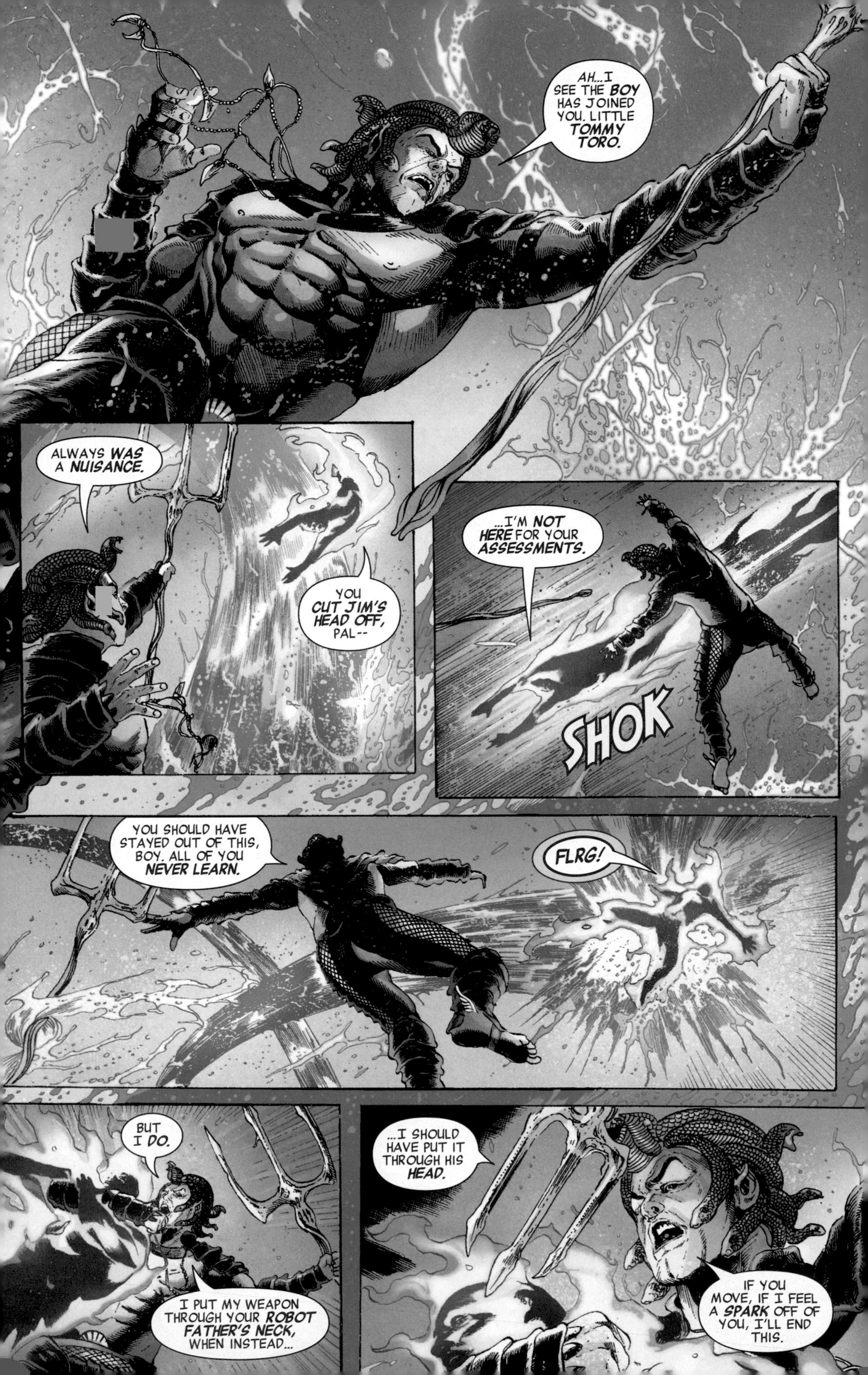
AH...I SEE THE BOY HAS JOINED YOU. LITTLE TOMMY TORO.
ALWAYS WAS A NUISANCE.
YOU CUT JIM'S HEAD OFF, PAL--
...I'M NOT HERE FOR YOUR ASSESSMENTS.
SHOK
YOU SHOULD HAVE STAYED OUT OF THIS, BOY. ALL OF YOU NEVER LEARN.
FLRG!
BUT I DO.
I PUT MY WEAPON THROUGH YOUR ROBOT FATHER'S NECK, WHEN INSTEAD...
...I SHOULD HAVE PUT IT THROUGH HIS HEAD.
IF YOU MOVE, IF I FEEL A SPARK OFF OF YOU, I'LL END THIS.

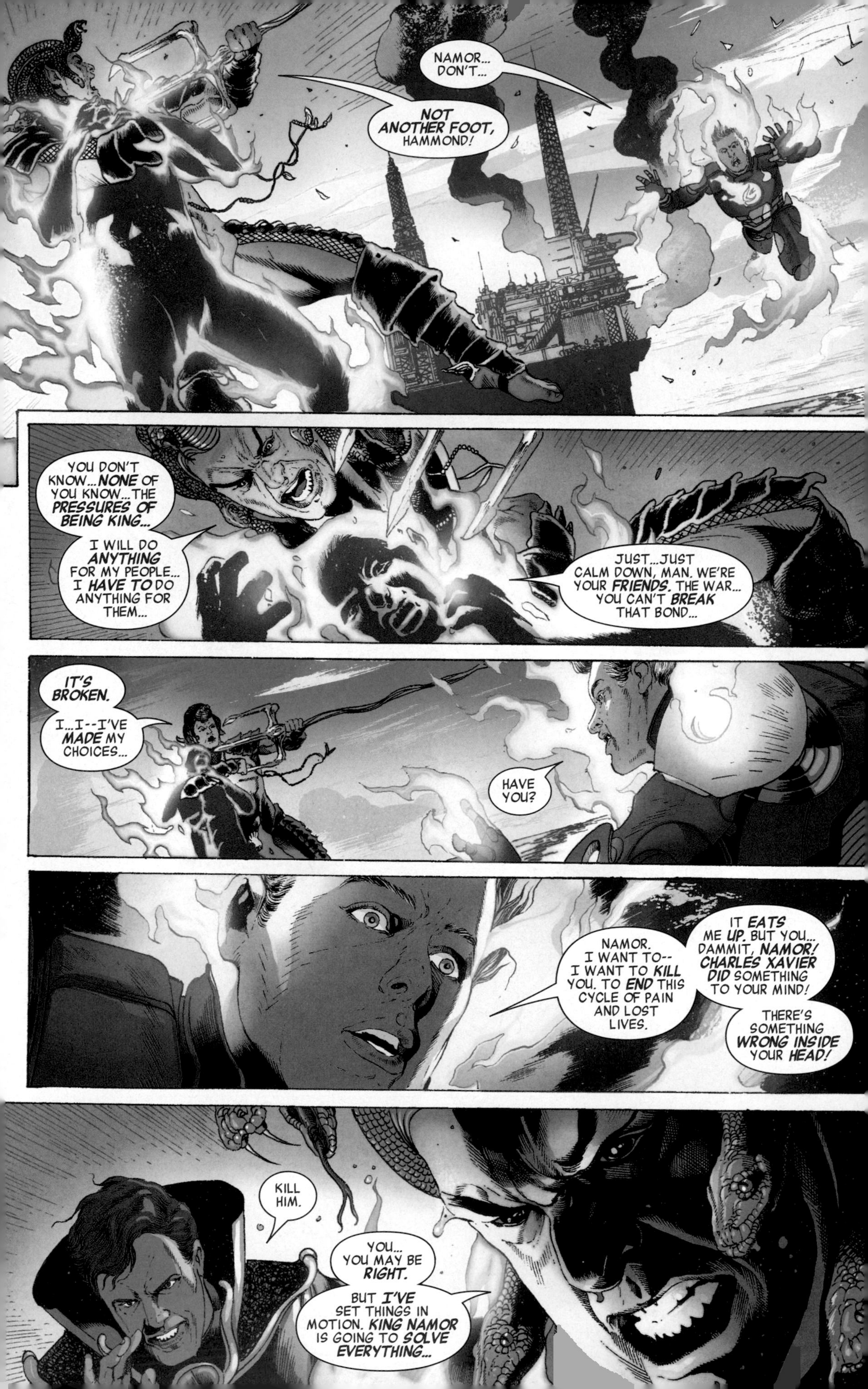
NAMOR... DON'T...
NOT ANOTHER FOOT, HAMMOND!
YOU DON'T KNOW...NONE OF YOU KNOW...THE PRESSURES OF BEING KING...
I WILL DO ANYTHING FOR MY PEOPLE... I HAVE TO DO ANYTHING FOR THEM...
JUST...JUST CALM DOWN, MAN. WE'RE YOUR FRIENDS. THE WAR... YOU CAN'T BREAK THAT BOND...
IT'S BROKEN.
I...I--I'VE MADE MY CHOICES...
HAVE YOU?
NAMOR. I WANT TO-- I WANT TO KILL YOU. TO END THIS CYCLE OF PAIN AND LOST LIVES.
IT EATS ME UP. BUT YOU... DAMMIT, NAMOR! CHARLES XAVIER DID SOMETHING TO YOUR MIND!
THERE'S SOMETHING WRONG INSIDE YOUR HEAD!
KILL HIM.
YOU... YOU MAY BE RIGHT.
BUT I'VE SET THINGS IN MOTION. KING NAMOR IS GOING TO SOLVE EVERYTHING...

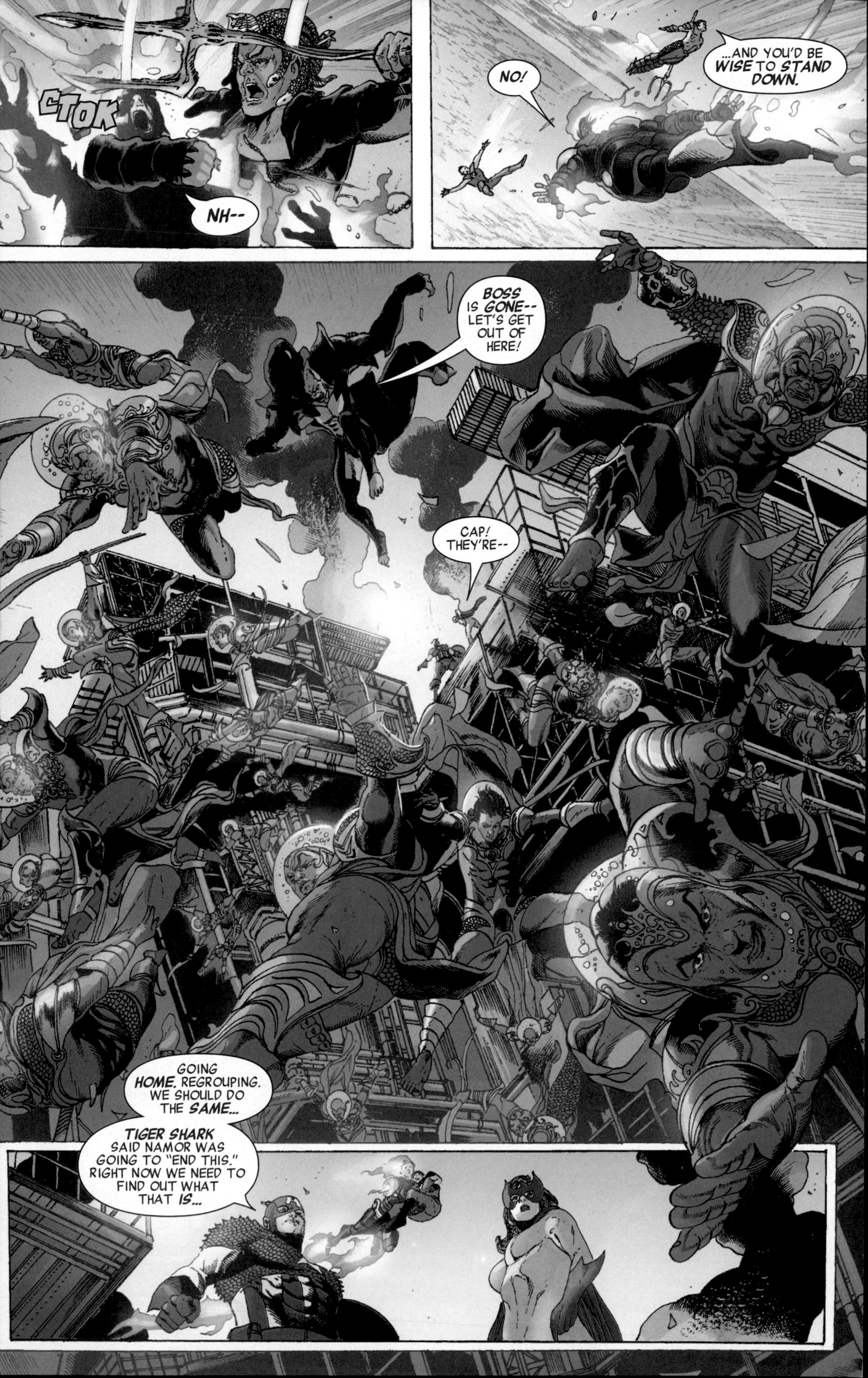
CTOK
NH--
NO!
...AND YOU'D BE WISE TO STAND DOWN.
BOSS IS GONE-- LET'S GET OUT OF HERE!
CAP! THEY'RE--
GOING HOME. REGROUPING. WE SHOULD DO THE SAME...
TIGER SHARK SAID NAMOR WAS GOING TO "END THIS." RIGHT NOW WE NEED TO FIND OUT WHAT THAT IS...

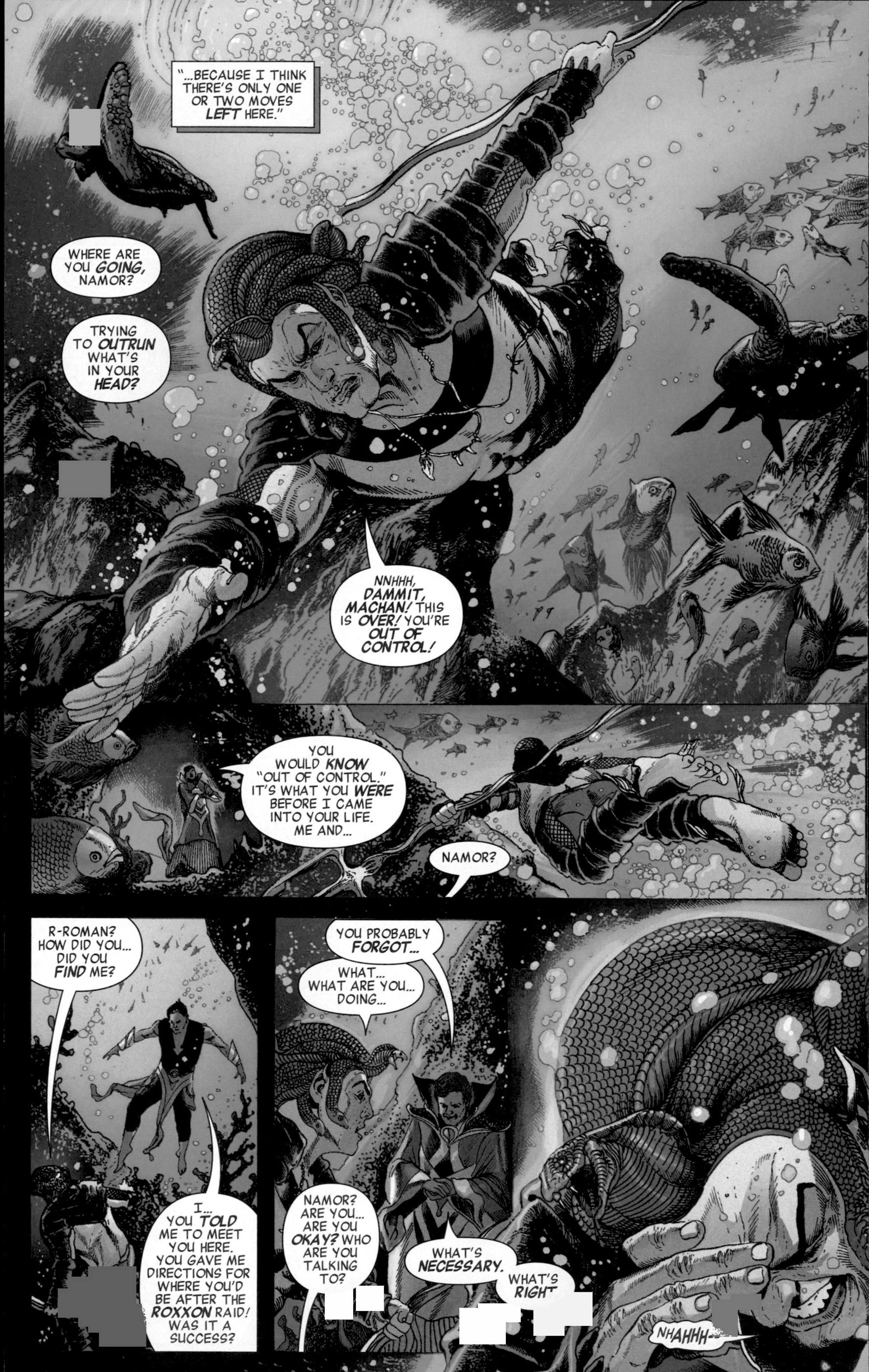
"...BECAUSE I THINK THERE'S ONLY ONE OR TWO MOVES *LEFT* HERE."
WHERE ARE YOU *GOING,* NAMOR?
TRYING TO *OUTRUN* WHAT'S IN YOUR *HEAD?*
NNHHH, *DAMMIT, MACHAN!* THIS IS *OVER!* YOU'RE *OUT OF CONTROL!*
YOU WOULD *KNOW* "OUT OF CONTROL." IT'S WHAT YOU *WERE* BEFORE I CAME INTO YOUR LIFE. ME AND...
NAMOR?
R-ROMAN? HOW DID YOU... DID YOU *FIND* ME?
I... YOU *TOLD* ME TO MEET YOU HERE. YOU GAVE ME DIRECTIONS FOR WHERE YOU'D BE AFTER THE *ROXXON* RAID! WAS IT A SUCCESS?
YOU PROBABLY *FORGOT...*
WHAT... WHAT ARE YOU... DOING...
NAMOR? ARE YOU... ARE YOU *OKAY?* WHO ARE YOU TALKING TO?
WHAT'S *NECESSARY.*
WHAT'S *RIGHT*
NHAHHH-

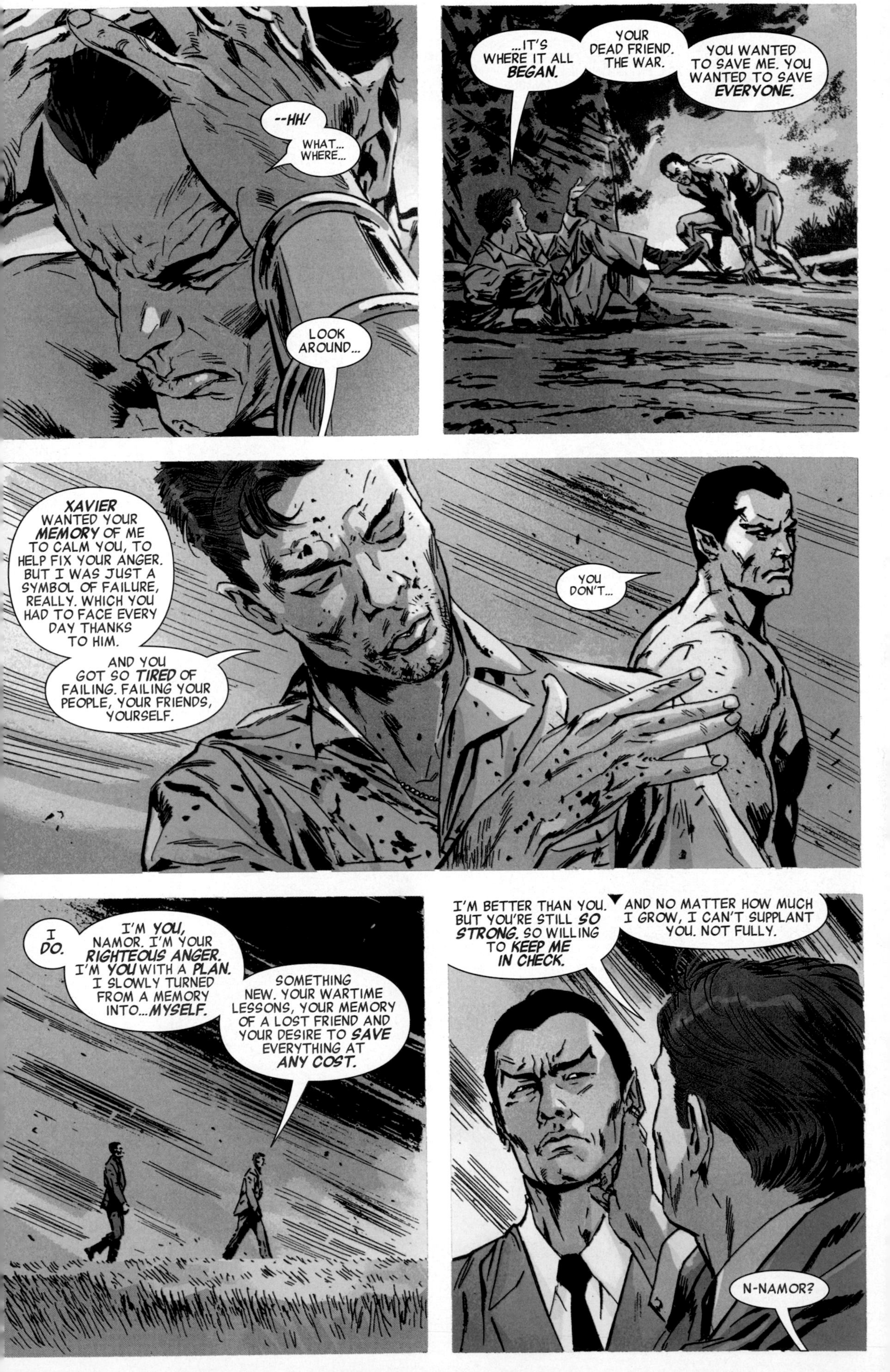
--HH!
WHAT... WHERE...
LOOK AROUND...
...IT'S WHERE IT ALL BEGAN.
YOUR DEAD FRIEND. THE WAR.
YOU WANTED TO SAVE ME. YOU WANTED TO SAVE EVERYONE.
XAVIER WANTED YOUR MEMORY OF ME TO CALM YOU, TO HELP FIX YOUR ANGER. BUT I WAS JUST A SYMBOL OF FAILURE, REALLY. WHICH YOU HAD TO FACE EVERY DAY THANKS TO HIM.
AND YOU GOT SO TIRED OF FAILING. FAILING YOUR PEOPLE, YOUR FRIENDS, YOURSELF.
YOU DON'T...
I DO.
I'M YOU, NAMOR. I'M YOUR RIGHTEOUS ANGER. I'M YOU WITH A PLAN. I SLOWLY TURNED FROM A MEMORY INTO...MYSELF.
SOMETHING NEW. YOUR WARTIME LESSONS, YOUR MEMORY OF A LOST FRIEND AND YOUR DESIRE TO SAVE EVERYTHING AT ANY COST.
I'M BETTER THAN YOU. BUT YOU'RE STILL SO STRONG. SO WILLING TO KEEP ME IN CHECK.
AND NO MATTER HOW MUCH I GROW, I CAN'T SUPPLANT YOU. NOT FULLY.
N-NAMOR?

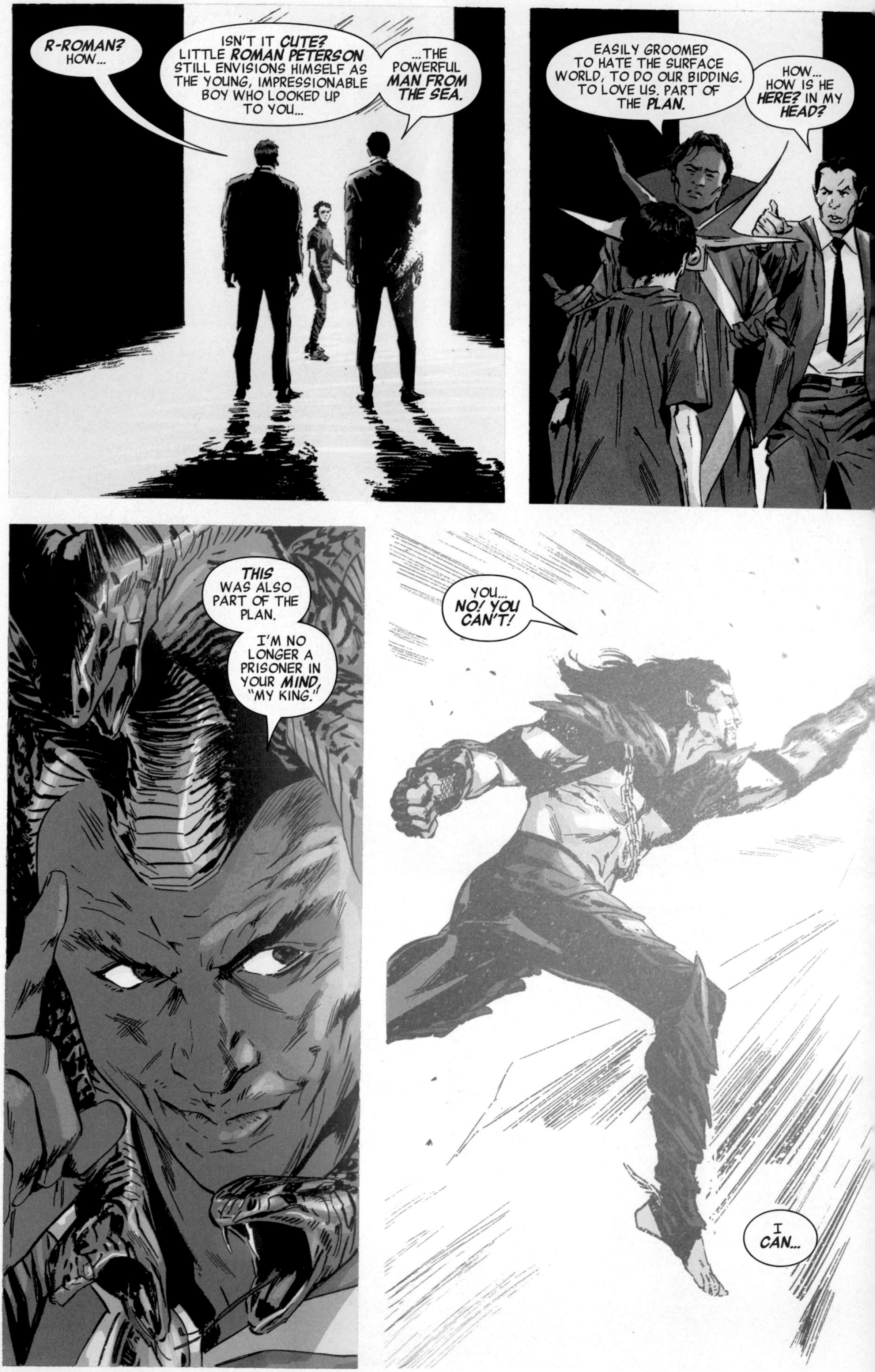
R-ROMAN? HOW...
ISN'T IT CUTE? LITTLE ROMAN PETERSON STILL ENVISIONS HIMSELF AS THE YOUNG, IMPRESSIONABLE BOY WHO LOOKED UP TO YOU...
...THE POWERFUL MAN FROM THE SEA.
EASILY GROOMED TO HATE THE SURFACE WORLD, TO DO OUR BIDDING. TO LOVE US. PART OF THE PLAN.
HOW... HOW IS HE HERE? IN MY HEAD?
THIS WAS ALSO PART OF THE PLAN.
I'M NO LONGER A PRISONER IN YOUR MIND, "MY KING."
YOU... NO! YOU CAN'T!
I CAN...

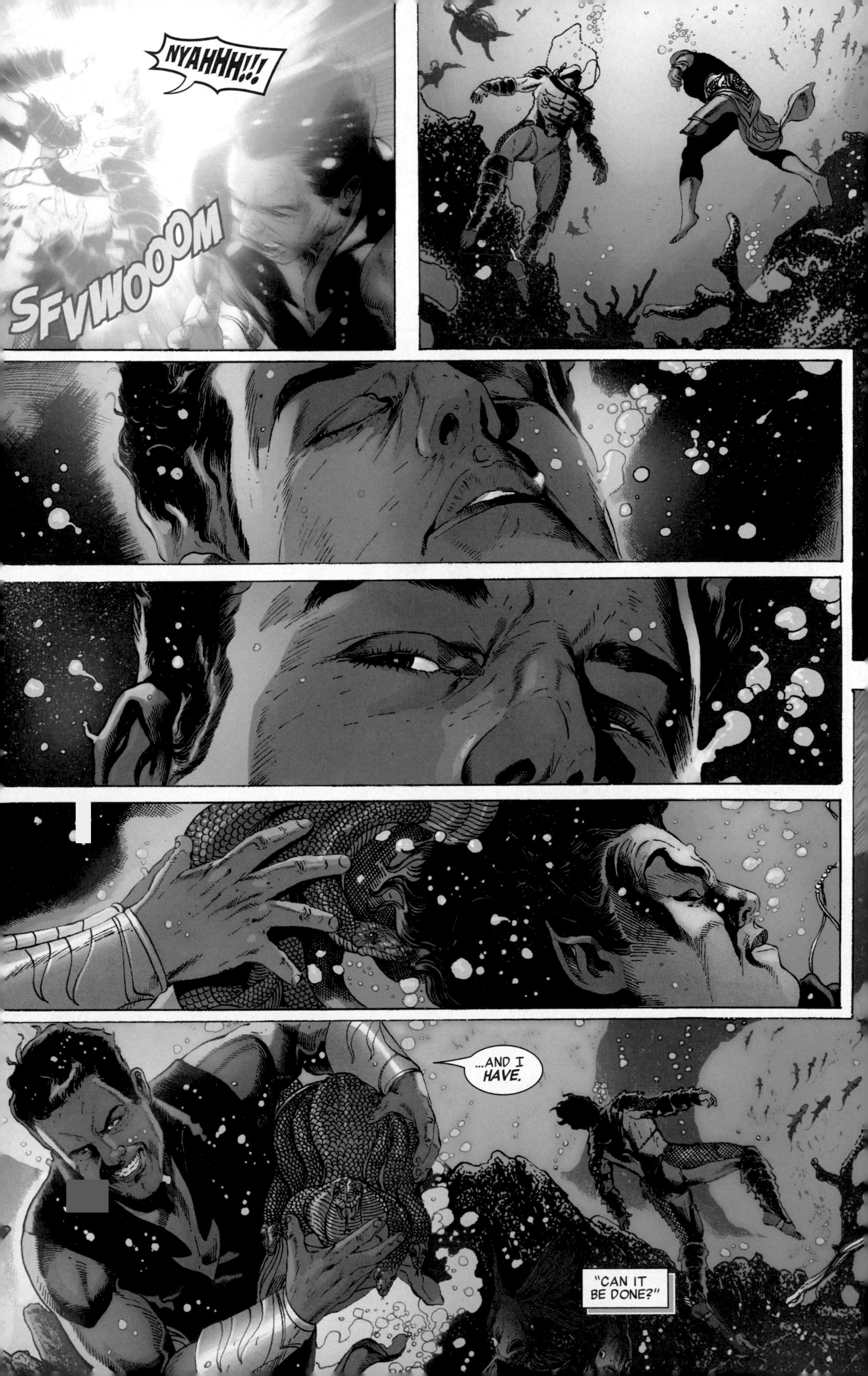
NYAHHH!!!
SFVWOOOM
...AND I HAVE.
"CAN IT BE DONE?"

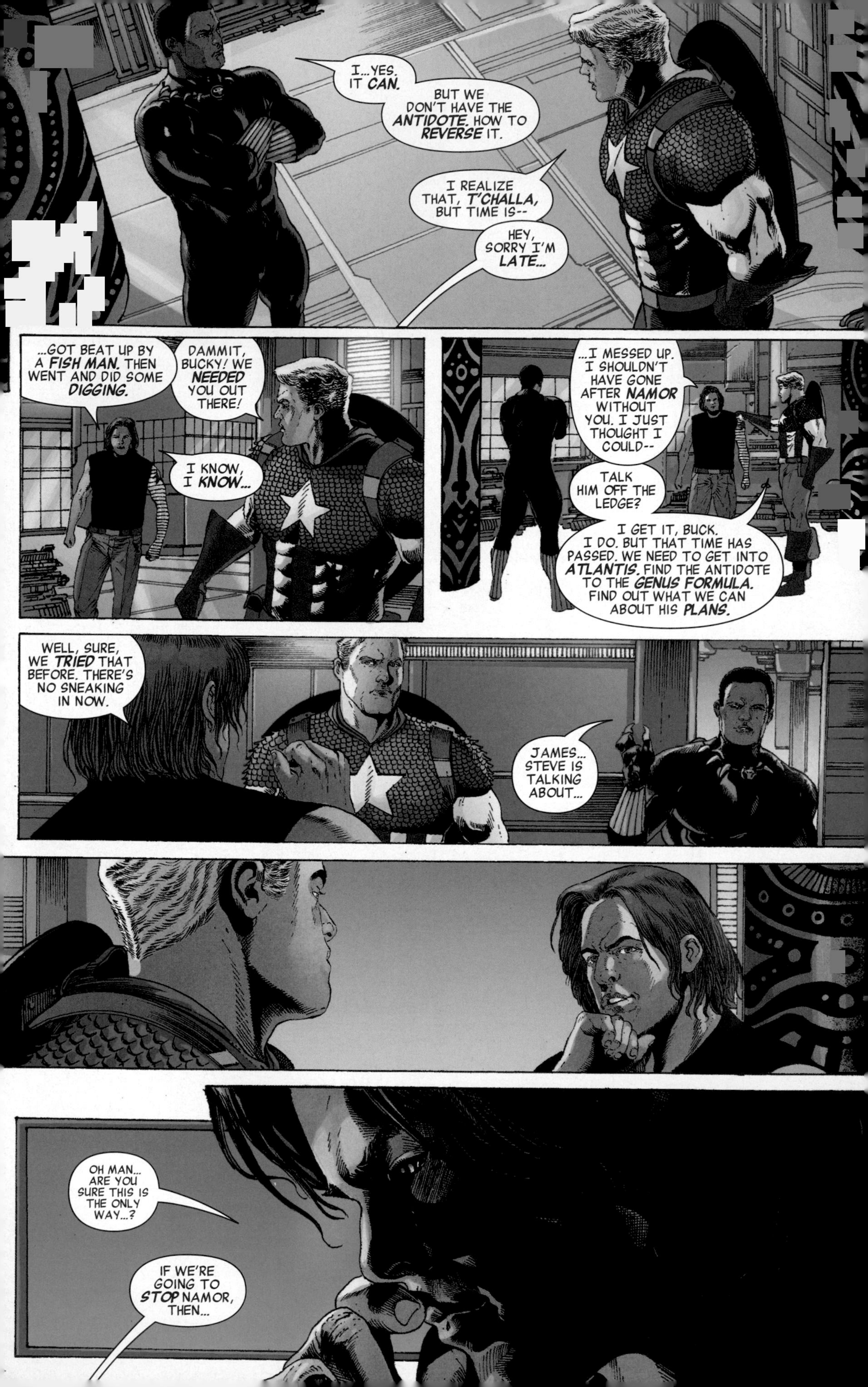

I...YES. IT CAN.
BUT WE DON'T HAVE THE ANTIDOTE. HOW TO REVERSE IT.
I REALIZE THAT, T'CHALLA, BUT TIME IS--
HEY, SORRY I'M LATE...
...GOT BEAT UP BY A FISH MAN. THEN WENT AND DID SOME DIGGING.
DAMMIT, BUCKY! WE NEEDED YOU OUT THERE!
I KNOW, I KNOW...
...I MESSED UP. I SHOULDN'T HAVE GONE AFTER NAMOR WITHOUT YOU. I JUST THOUGHT I COULD--
TALK HIM OFF THE LEDGE?
I GET IT, BUCK. I DO. BUT THAT TIME HAS PASSED. WE NEED TO GET INTO ATLANTIS. FIND THE ANTIDOTE TO THE GENUS FORMULA. FIND OUT WHAT WE CAN ABOUT HIS PLANS.
WELL, SURE, WE TRIED THAT BEFORE. THERE'S NO SNEAKING IN NOW.
JAMES... STEVE IS TALKING ABOUT...
OH MAN... ARE YOU SURE THIS IS THE ONLY WAY...?
IF WE'RE GOING TO STOP NAMOR, THEN...

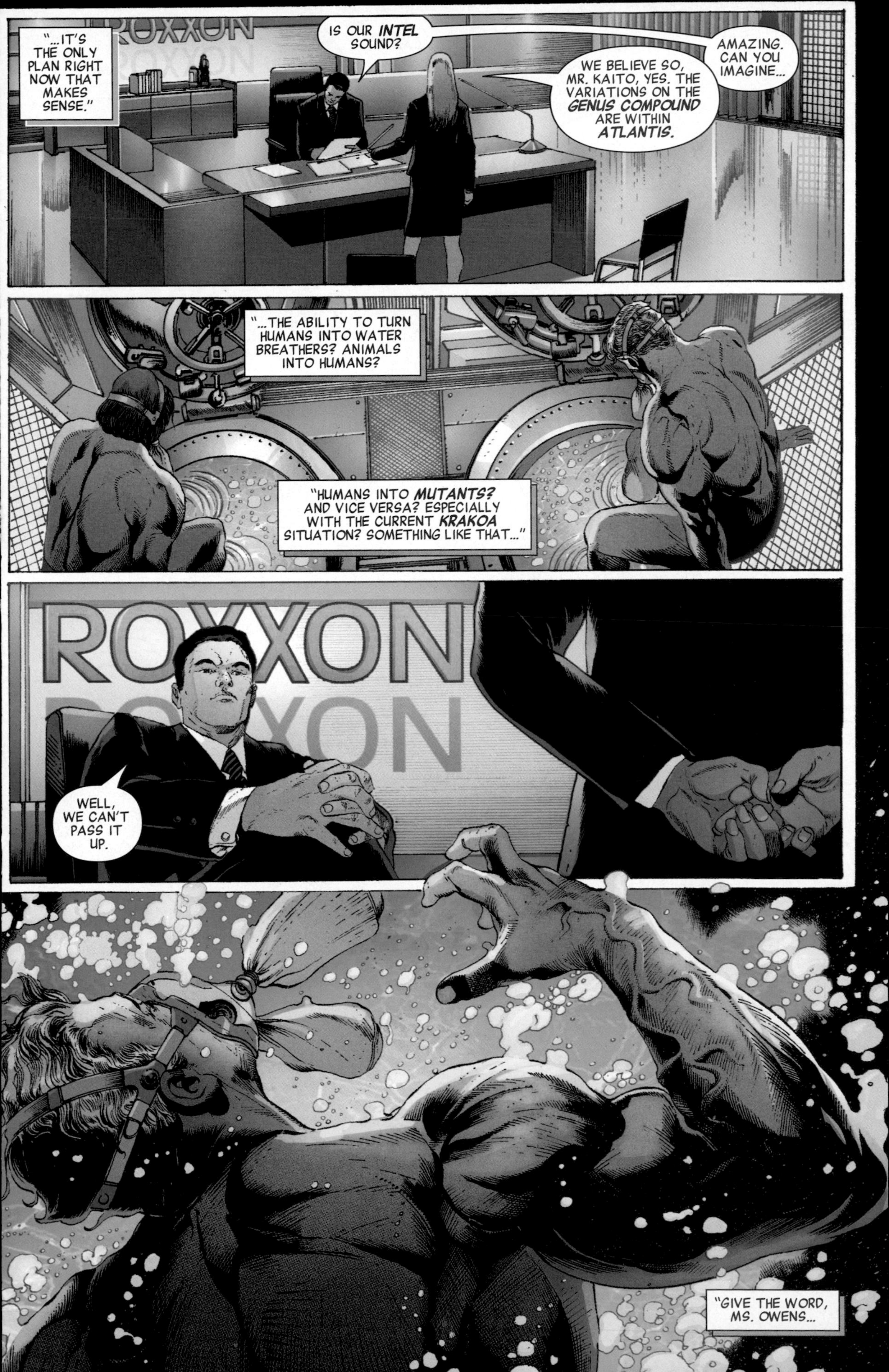
"...IT'S THE ONLY PLAN RIGHT NOW THAT MAKES SENSE."
IS OUR INTEL SOUND?
WE BELIEVE SO, MR. KAITO, YES. THE VARIATIONS ON THE GENUS COMPOUND ARE WITHIN ATLANTIS.
AMAZING. CAN YOU IMAGINE...
"...THE ABILITY TO TURN HUMANS INTO WATER BREATHERS? ANIMALS INTO HUMANS?
"HUMANS INTO MUTANTS? AND VICE VERSA? ESPECIALLY WITH THE CURRENT KRAKOA SITUATION? SOMETHING LIKE THAT..."
ROXXON
WELL, WE CAN'T PASS IT UP.
"GIVE THE WORD, MS. OWENS...

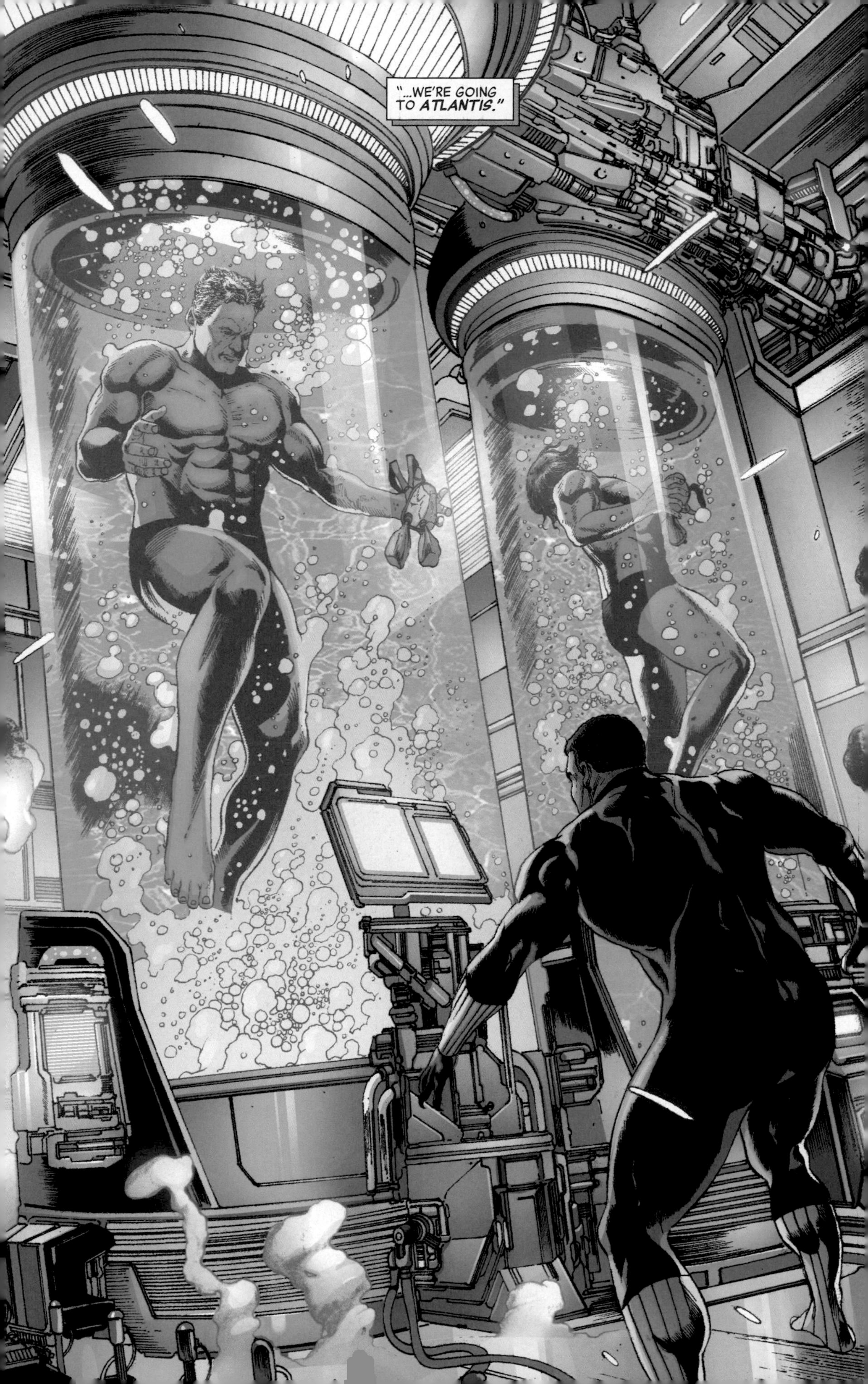
"...WE'RE GOING TO ATLANTIS."

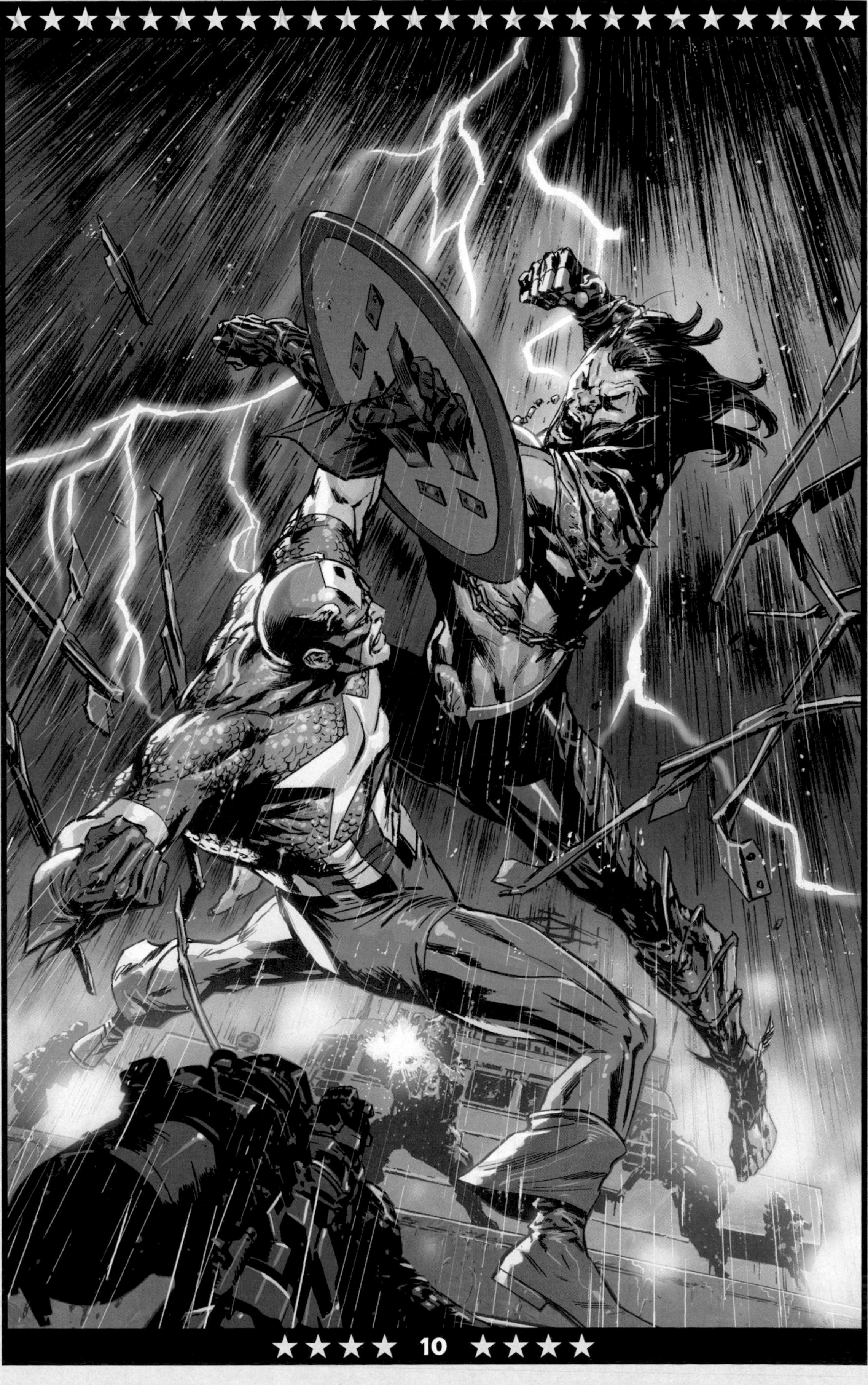

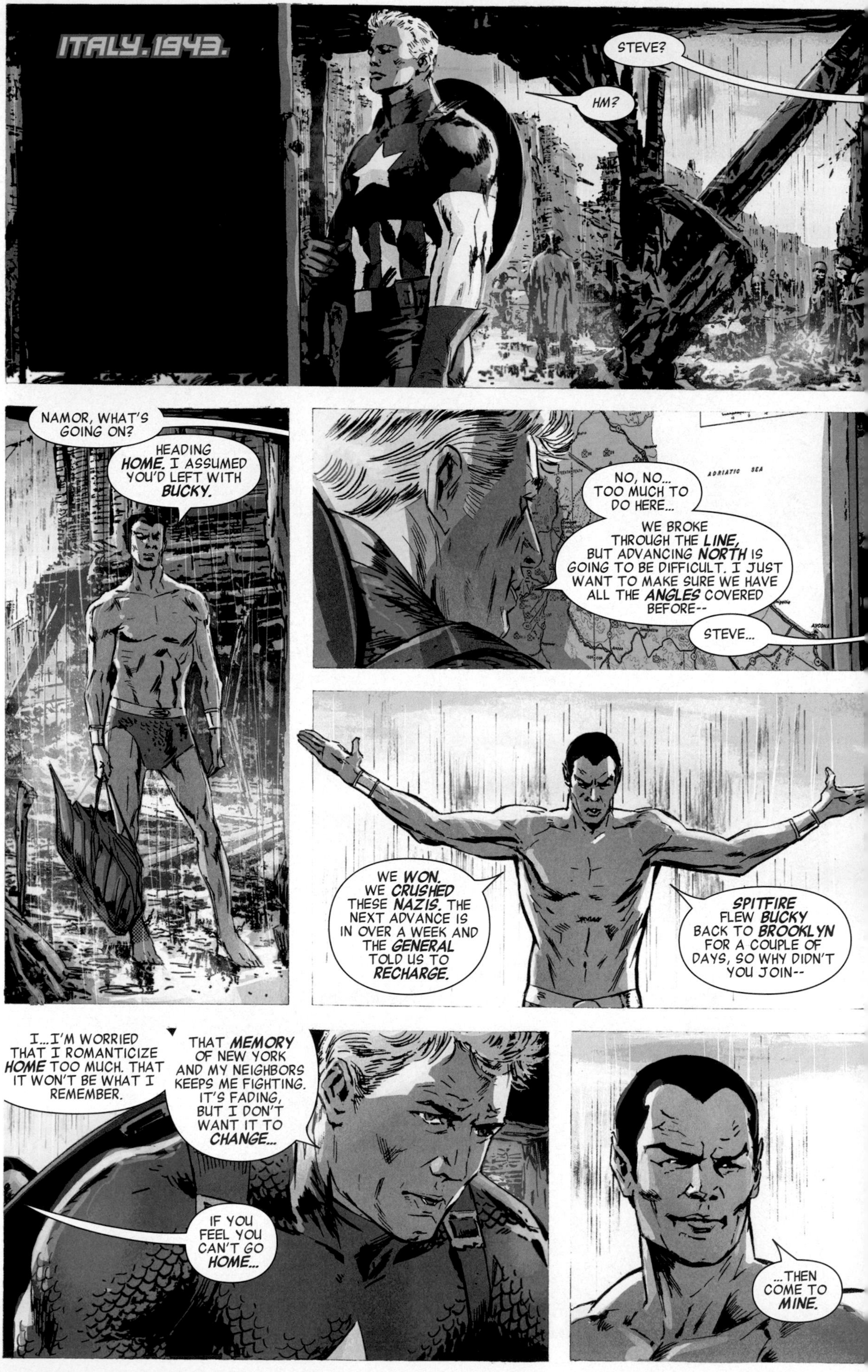
ITALY. 1943.
STEVE?
HM?
NAMOR, WHAT'S GOING ON?
HEADING HOME. I ASSUMED YOU'D LEFT WITH BUCKY.
NO, NO... TOO MUCH TO DO HERE...
WE BROKE THROUGH THE LINE, BUT ADVANCING NORTH IS GOING TO BE DIFFICULT. I JUST WANT TO MAKE SURE WE HAVE ALL THE ANGLES COVERED BEFORE--
STEVE...
ADRIATIC SEA
ANCONA
WE WON. WE CRUSHED THESE NAZIS. THE NEXT ADVANCE IS IN OVER A WEEK AND THE GENERAL TOLD US TO RECHARGE.
SPITFIRE FLEW BUCKY BACK TO BROOKLYN FOR A COUPLE OF DAYS, SO WHY DIDN'T YOU JOIN--
I...I'M WORRIED THAT I ROMANTICIZE HOME TOO MUCH. THAT IT WON'T BE WHAT I REMEMBER.
THAT MEMORY OF NEW YORK AND MY NEIGHBORS KEEPS ME FIGHTING. IT'S FADING, BUT I DON'T WANT IT TO CHANGE...
IF YOU FEEL YOU CAN'T GO HOME...
...THEN COME TO MINE.

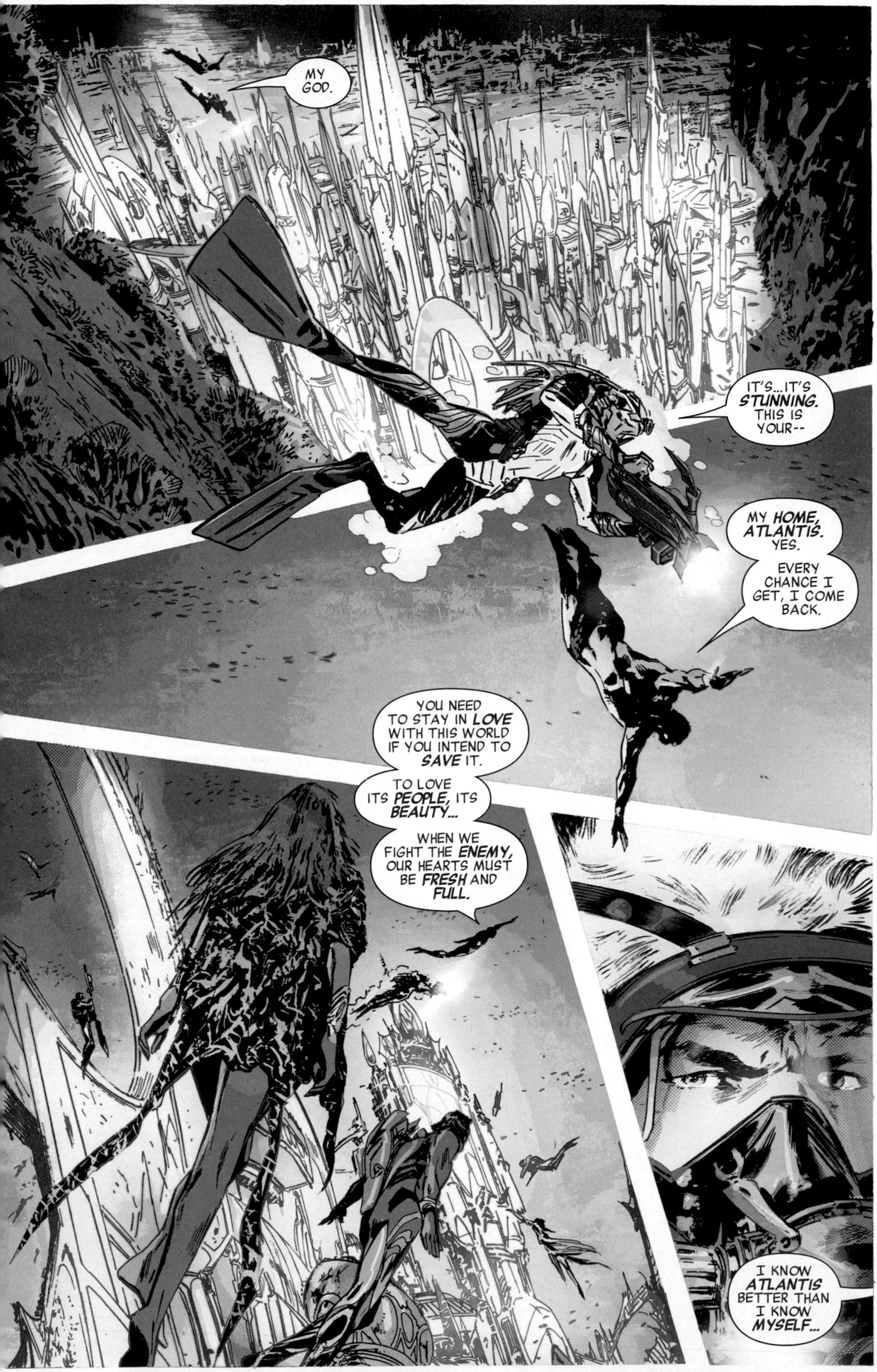
MY GOD.
IT'S...IT'S STUNNING. THIS IS YOUR--
MY HOME, ATLANTIS. YES.
EVERY CHANCE I GET, I COME BACK.
YOU NEED TO STAY IN LOVE WITH THIS WORLD IF YOU INTEND TO SAVE IT.
TO LOVE ITS PEOPLE, ITS BEAUTY...
WHEN WE FIGHT THE ENEMY, OUR HEARTS MUST BE FRESH AND FULL.
I KNOW ATLANTIS BETTER THAN I KNOW MYSELF...

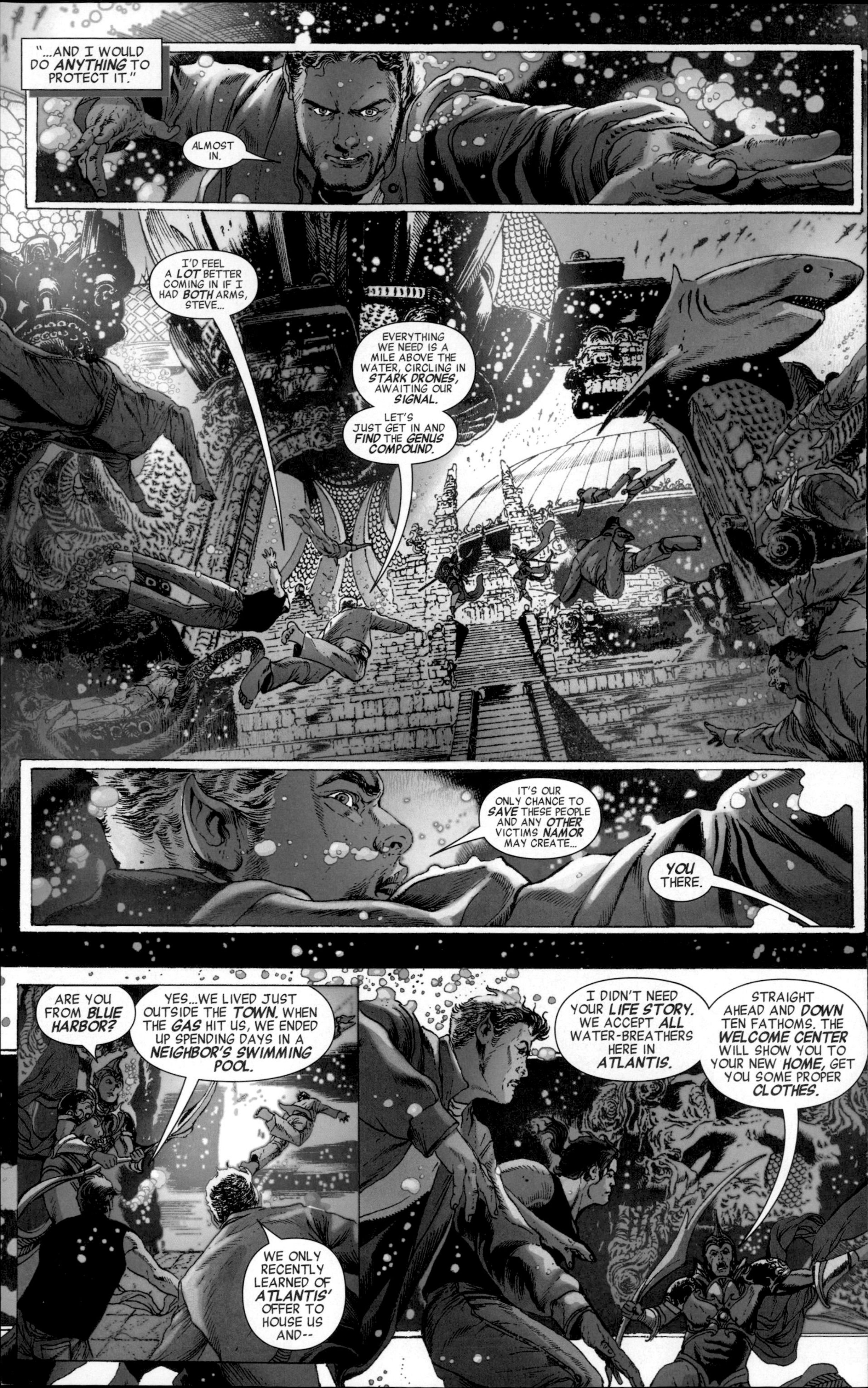
"...AND I WOULD DO ANYTHING TO PROTECT IT."
ALMOST IN.
I'D FEEL A LOT BETTER COMING IN IF I HAD BOTH ARMS, STEVE...
EVERYTHING WE NEED IS A MILE ABOVE THE WATER, CIRCLING IN STARK DRONES, AWAITING OUR SIGNAL.
LET'S JUST GET IN AND FIND THE GENUS COMPOUND.
IT'S OUR ONLY CHANCE TO SAVE THESE PEOPLE AND ANY OTHER VICTIMS NAMOR MAY CREATE...
YOU THERE.
ARE YOU FROM BLUE HARBOR?
YES...WE LIVED JUST OUTSIDE THE TOWN. WHEN THE GAS HIT US, WE ENDED UP SPENDING DAYS IN A NEIGHBOR'S SWIMMING POOL.
WE ONLY RECENTLY LEARNED OF ATLANTIS' OFFER TO HOUSE US AND--
I DIDN'T NEED YOUR LIFE STORY. WE ACCEPT ALL WATER-BREATHERS HERE IN ATLANTIS.
STRAIGHT AHEAD AND DOWN TEN FATHOMS. THE WELCOME CENTER WILL SHOW YOU TO YOUR NEW HOME, GET YOU SOME PROPER CLOTHES.

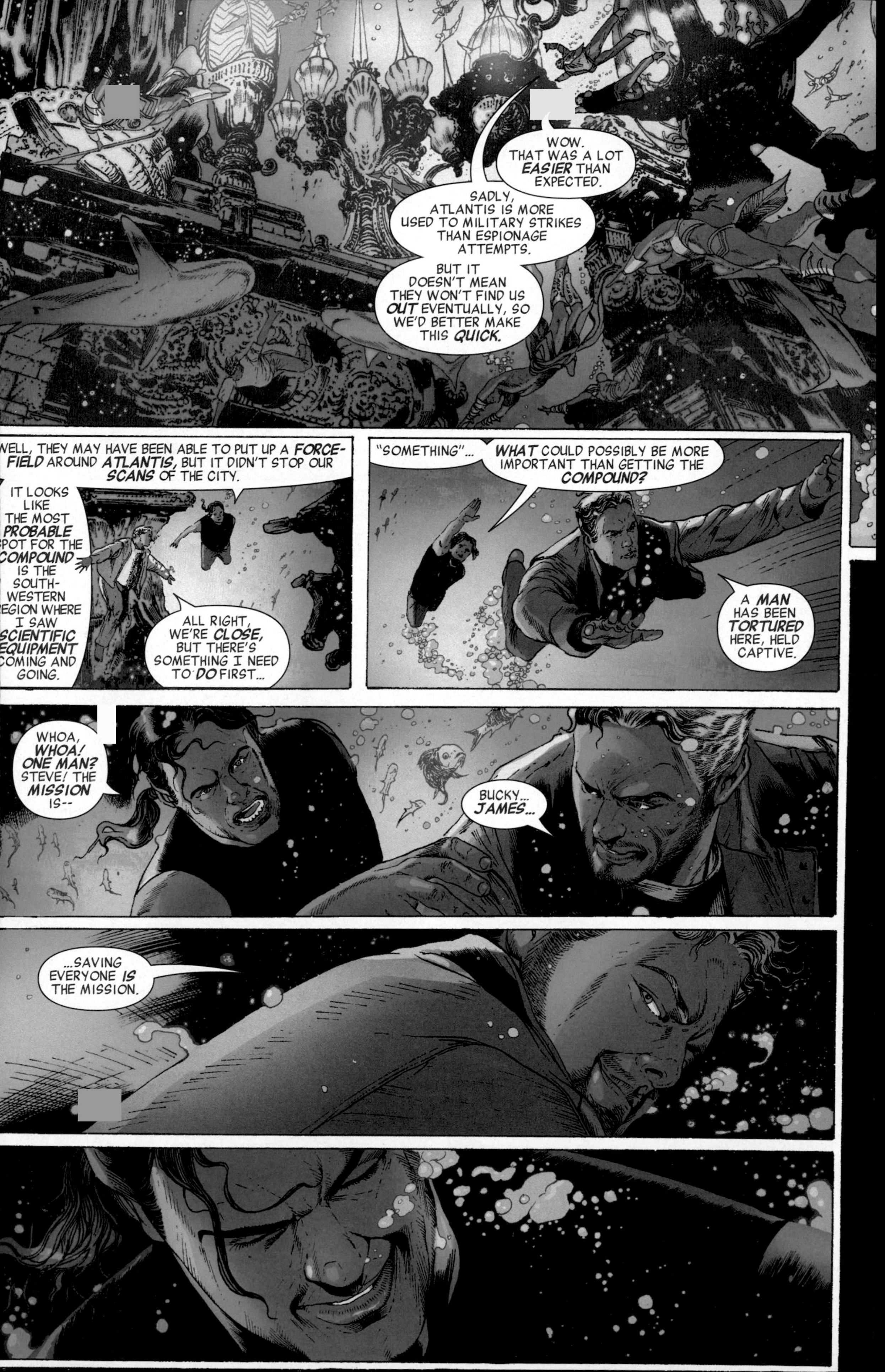
WOW. THAT WAS A LOT EASIER THAN EXPECTED.
SADLY, ATLANTIS IS MORE USED TO MILITARY STRIKES THAN ESPIONAGE ATTEMPTS.
BUT IT DOESN'T MEAN THEY WON'T FIND US OUT EVENTUALLY, SO WE'D BETTER MAKE THIS QUICK.
WELL, THEY MAY HAVE BEEN ABLE TO PUT UP A FORCE-FIELD AROUND ATLANTIS, BUT IT DIDN'T STOP OUR SCANS OF THE CITY.
IT LOOKS LIKE THE MOST PROBABLE SPOT FOR THE COMPOUND IS THE SOUTH-WESTERN REGION WHERE I SAW SCIENTIFIC EQUIPMENT COMING AND GOING.
ALL RIGHT, WE'RE CLOSE, BUT THERE'S SOMETHING I NEED TO DO FIRST...
"SOMETHING"...
WHAT COULD POSSIBLY BE MORE IMPORTANT THAN GETTING THE COMPOUND?
A MAN HAS BEEN TORTURED HERE, HELD CAPTIVE.
WHOA, WHOA! ONE MAN? STEVE! THE MISSION IS--
BUCKY... JAMES...
...SAVING EVERYONE IS THE MISSION.

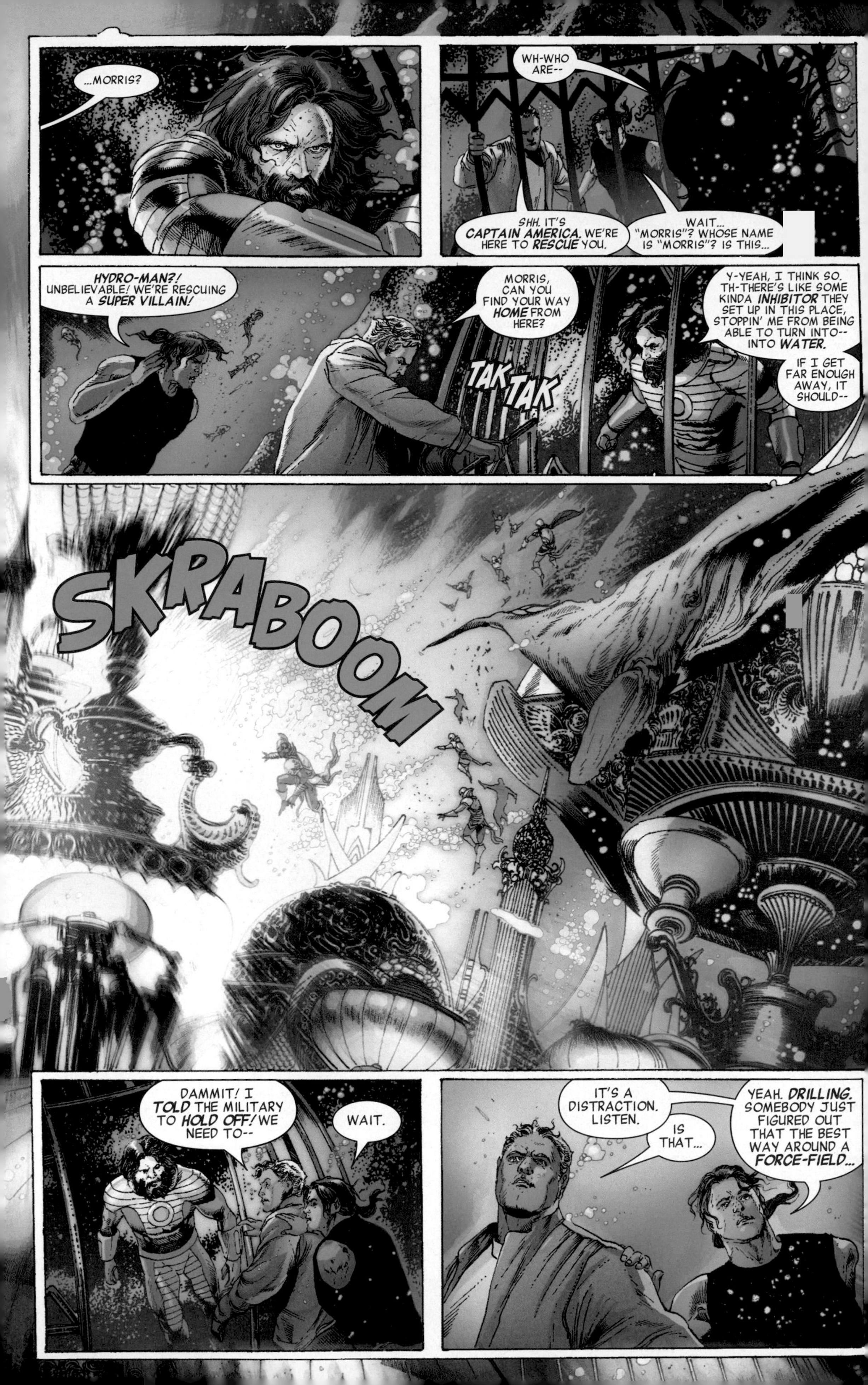

...MORRIS?
WH-WHO ARE--
SHH. IT'S CAPTAIN AMERICA. WE'RE HERE TO RESCUE YOU.
WAIT... "MORRIS"? WHOSE NAME IS "MORRIS"? IS THIS...
HYDRO-MAN?! UNBELIEVABLE! WE'RE RESCUING A SUPER VILLAIN!
MORRIS, CAN YOU FIND YOUR WAY HOME FROM HERE?
TAK TAK
Y-YEAH, I THINK SO. TH-THERE'S LIKE SOME KINDA INHIBITOR THEY SET UP IN THIS PLACE, STOPPIN' ME FROM BEING ABLE TO TURN INTO-- INTO WATER.
IF I GET FAR ENOUGH AWAY, IT SHOULD--
SKRABOOM
DAMMIT! I TOLD THE MILITARY TO HOLD OFF! WE NEED TO--
WAIT.
IT'S A DISTRACTION. LISTEN.
IS THAT...
YEAH. DRILLING. SOMEBODY JUST FIGURED OUT THAT THE BEST WAY AROUND A FORCE-FIELD...

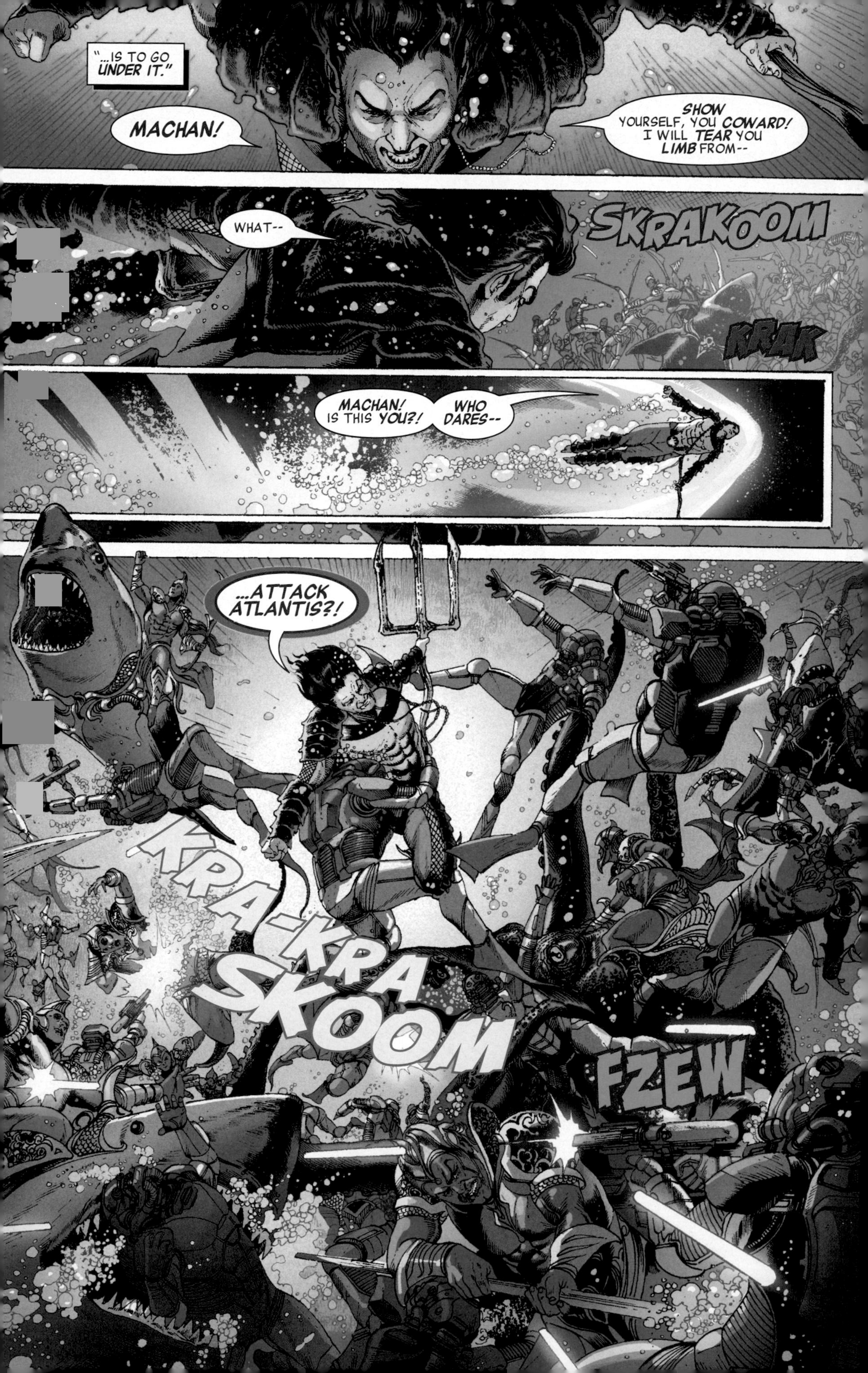
"...IS TO GO UNDER IT."
MACHAN!
SHOW YOURSELF, YOU COWARD! I WILL TEAR YOU LIMB FROM--
WHAT--
SKRAKOOM
KRAK
MACHAN! IS THIS YOU?!
WHO DARES--
...ATTACK ATLANTIS?!
KRA-KRA SKOOM
FZEW

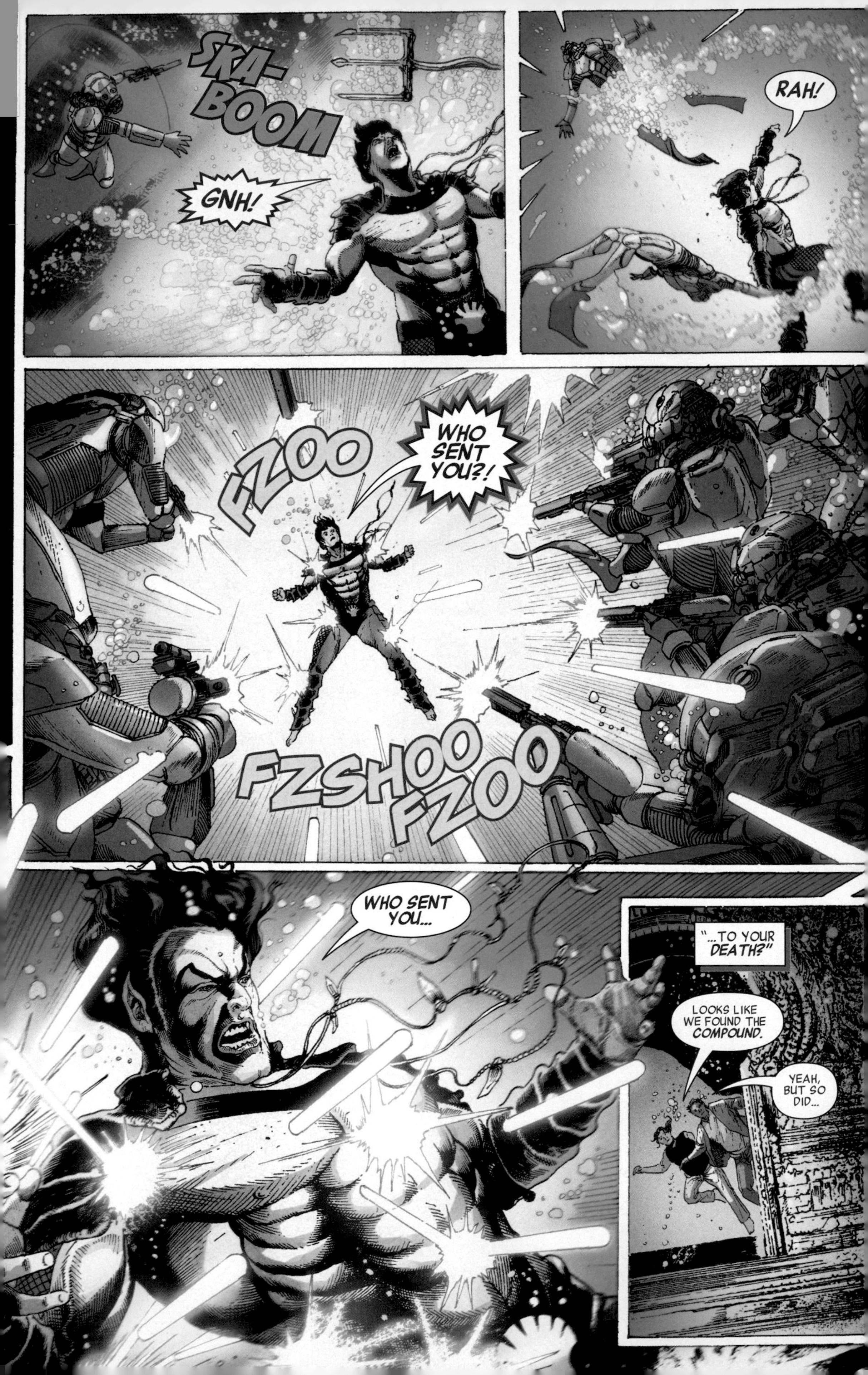
SKA-BOOM
GNH!
RAH!
FZOO
WHO SENT YOU?!
FZSHOO
FZOO
WHO SENT YOU...
"...TO YOUR DEATH?"
LOOKS LIKE WE FOUND THE COMPOUND.
YEAH, BUT SO DID...

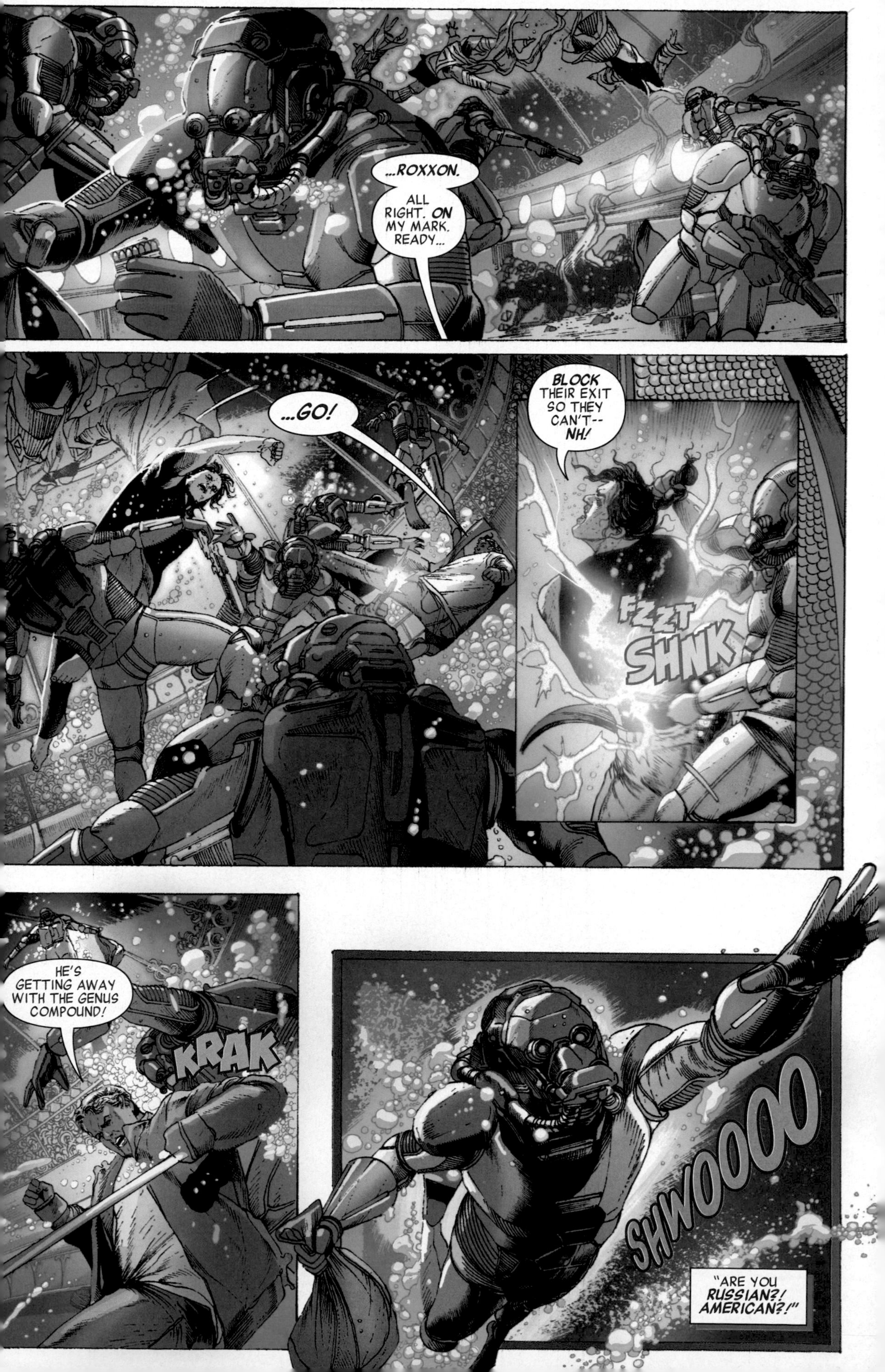
...ROXXON.
ALL RIGHT. ON MY MARK. READY...
...GO!
BLOCK THEIR EXIT SO THEY CAN'T-- NH!
FZZT
SHNK
HE'S GETTING AWAY WITH THE GENUS COMPOUND!
KRAK
SHWOOOO
"ARE YOU RUSSIAN?! AMERICAN?!"

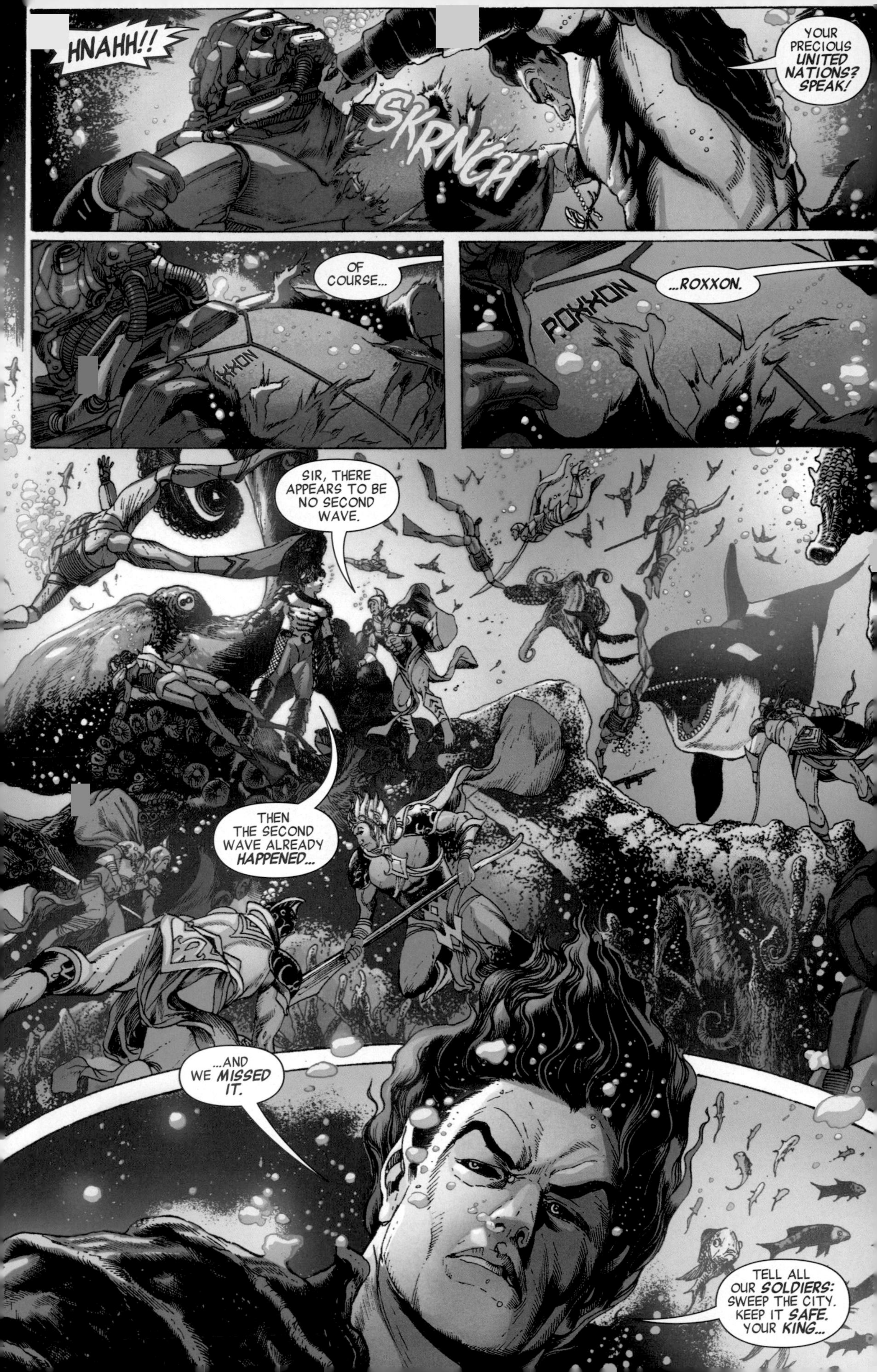
HNAHH!!
SKRNCH
YOUR PRECIOUS UNITED NATIONS? SPEAK!
OF COURSE...
...ROXXON.
ROXXON
SIR, THERE APPEARS TO BE NO SECOND WAVE.
THEN THE SECOND WAVE ALREADY HAPPENED...
...AND WE MISSED IT.
TELL ALL OUR SOLDIERS: SWEEP THE CITY. KEEP IT SAFE. YOUR KING...

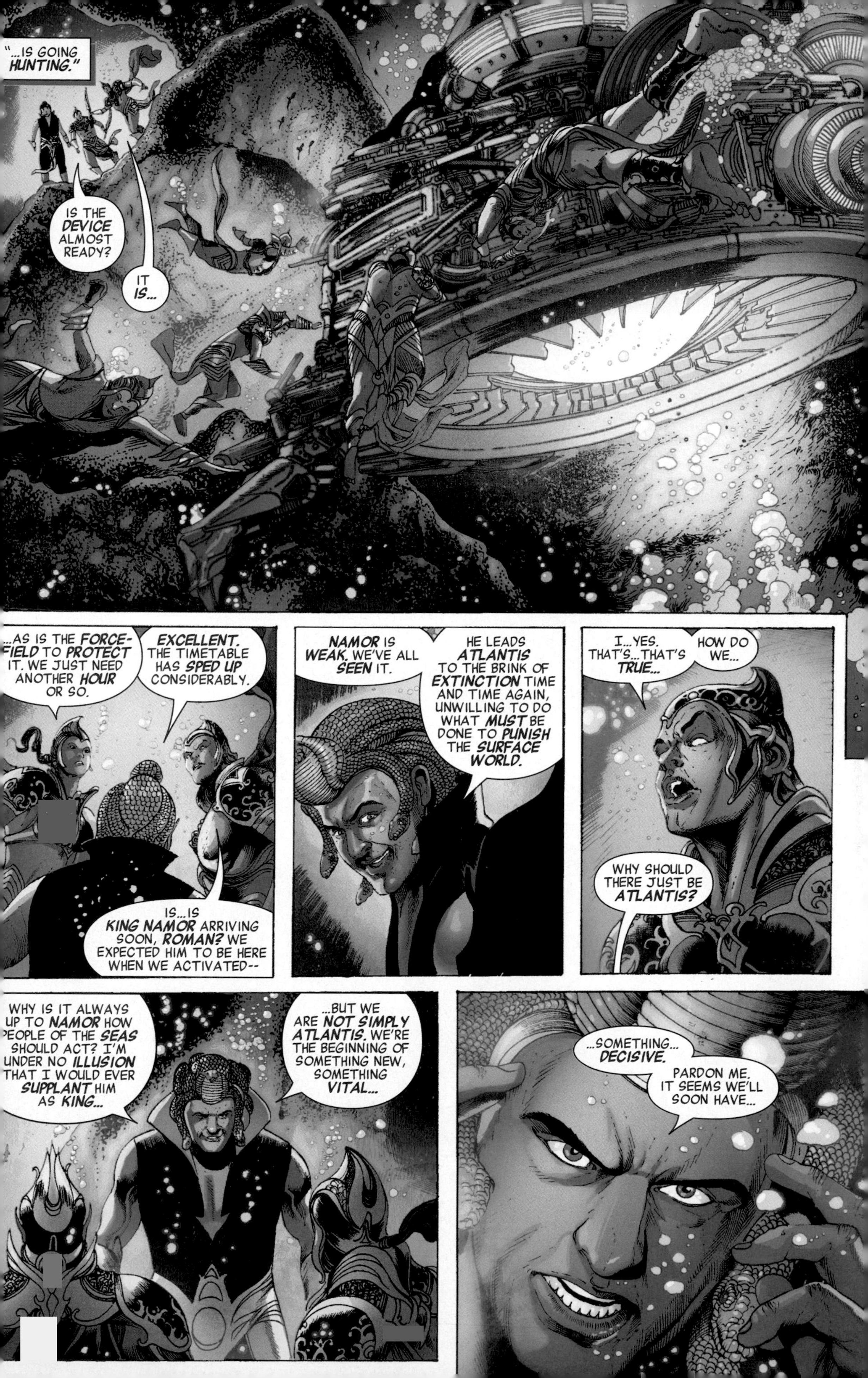
"...IS GOING HUNTING."
IS THE DEVICE ALMOST READY?
IT IS...
...AS IS THE FORCE-FIELD TO PROTECT IT. WE JUST NEED ANOTHER HOUR OR SO.
EXCELLENT. THE TIMETABLE HAS SPED UP CONSIDERABLY.
IS...IS KING NAMOR ARRIVING SOON, ROMAN? WE EXPECTED HIM TO BE HERE WHEN WE ACTIVATED--
NAMOR IS WEAK. WE'VE ALL SEEN IT.
HE LEADS ATLANTIS TO THE BRINK OF EXTINCTION TIME AND TIME AGAIN, UNWILLING TO DO WHAT MUST BE DONE TO PUNISH THE SURFACE WORLD.
I...YES. THAT'S...THAT'S TRUE...
HOW DO WE...
WHY SHOULD THERE JUST BE ATLANTIS?
WHY IS IT ALWAYS UP TO NAMOR HOW PEOPLE OF THE SEAS SHOULD ACT? I'M UNDER NO ILLUSION THAT I WOULD EVER SUPPLANT HIM AS KING...
...BUT WE ARE NOT SIMPLY ATLANTIS. WE'RE THE BEGINNING OF SOMETHING NEW, SOMETHING VITAL...
...SOMETHING... DECISIVE.
PARDON ME. IT SEEMS WE'LL SOON HAVE...

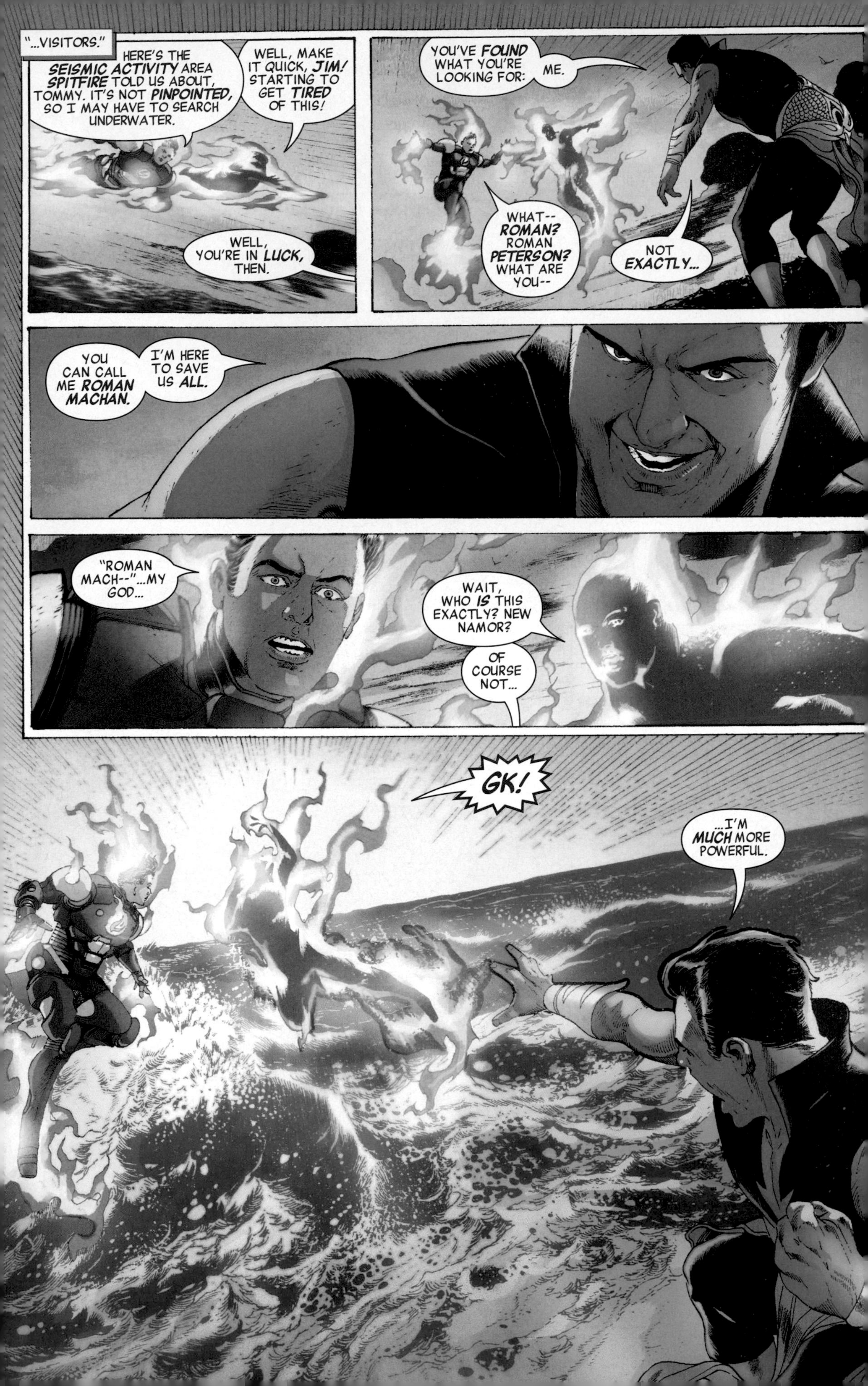
"...VISITORS."
HERE'S THE SEISMIC ACTIVITY AREA SPITFIRE TOLD US ABOUT, TOMMY. IT'S NOT PINPOINTED, SO I MAY HAVE TO SEARCH UNDERWATER.
WELL, MAKE IT QUICK, JIM! STARTING TO GET TIRED OF THIS!
WELL, YOU'RE IN LUCK, THEN.
YOU'VE FOUND WHAT YOU'RE LOOKING FOR:
ME.
WHAT-- ROMAN? ROMAN PETERSON? WHAT ARE YOU--
NOT EXACTLY...
YOU CAN CALL ME ROMAN MACHAN.
I'M HERE TO SAVE US ALL.
"ROMAN MACH--"...MY GOD...
WAIT, WHO IS THIS EXACTLY? NEW NAMOR?
OF COURSE NOT...
GK!
...I'M MUCH MORE POWERFUL.

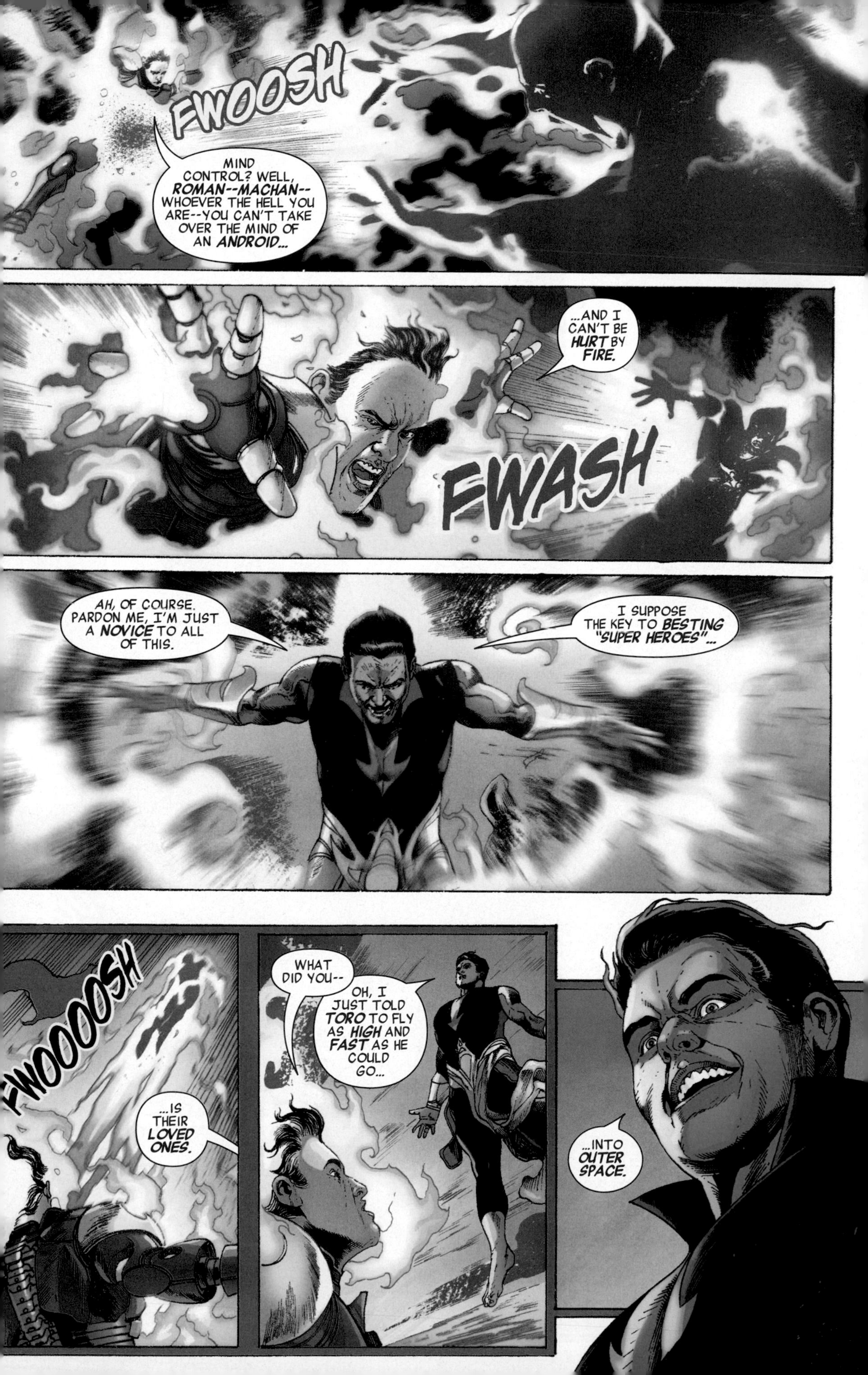
FWOOSH
MIND CONTROL? WELL, ROMAN--MACHAN--WHOEVER THE HELL YOU ARE--YOU CAN'T TAKE OVER THE MIND OF AN ANDROID...
...AND I CAN'T BE HURT BY FIRE.
FWASH
AH, OF COURSE. PARDON ME, I'M JUST A NOVICE TO ALL OF THIS.
I SUPPOSE THE KEY TO BESTING "SUPER HEROES"...
FWOOOOSH
...IS THEIR LOVED ONES.
WHAT DID YOU--
OH, I JUST TOLD TORO TO FLY AS HIGH AND FAST AS HE COULD GO...
...INTO OUTER SPACE.

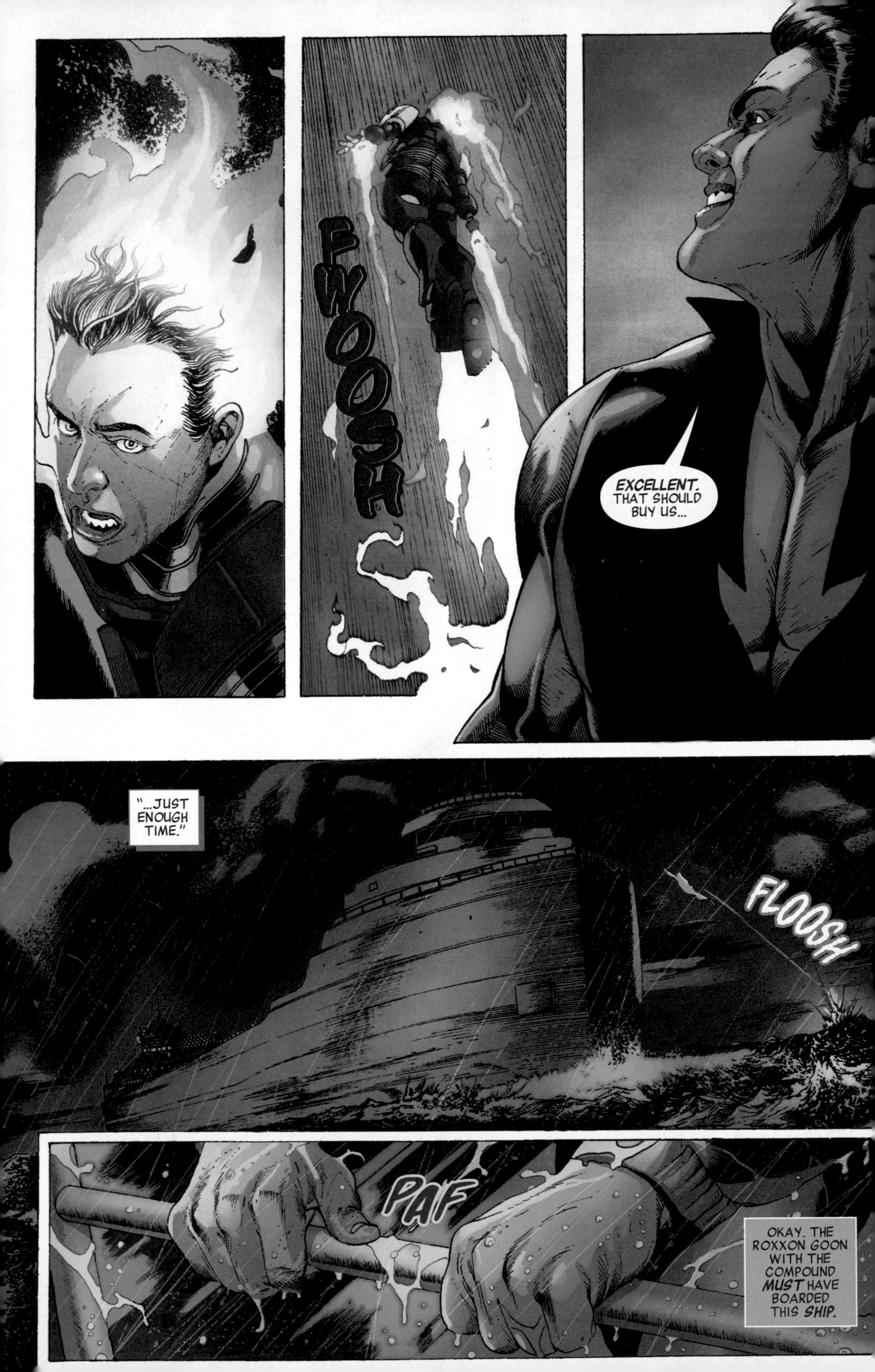
FWOOSH
EXCELLENT. THAT SHOULD BUY US...
"...JUST ENOUGH TIME."
FLOOSH
PAF
OKAY. THE ROXXON GOON WITH THE COMPOUND MUST HAVE BOARDED THIS SHIP.

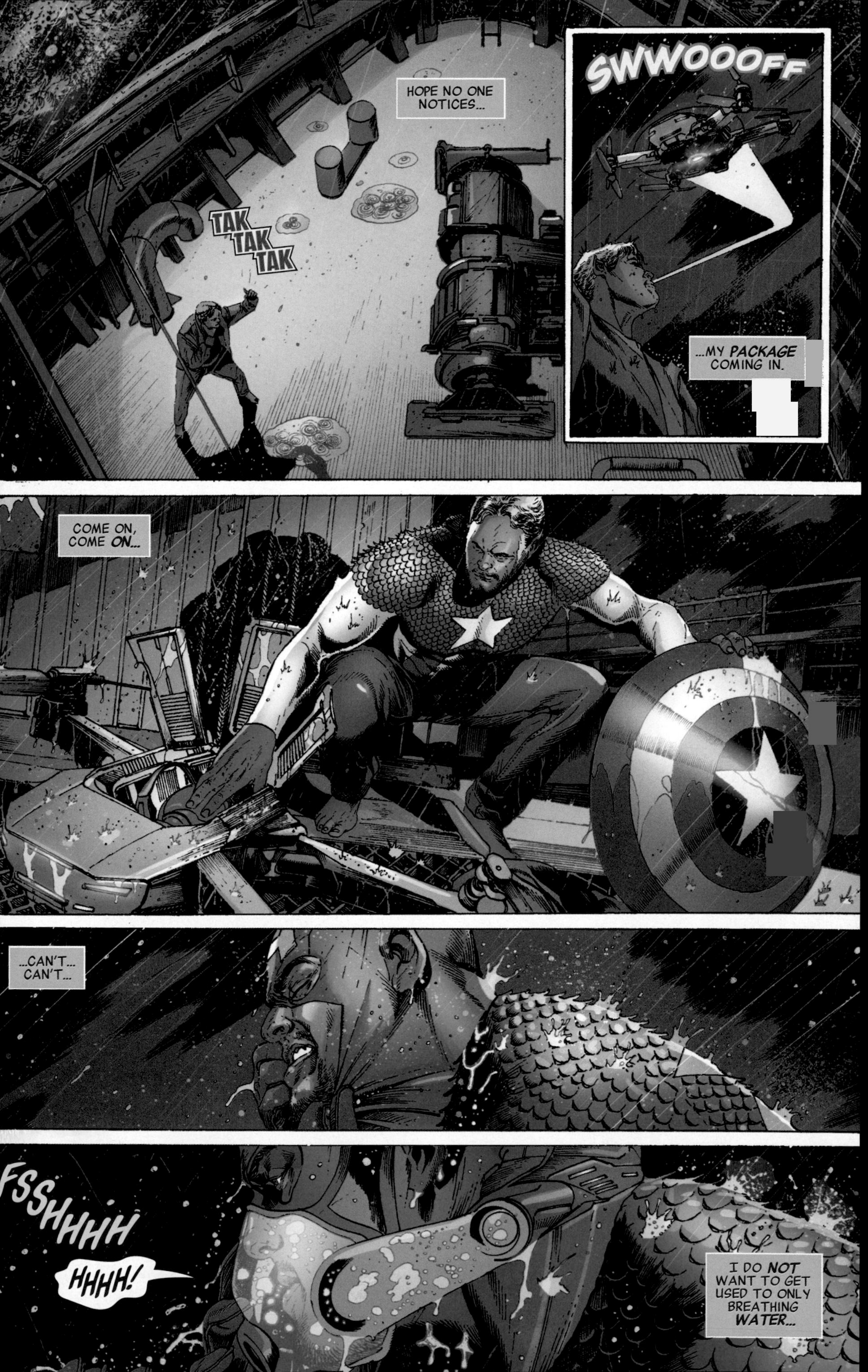
HOPE NO ONE NOTICES...
TAK TAK TAK
SWWOOOFF
...MY PACKAGE COMING IN.
COME ON, COME ON...
...CAN'T... CAN'T...
FSSHHHHH
HHHH!
I DO NOT WANT TO GET USED TO ONLY BREATHING WATER...

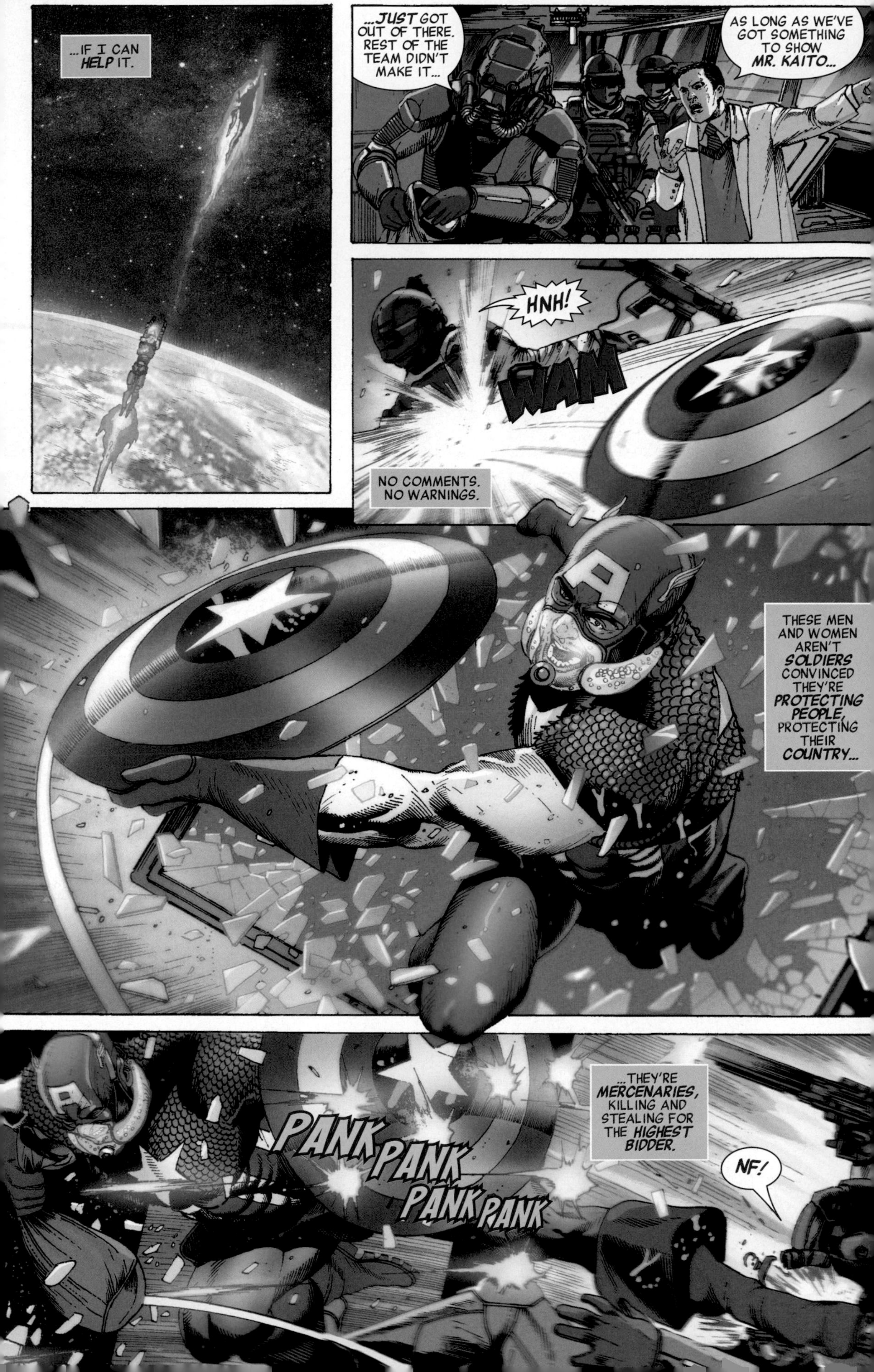
...IF I CAN HELP IT.
...JUST GOT OUT OF THERE. REST OF THE TEAM DIDN'T MAKE IT...
AS LONG AS WE'VE GOT SOMETHING TO SHOW MR. KAITO...
HNH!
WAM
NO COMMENTS. NO WARNINGS.
THESE MEN AND WOMEN AREN'T SOLDIERS CONVINCED THEY'RE PROTECTING PEOPLE, PROTECTING THEIR COUNTRY...
...THEY'RE MERCENARIES, KILLING AND STEALING FOR THE HIGHEST BIDDER.
PANK PANK PANK PANK
NF!

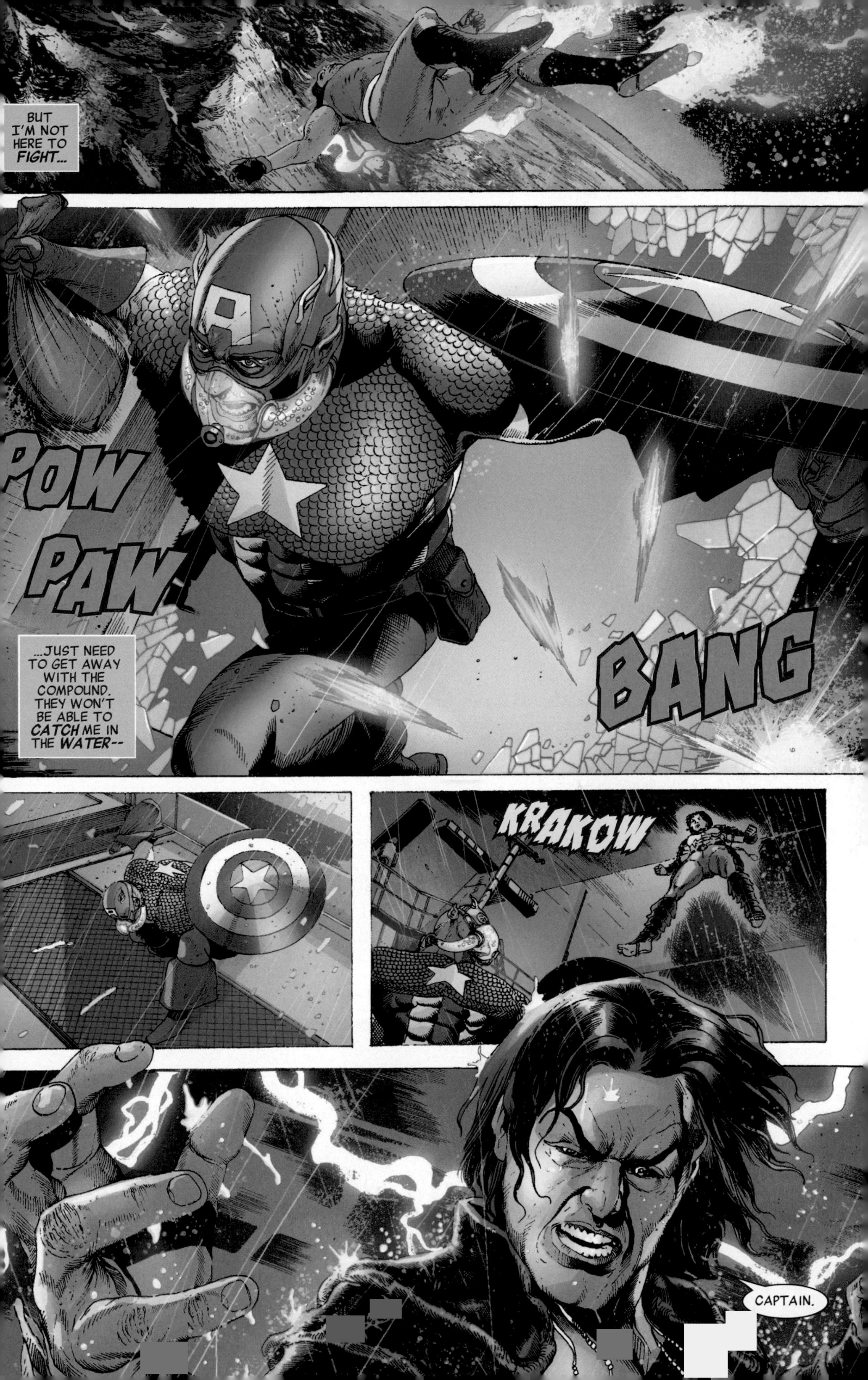
BUT I'M NOT HERE TO FIGHT...
POW
PAW
...JUST NEED TO GET AWAY WITH THE COMPOUND. THEY WON'T BE ABLE TO CATCH ME IN THE WATER--
BANG
KRAKOW
CAPTAIN.

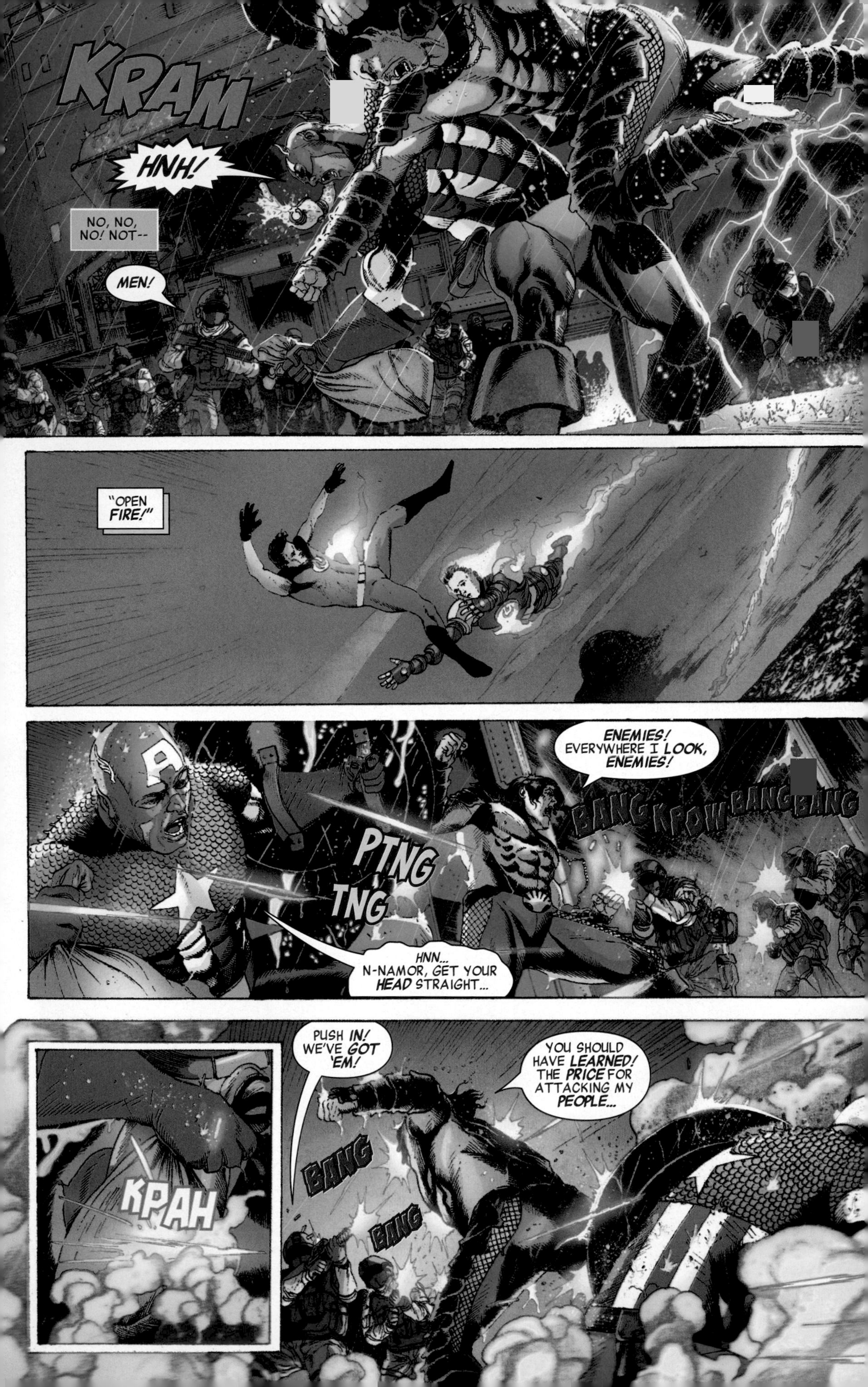
KRAM
HNH!
NO, NO, NO! NOT--
MEN!
"OPEN FIRE!"
ENEMIES! EVERYWHERE I LOOK, ENEMIES!
PTNG
TNG
BANG KRAW BANG BANG
HNN... N-NAMOR, GET YOUR HEAD STRAIGHT...
KPAH
PUSH IN! WE'VE GOT 'EM!
YOU SHOULD HAVE LEARNED! THE PRICE FOR ATTACKING MY PEOPLE...
BANG
BANG

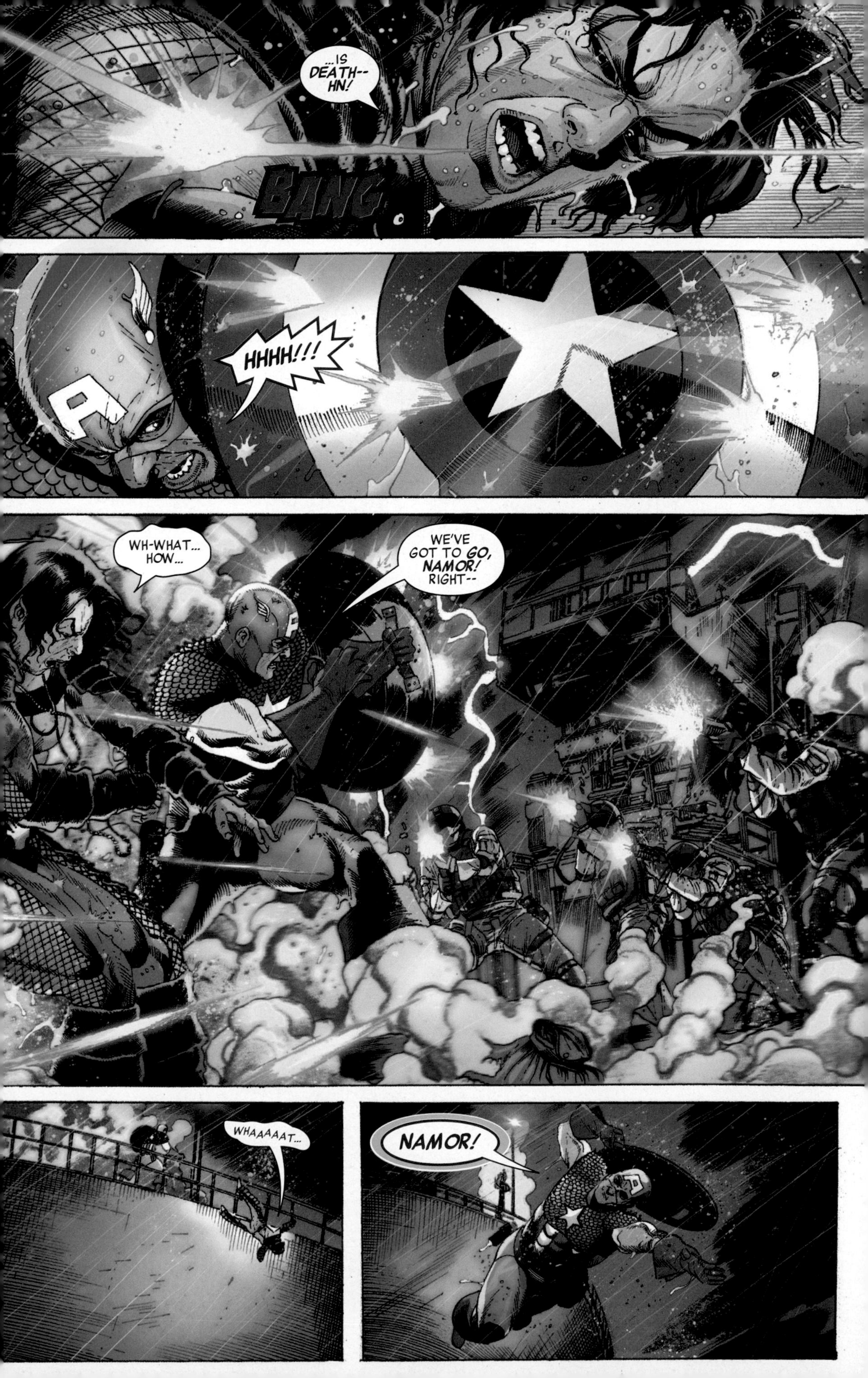
...IS DEATH-- HN!
BANG
HHHH!!!
WH-WHAT... HOW...
WE'VE GOT TO GO, NAMOR! RIGHT--
WHAAAAAT...
NAMOR!

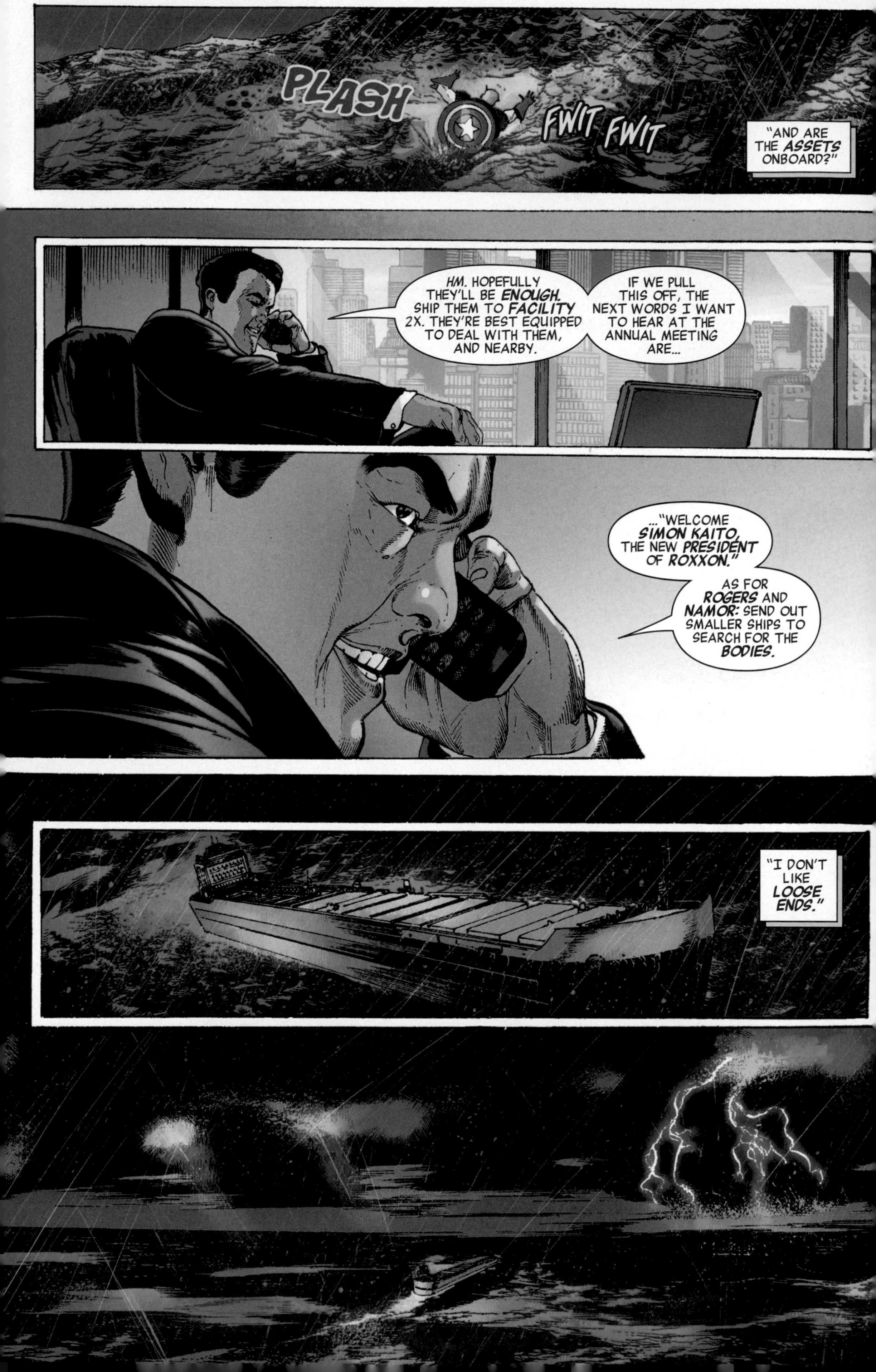
PLASH
FWIT FWIT
"AND ARE THE ASSETS ONBOARD?"
HM. HOPEFULLY THEY'LL BE ENOUGH. SHIP THEM TO FACILITY 2X. THEY'RE BEST EQUIPPED TO DEAL WITH THEM, AND NEARBY.
IF WE PULL THIS OFF, THE NEXT WORDS I WANT TO HEAR AT THE ANNUAL MEETING ARE...
..."WELCOME SIMON KAITO, THE NEW PRESIDENT OF ROXXON."
AS FOR ROGERS AND NAMOR: SEND OUT SMALLER SHIPS TO SEARCH FOR THE BODIES.
"I DON'T LIKE LOOSE ENDS."

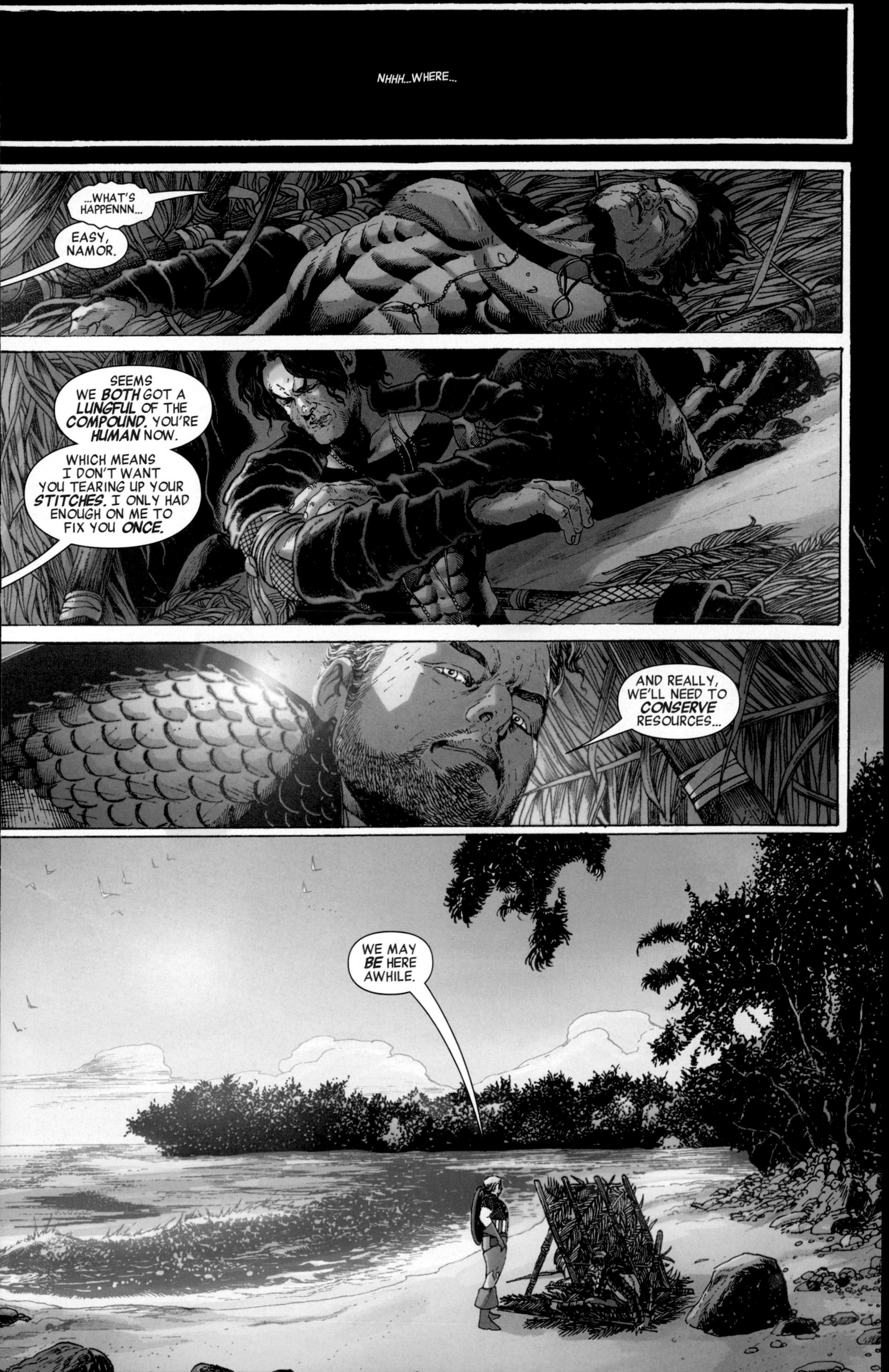
NHHH...WHERE...
...WHAT'S HAPPENNN...
EASY, NAMOR.
SEEMS WE **BOTH** GOT A **LUNGFUL** OF THE **COMPOUND.** YOU'RE **HUMAN** NOW.
WHICH MEANS I DON'T WANT YOU TEARING UP YOUR **STITCHES.** I ONLY HAD ENOUGH ON ME TO FIX YOU **ONCE.**
AND REALLY, WE'LL NEED TO **CONSERVE** RESOURCES...
WE MAY **BE** HERE AWHILE.

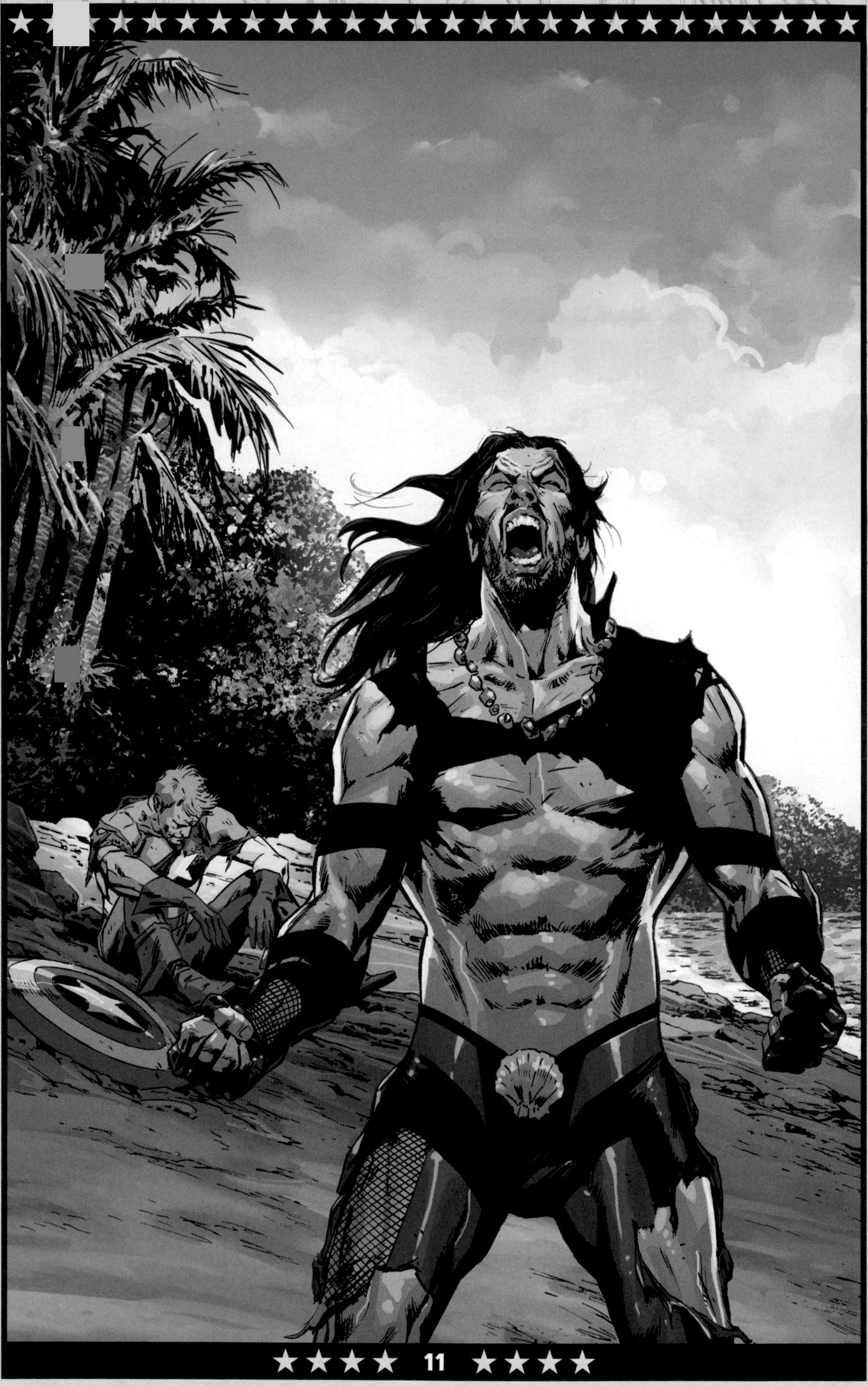

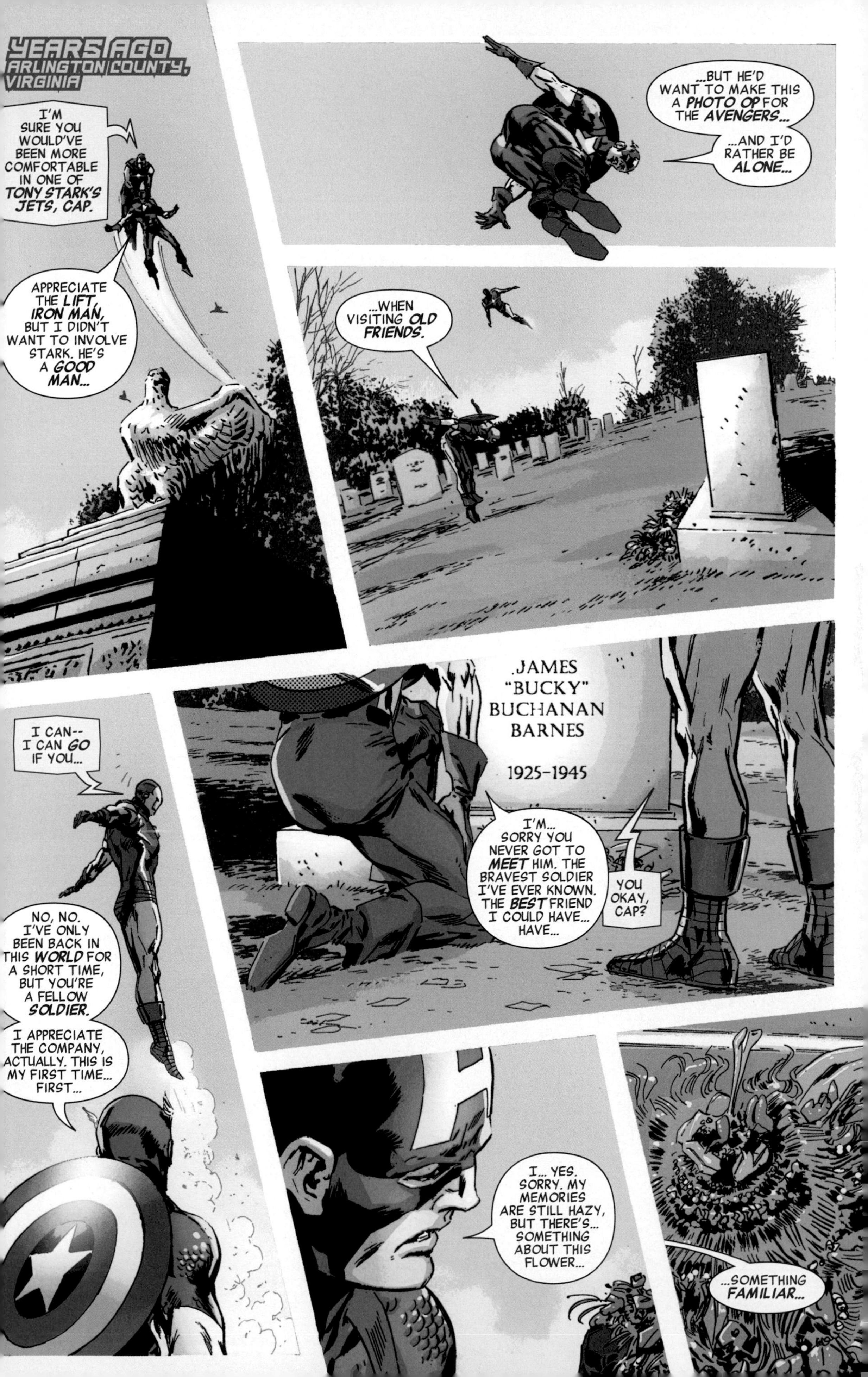

YEARS AGO ARLINGTON COUNTY, VIRGINIA
I'M SURE YOU WOULD'VE BEEN MORE COMFORTABLE IN ONE OF TONY STARK'S JETS, CAP.
APPRECIATE THE LIFT, IRON MAN, BUT I DIDN'T WANT TO INVOLVE STARK. HE'S A GOOD MAN...
...BUT HE'D WANT TO MAKE THIS A PHOTO OP FOR THE AVENGERS...
...AND I'D RATHER BE ALONE...
...WHEN VISITING OLD FRIENDS.
I CAN-- I CAN GO IF YOU...
NO, NO. I'VE ONLY BEEN BACK IN THIS WORLD FOR A SHORT TIME, BUT YOU'RE A FELLOW SOLDIER.
I APPRECIATE THE COMPANY, ACTUALLY. THIS IS MY FIRST TIME... FIRST...
JAMES "BUCKY" BUCHANAN BARNES
1925–1945
I'M... SORRY YOU NEVER GOT TO MEET HIM. THE BRAVEST SOLDIER I'VE EVER KNOWN. THE BEST FRIEND I COULD HAVE... HAVE...
YOU OKAY, CAP?
I... YES. SORRY. MY MEMORIES ARE STILL HAZY, BUT THERE'S... SOMETHING ABOUT THIS FLOWER...
...SOMETHING FAMILIAR...

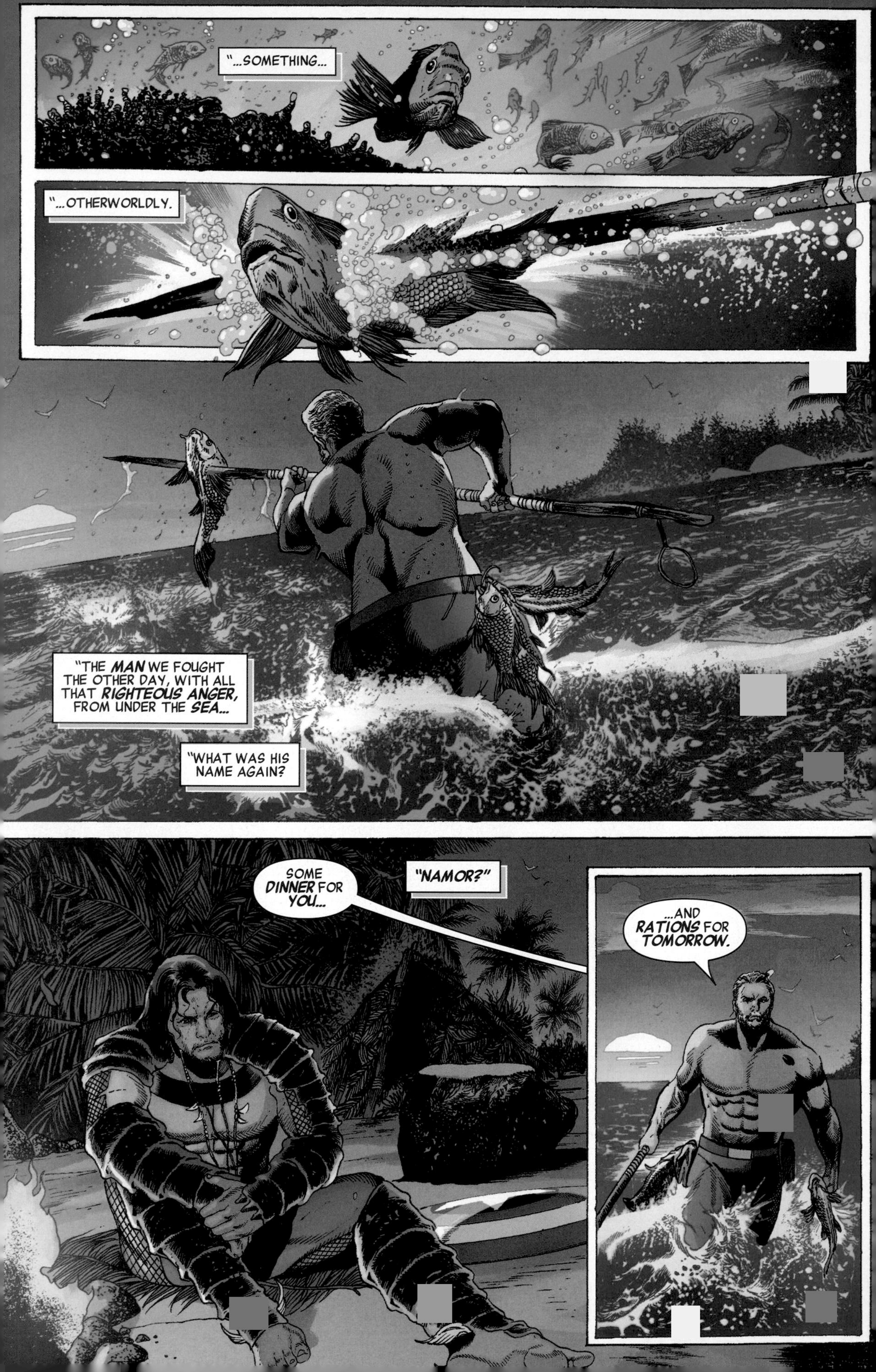
"...SOMETHING...
"...OTHERWORLDLY.
"THE MAN WE FOUGHT THE OTHER DAY, WITH ALL THAT RIGHTEOUS ANGER, FROM UNDER THE SEA...
"WHAT WAS HIS NAME AGAIN?
SOME DINNER FOR YOU...
"NAMOR?"
...AND RATIONS FOR TOMORROW.

I THINK CHARTING **NORTHWEST** IS OUR BEST BET IN THE MORNING. THE SOUNDS I HEARD YESTERDAY SEEMED TO BE COMING FROM THAT DIRECTION.

IF WE CAN FIND OTHERS, THERE'S A CHANCE WE CAN FIGURE OUT A WAY OFF THIS--

DO YOU EVER **TIRE...**

...OF BEING **UNRELENTINGLY** OPTIMISTIC?

WE ARE STRANDED. I AM NOW **HUMAN.**

THE "MAN" WHO INFECTED MY BRAIN IS **HOURS** AWAY FROM SETTING OFF AN **EARTH-CHANGING** DEVICE.

AND HERE YOU ARE, THE GREAT "CAPTAIN AMERICA," PLANNING HIS NEXT MOVES, WHEN THE NEXT MOVE FOR BOTH OF US...

...IS **DEATH.**

NAMOR, YOU'RE CONSTANTLY REMINDING ME-- **ALL** OF US-- THAT YOU'RE A **KING.**

BUT A **KING,** A **LEADER,** DOESN'T GIVE UP. ESPECIALLY WHEN PEOPLE ARE IN DANGER.

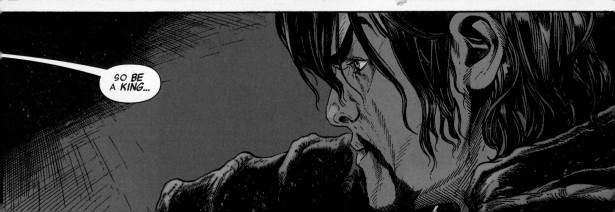

SO **BE** A KING...

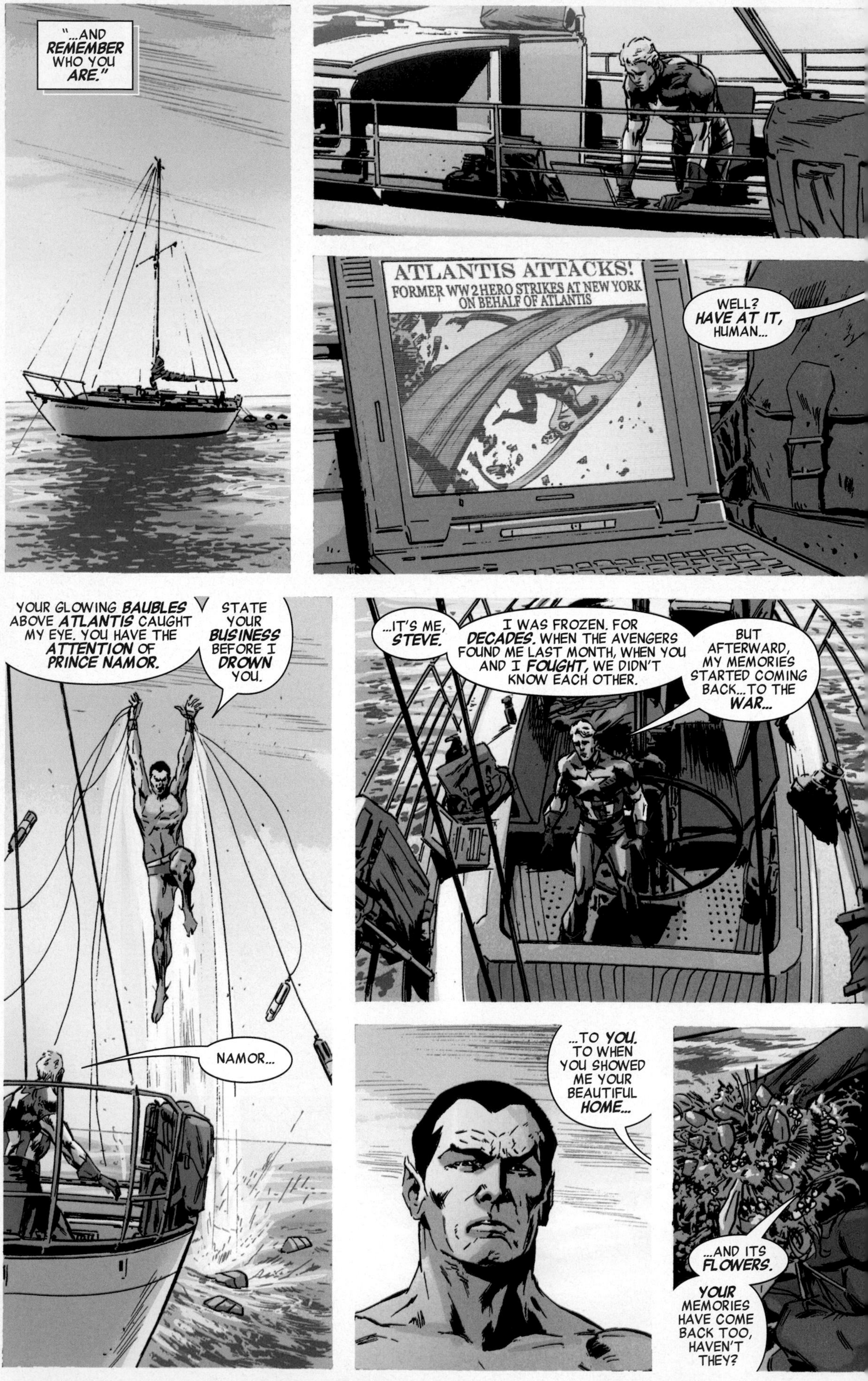
"...AND REMEMBER WHO YOU ARE."
ATLANTIS ATTACKS!
FORMER WW 2 HERO STRIKES AT NEW YORK ON BEHALF OF ATLANTIS
WELL? HAVE AT IT, HUMAN...
YOUR GLOWING BAUBLES ABOVE ATLANTIS CAUGHT MY EYE. YOU HAVE THE ATTENTION OF PRINCE NAMOR.
STATE YOUR BUSINESS BEFORE I DROWN YOU.
NAMOR...
...IT'S ME, STEVE.
I WAS FROZEN. FOR DECADES. WHEN THE AVENGERS FOUND ME LAST MONTH, WHEN YOU AND I FOUGHT, WE DIDN'T KNOW EACH OTHER.
BUT AFTERWARD, MY MEMORIES STARTED COMING BACK...TO THE WAR...
...TO YOU. TO WHEN YOU SHOWED ME YOUR BEAUTIFUL HOME...
...AND ITS FLOWERS.
YOUR MEMORIES HAVE COME BACK TOO, HAVEN'T THEY?

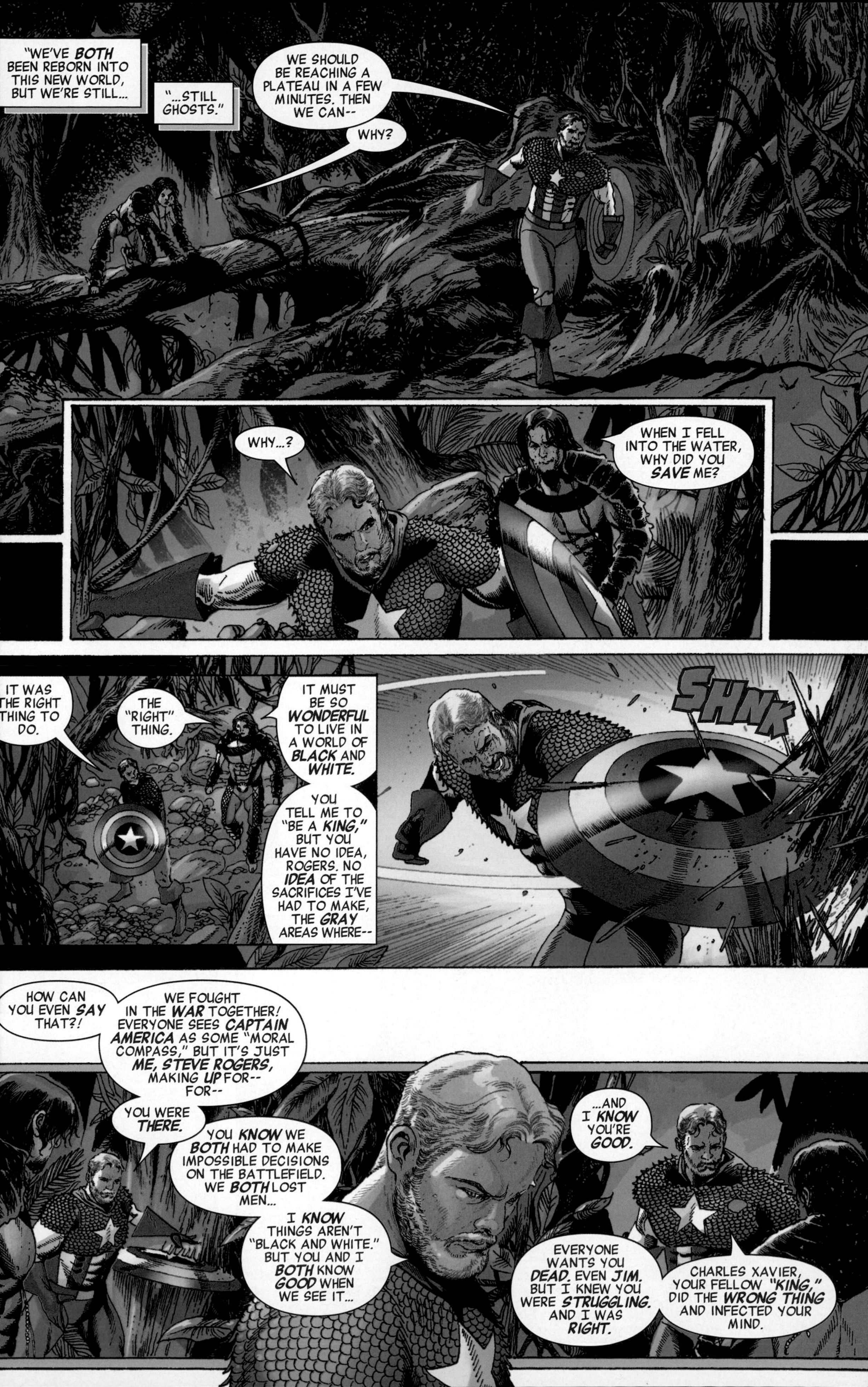
"WE'VE BOTH BEEN REBORN INTO THIS NEW WORLD, BUT WE'RE STILL...
"...STILL GHOSTS."
WE SHOULD BE REACHING A PLATEAU IN A FEW MINUTES. THEN WE CAN--
WHY?
WHY...?
WHEN I FELL INTO THE WATER, WHY DID YOU SAVE ME?
IT WAS THE RIGHT THING TO DO.
THE "RIGHT" THING.
IT MUST BE SO WONDERFUL TO LIVE IN A WORLD OF BLACK AND WHITE.
YOU TELL ME TO "BE A KING," BUT YOU HAVE NO IDEA, ROGERS. NO IDEA OF THE SACRIFICES I'VE HAD TO MAKE, THE GRAY AREAS WHERE--
SHNK
HOW CAN YOU EVEN SAY THAT?!
WE FOUGHT IN THE WAR TOGETHER! EVERYONE SEES CAPTAIN AMERICA AS SOME "MORAL COMPASS," BUT IT'S JUST ME, STEVE ROGERS, MAKING UP FOR-- FOR--
YOU WERE THERE.
YOU KNOW WE BOTH HAD TO MAKE IMPOSSIBLE DECISIONS ON THE BATTLEFIELD. WE BOTH LOST MEN...
I KNOW THINGS AREN'T "BLACK AND WHITE." BUT YOU AND I BOTH KNOW GOOD WHEN WE SEE IT...
...AND I KNOW YOU'RE GOOD.
EVERYONE WANTS YOU DEAD, EVEN JIM. BUT I KNEW YOU WERE STRUGGLING. AND I WAS RIGHT.
CHARLES XAVIER, YOUR FELLOW "KING," DID THE WRONG THING AND INFECTED YOUR MIND.

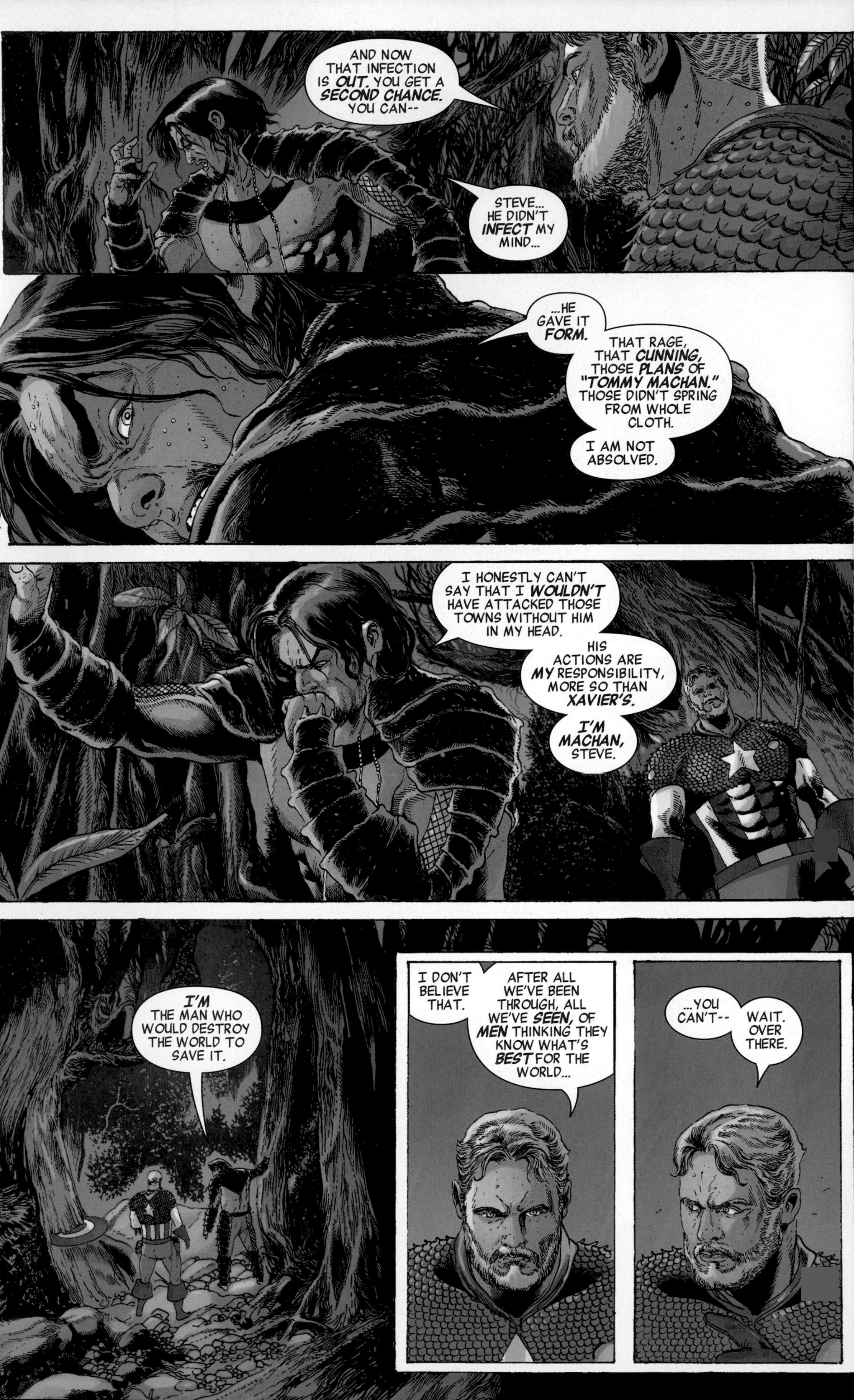
AND NOW THAT INFECTION IS OUT. YOU GET A SECOND CHANCE. YOU CAN--
STEVE... HE DIDN'T INFECT MY MIND...
...HE GAVE IT FORM.
THAT RAGE, THAT CUNNING, THOSE PLANS OF "TOMMY MACHAN." THOSE DIDN'T SPRING FROM WHOLE CLOTH.
I AM NOT ABSOLVED.
I HONESTLY CAN'T SAY THAT I WOULDN'T HAVE ATTACKED THOSE TOWNS WITHOUT HIM IN MY HEAD.
HIS ACTIONS ARE MY RESPONSIBILITY, MORE SO THAN XAVIER'S.
I'M MACHAN, STEVE.
I'M THE MAN WHO WOULD DESTROY THE WORLD TO SAVE IT.
I DON'T BELIEVE THAT.
AFTER ALL WE'VE BEEN THROUGH, ALL WE'VE SEEN, OF MEN THINKING THEY KNOW WHAT'S BEST FOR THE WORLD...
...YOU CAN'T--
WAIT. OVER THERE.

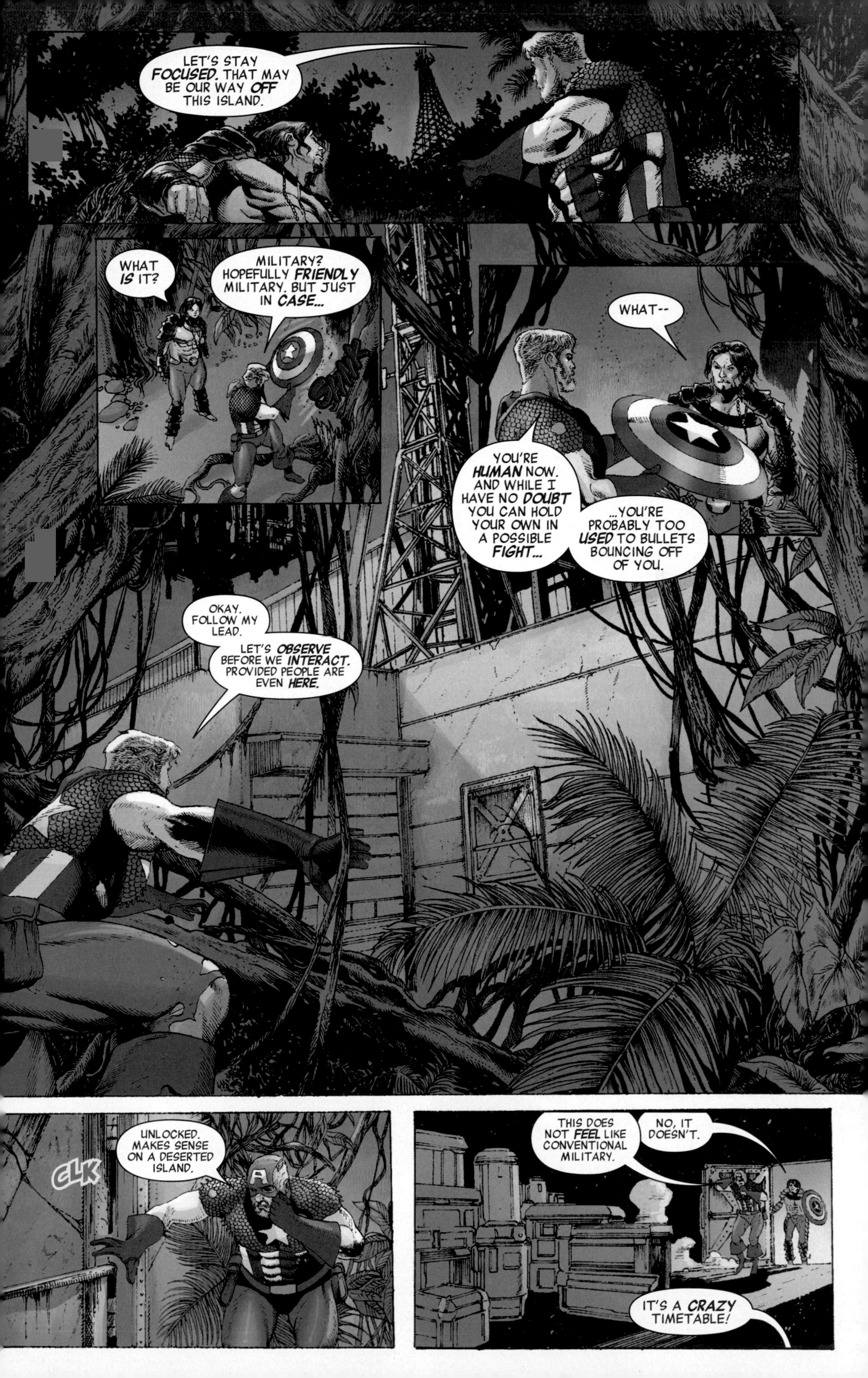

LET'S STAY FOCUSED. THAT MAY BE OUR WAY OFF THIS ISLAND.
WHAT IS IT?
MILITARY? HOPEFULLY FRIENDLY MILITARY. BUT JUST IN CASE...
SHNK
WHAT--
YOU'RE HUMAN NOW. AND WHILE I HAVE NO DOUBT YOU CAN HOLD YOUR OWN IN A POSSIBLE FIGHT...
...YOU'RE PROBABLY TOO USED TO BULLETS BOUNCING OFF OF YOU.
OKAY. FOLLOW MY LEAD.
LET'S OBSERVE BEFORE WE INTERACT. PROVIDED PEOPLE ARE EVEN HERE.
CLK
UNLOCKED. MAKES SENSE ON A DESERTED ISLAND.
THIS DOES NOT FEEL LIKE CONVENTIONAL MILITARY.
NO, IT DOESN'T.
IT'S A CRAZY TIMETABLE!

WE CAN'T JUST **ABANDON** OUR HYBRID RESEARCH TO TACKLE THOSE--THOSE--

HIGH-PRIORITY SPECIMENS FROM **HEAD OFFICE.**

LOOK, IF THESE ARE WHAT THEY'RE **SUPPOSED** TO BE, THEY'LL MAKE OUR WORK **OBSOLETE...**

...WHICH MEANS WE CAN GO **HOME** FINALLY. AND **ROXXON** CAN MAKE MEN INTO MUTANTS OR TIGERS OR WHATEVER THEY **WANT!**

SO LET'S GET **TO** IT, ALAN, YOU WORK ON THE **MUTANT** COMPOUND WITH DON. IT'S THE NUMBER ONE PRIORITY, ACCORDING TO MR. **KAITO.**

ROXXON. **WITH** THE COMPOUNDS, THIS IS **PERFECT.**

WE **JUST** NEED TO CHECK FOR--

THESE **MONSTERS!**

NAMOR! DON'T!

DO YOUR **ETHICS ESCAPE** YOU SO FAR REMOVED FROM PRYING **EYES?!** CREATING **ABOMINATIONS** FOR **WHAT?**

TO **TORTURE?** TO TORTURE **OTHERS?!**

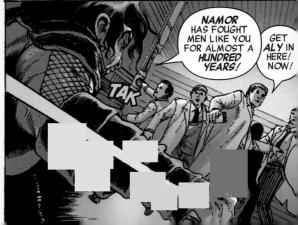

NAMOR HAS FOUGHT MEN LIKE YOU FOR ALMOST A **HUNDRED YEARS!**

GET **ALY** IN HERE! **NOW!**

TAK

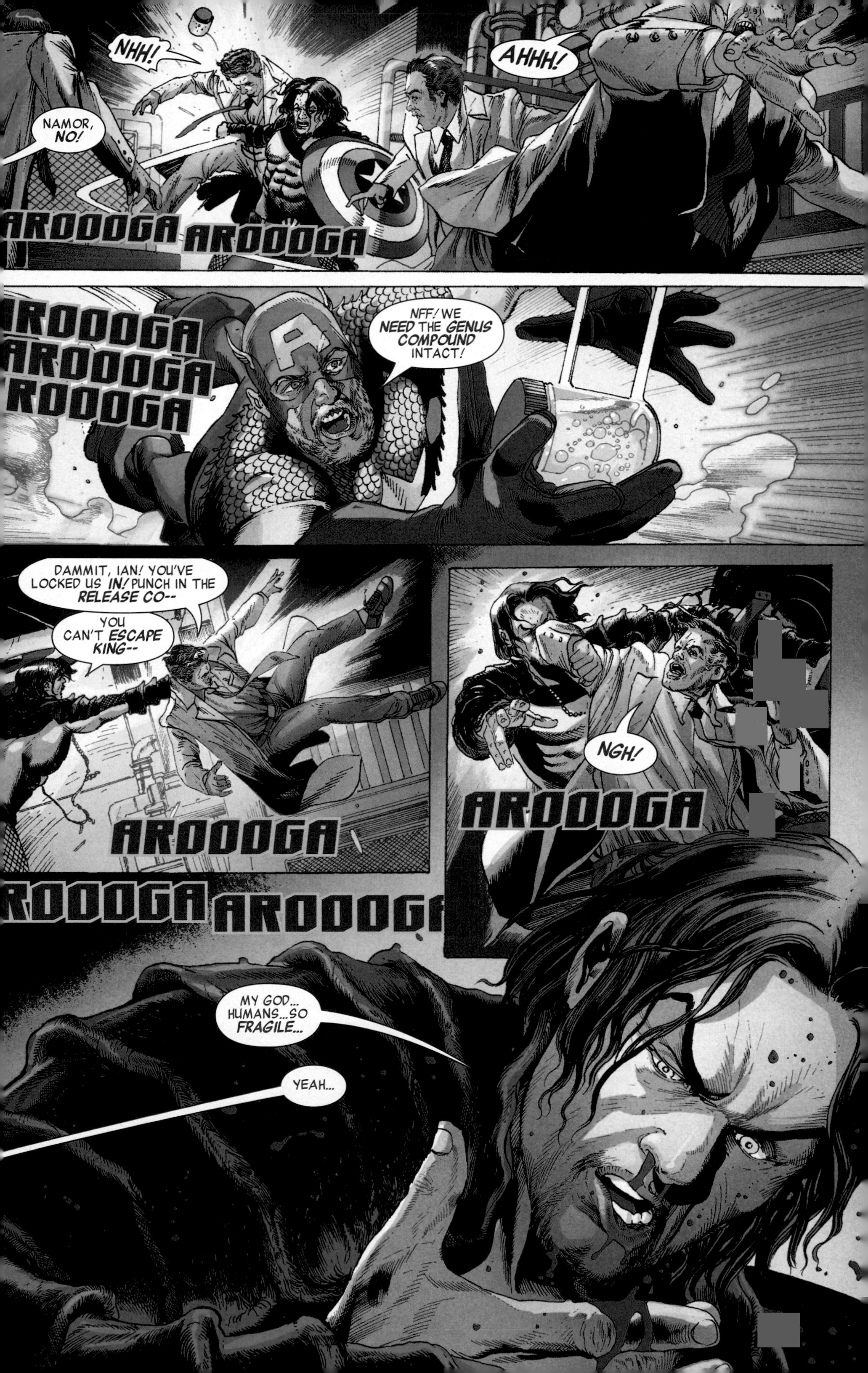
NHH!
NAMOR, NO!
AHHH!
AROOOGA AROOOGA
AROOOGA
AROOOGA
AROOOGA
NFF! WE NEED THE GENUS COMPOUND INTACT!
DAMMIT, IAN! YOU'VE LOCKED US IN! PUNCH IN THE RELEASE CO--
YOU CAN'T ESCAPE KING--
AROOOGA
NGH!
AROOOGA
AROOOGA AROOOGA
MY GOD... HUMANS...SO FRAGILE...
YEAH...

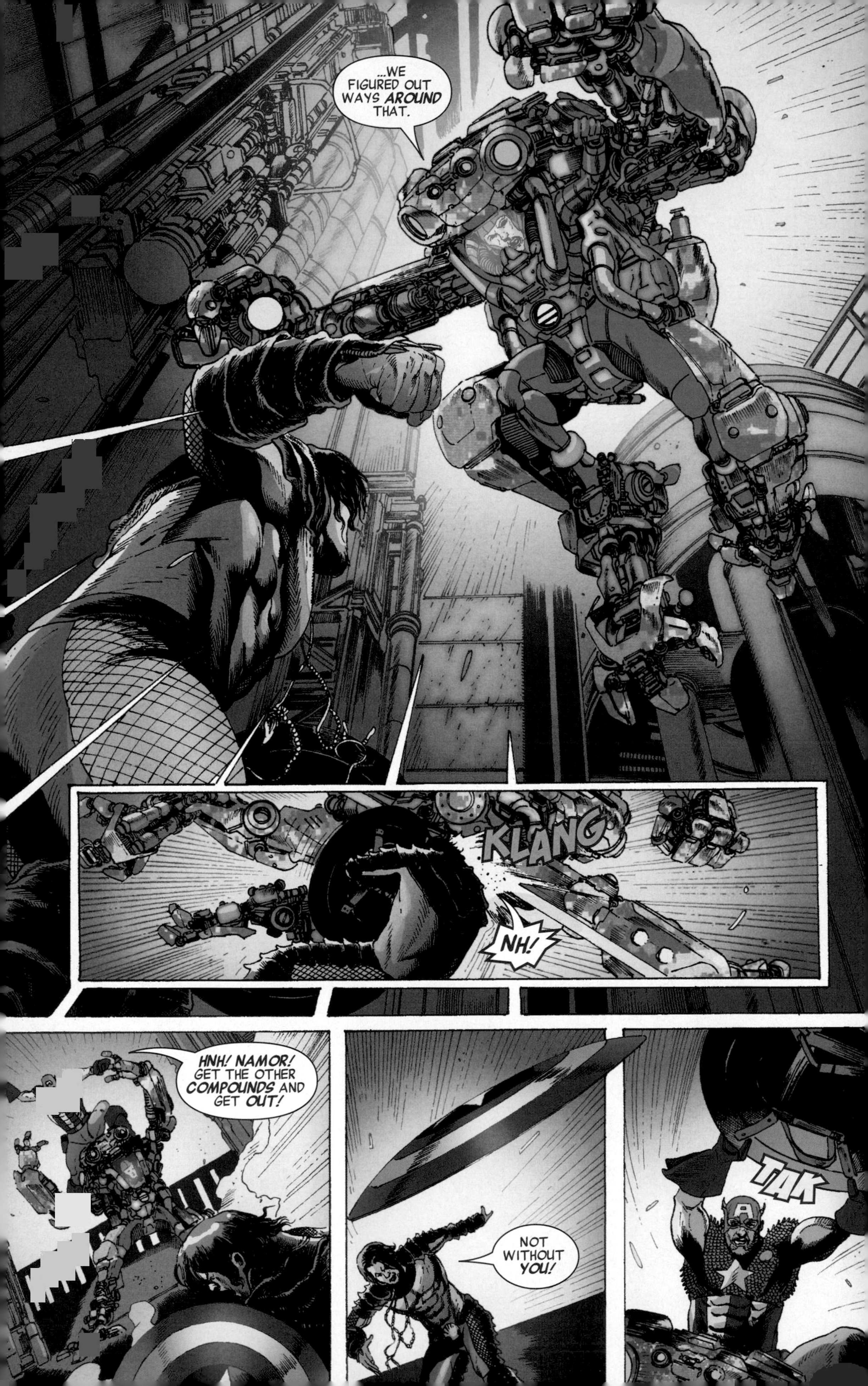
...WE FIGURED OUT WAYS AROUND THAT.
KLANG
NH!
HNH! NAMOR! GET THE OTHER COMPOUNDS AND GET OUT!
NOT WITHOUT YOU!
TAK

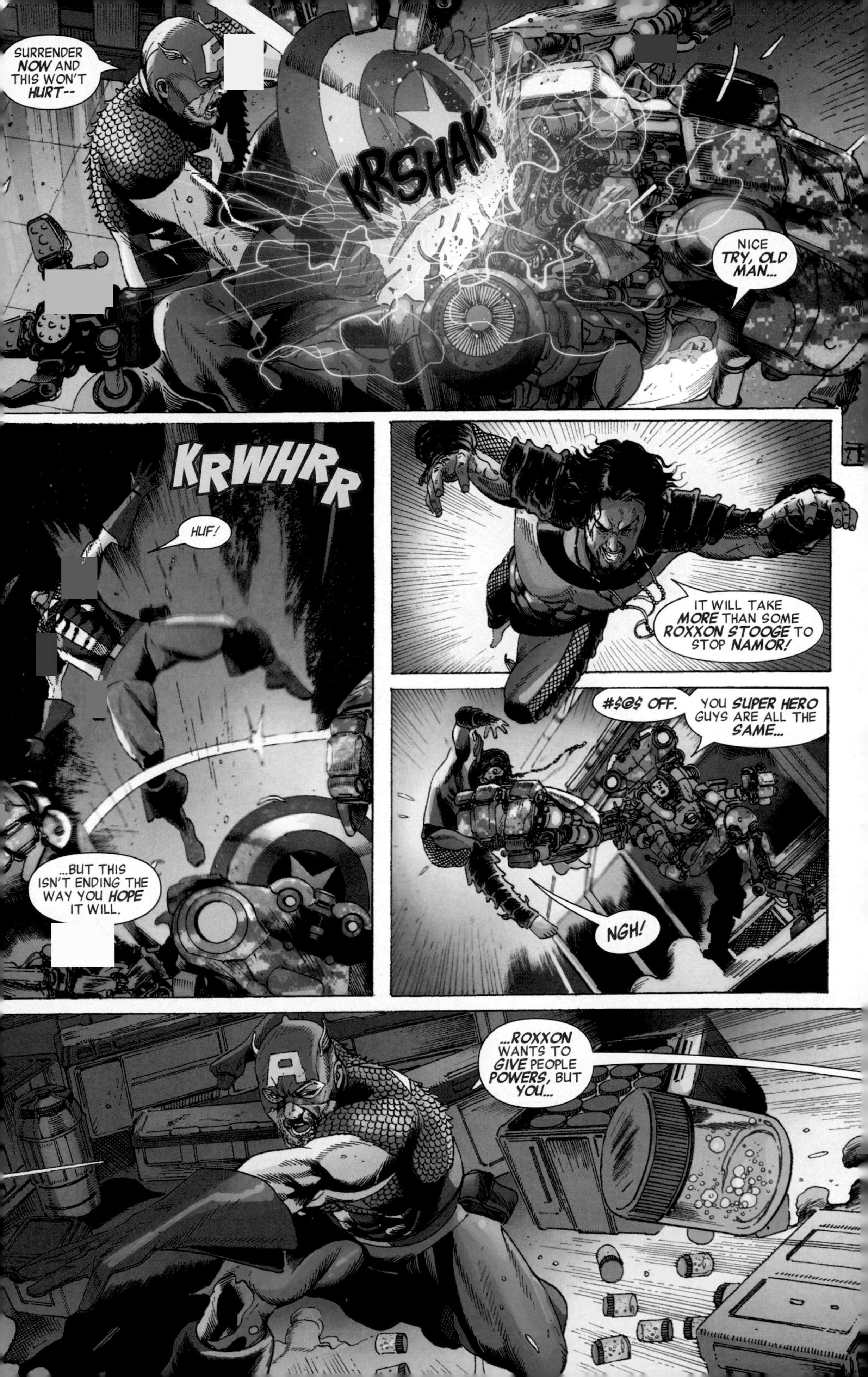
SURRENDER NOW AND THIS WON'T HURT--
KRSHAK
NICE TRY, OLD MAN...
KRWHRR
HUF!
...BUT THIS ISN'T ENDING THE WAY YOU HOPE IT WILL.
IT WILL TAKE MORE THAN SOME ROXXON STOOGE TO STOP NAMOR!
#$@$ OFF.
YOU SUPER HERO GUYS ARE ALL THE SAME...
NGH!
...ROXXON WANTS TO GIVE PEOPLE POWERS, BUT YOU...

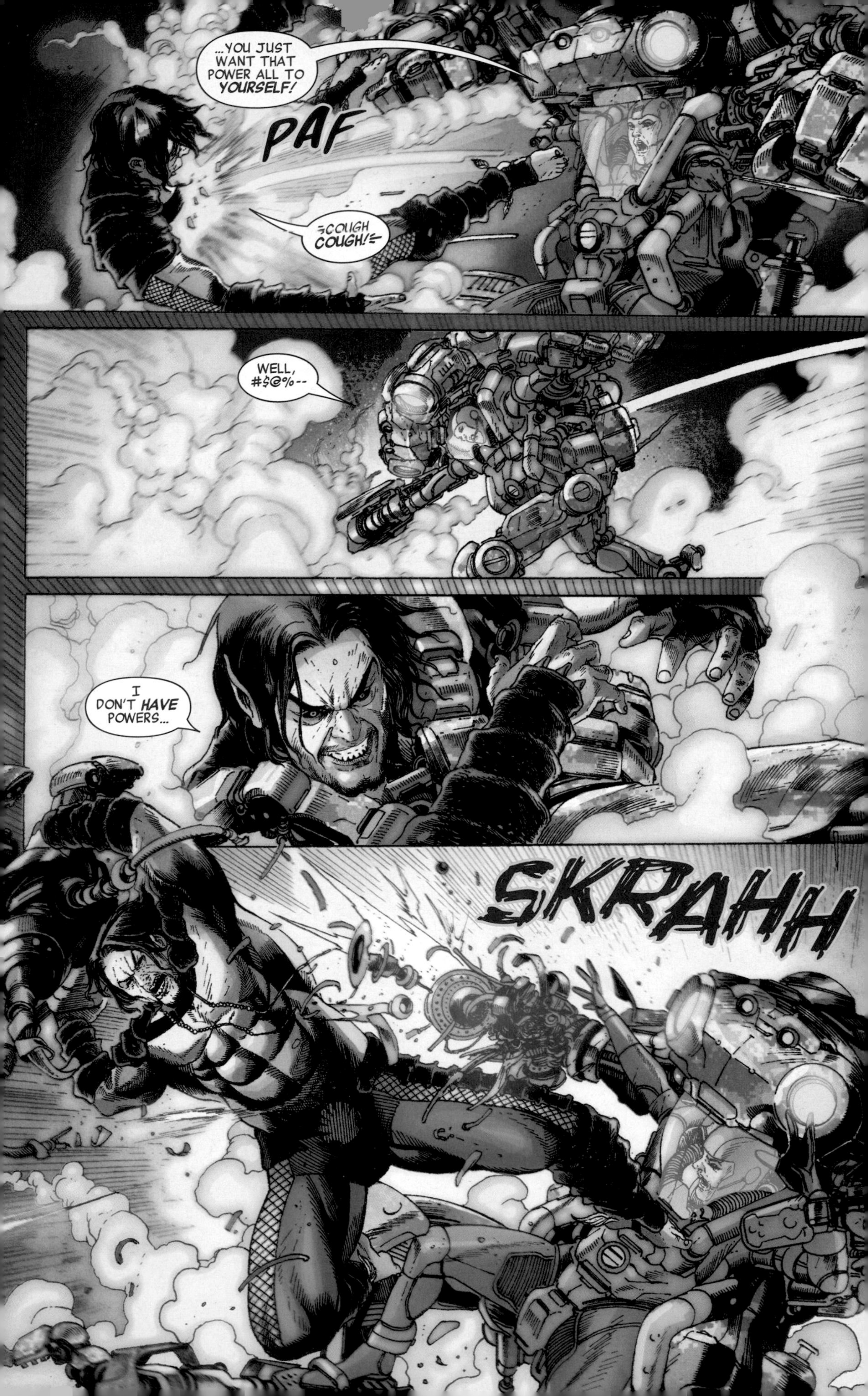
...YOU JUST WANT THAT POWER ALL TO YOURSELF!
PAF
=COUGH COUGH!=
WELL, #$@%--
I DON'T HAVE POWERS...
SKRAHH

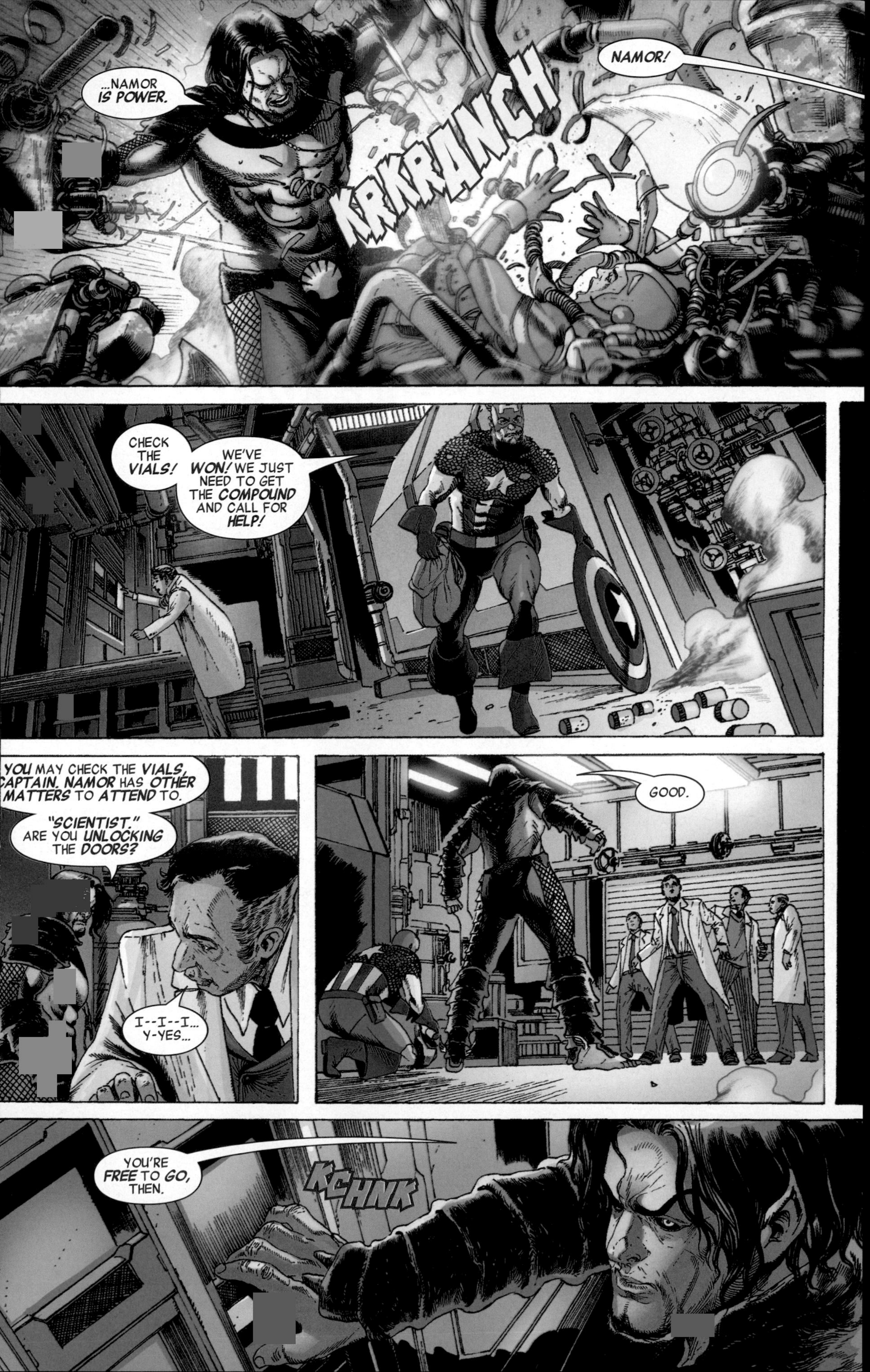
...NAMOR IS POWER.
KRKRANCH
NAMOR!
CHECK THE VIALS!
WE'VE WON! WE JUST NEED TO GET THE COMPOUND AND CALL FOR HELP!
YOU MAY CHECK THE VIALS, CAPTAIN. NAMOR HAS OTHER MATTERS TO ATTEND TO.
"SCIENTIST." ARE YOU UNLOCKING THE DOORS?
I--I--I... Y-YES...
GOOD.
YOU'RE FREE TO GO, THEN.
KCHNK

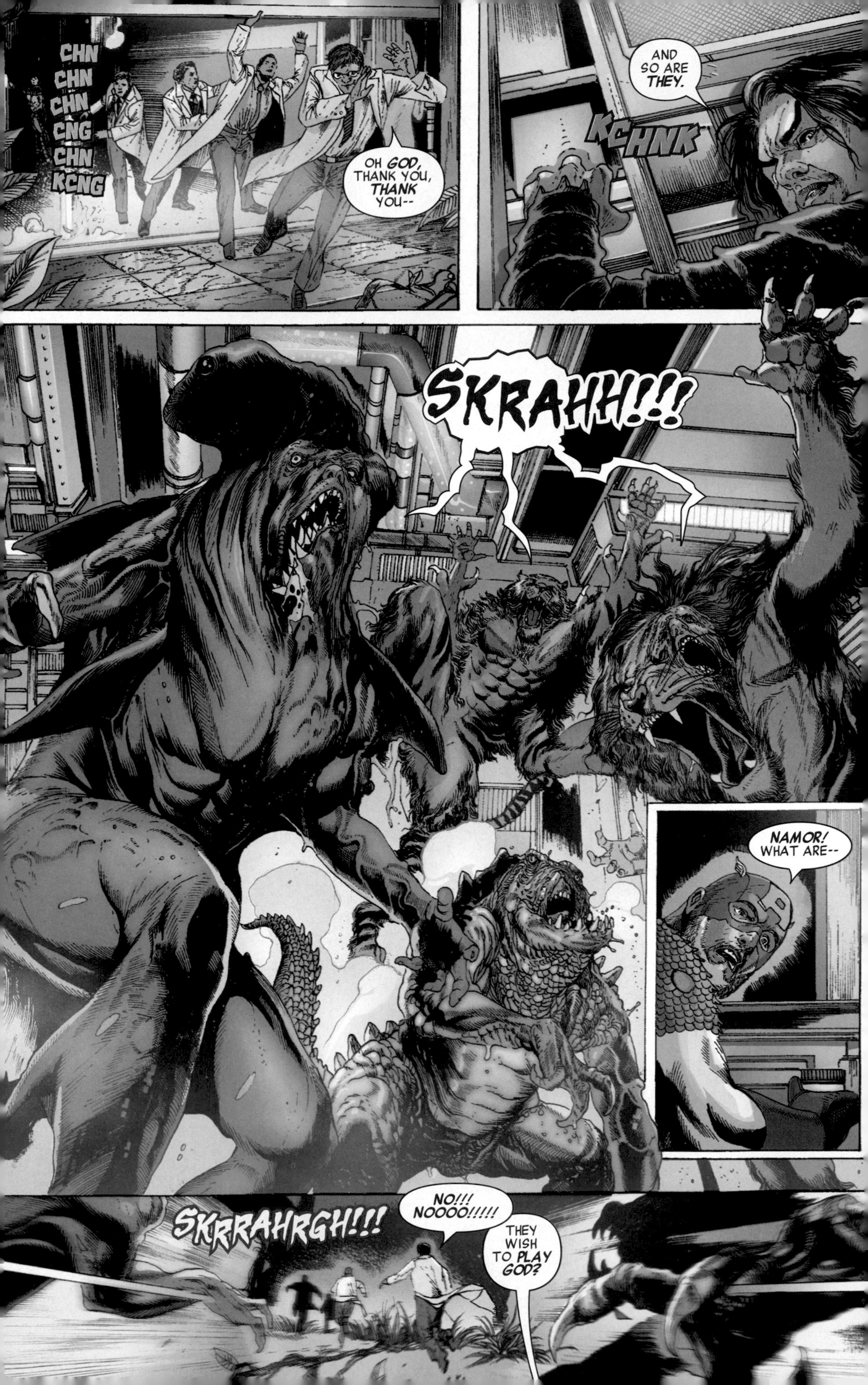
CHN CHN CHN CNG CHN KCNG
OH GOD, THANK YOU, THANK YOU--
AND SO ARE THEY.
KCHNK
SKRAHH!!!
NAMOR! WHAT ARE--
SKRRAHRGH!!!
NO!!! NOOOO!!!!!
THEY WISH TO PLAY GOD?

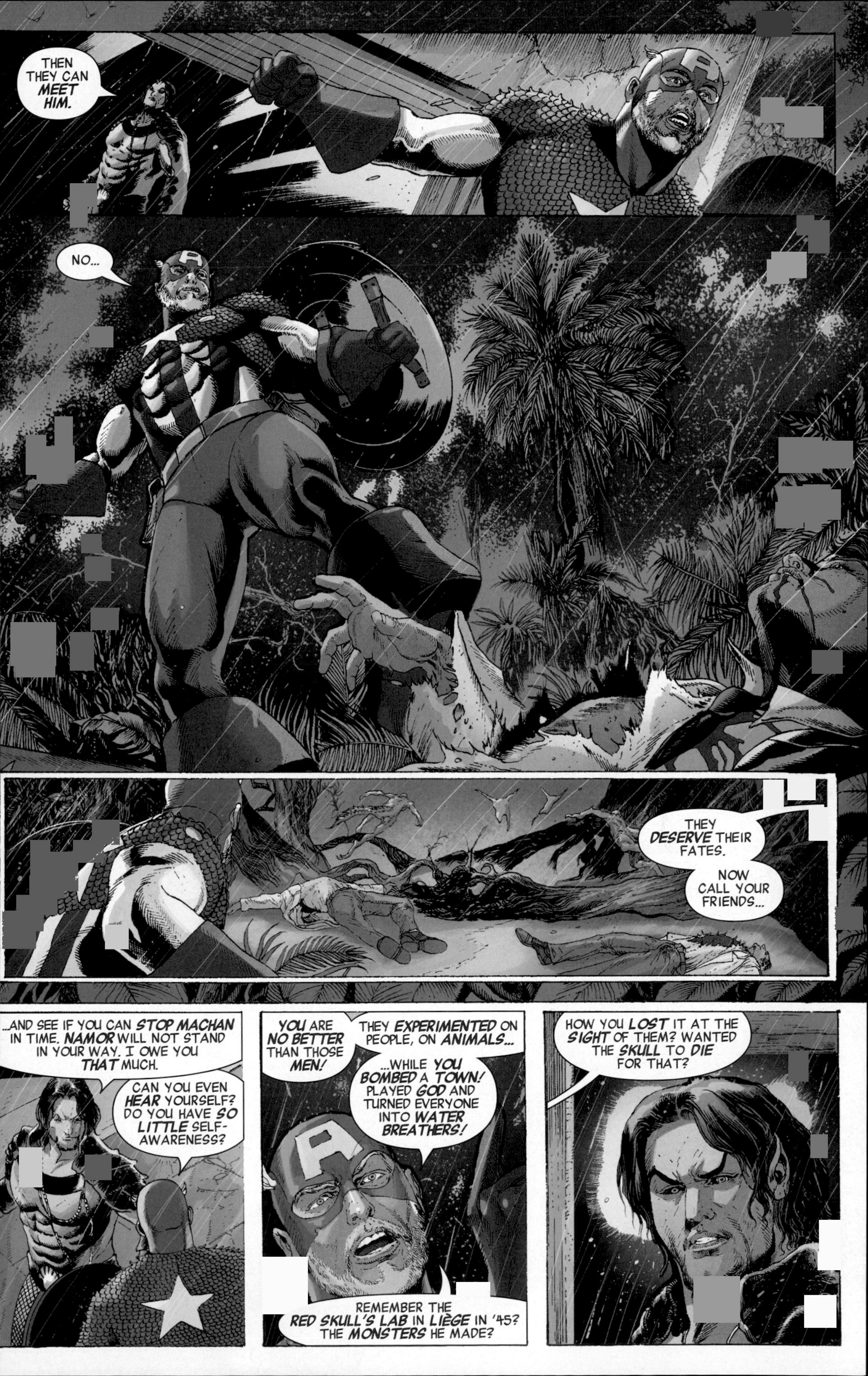
THEN THEY CAN MEET HIM.
NO...
THEY DESERVE THEIR FATES.
NOW CALL YOUR FRIENDS...
...AND SEE IF YOU CAN STOP MACHAN IN TIME. NAMOR WILL NOT STAND IN YOUR WAY. I OWE YOU THAT MUCH.
CAN YOU EVEN HEAR YOURSELF? DO YOU HAVE SO LITTLE SELF-AWARENESS?
YOU ARE NO BETTER THAN THOSE MEN!
THEY EXPERIMENTED ON PEOPLE, ON ANIMALS...
...WHILE YOU BOMBED A TOWN! PLAYED GOD AND TURNED EVERYONE INTO WATER BREATHERS!
REMEMBER THE RED SKULL'S LAB IN LIÈGE IN '45? THE MONSTERS HE MADE?
HOW YOU LOST IT AT THE SIGHT OF THEM? WANTED THE SKULL TO DIE FOR THAT?

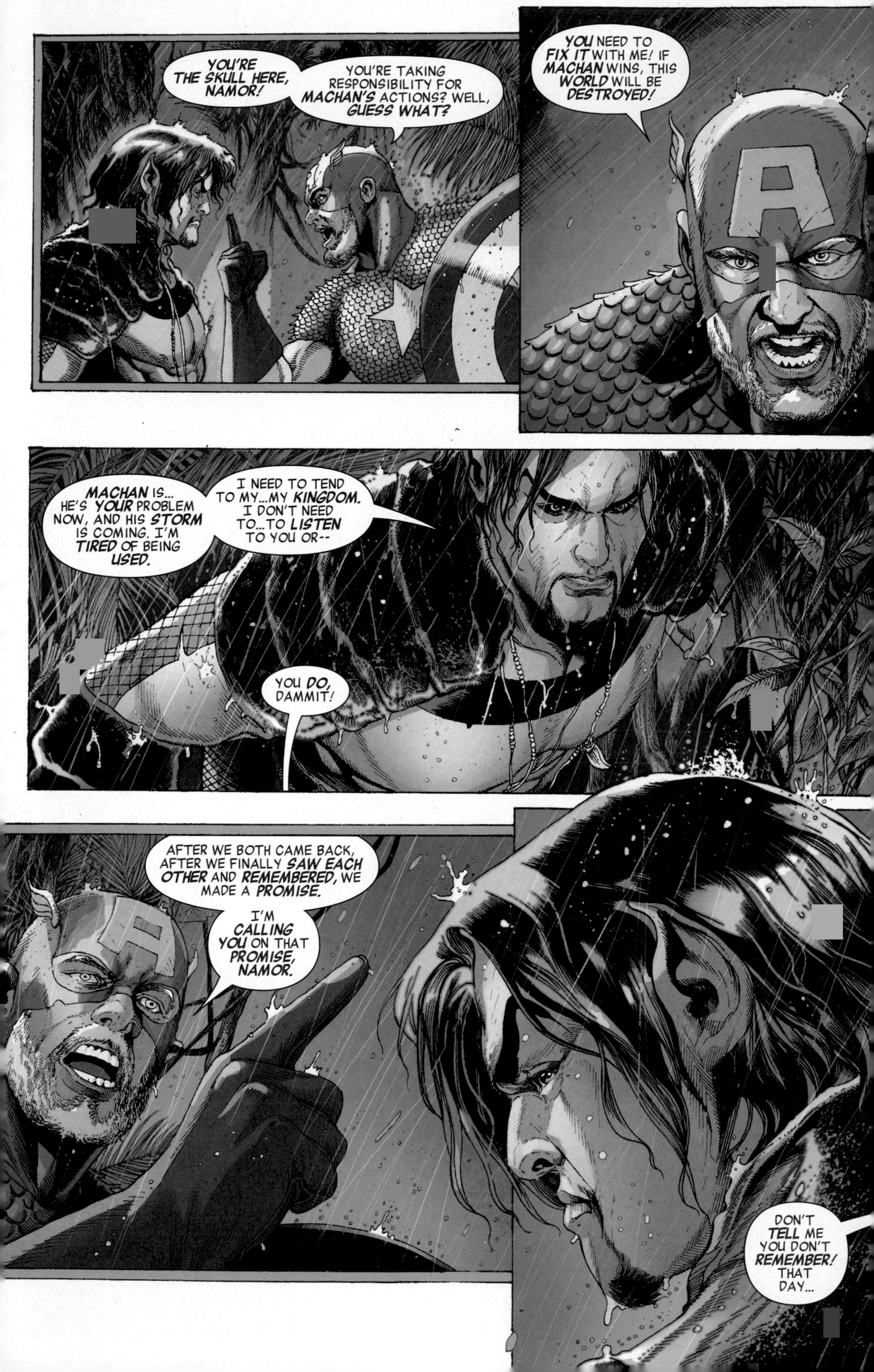
YOU'RE THE SKULL HERE, NAMOR!
YOU'RE TAKING RESPONSIBILITY FOR MACHAN'S ACTIONS? WELL, GUESS WHAT?
YOU NEED TO FIX IT WITH ME! IF MACHAN WINS, THIS WORLD WILL BE DESTROYED!
MACHAN IS... HE'S YOUR PROBLEM NOW, AND HIS STORM IS COMING. I'M TIRED OF BEING USED.
I NEED TO TEND TO MY...MY KINGDOM. I DON'T NEED TO...TO LISTEN TO YOU OR--
YOU DO, DAMMIT!
AFTER WE BOTH CAME BACK, AFTER WE FINALLY SAW EACH OTHER AND REMEMBERED, WE MADE A PROMISE.
I'M CALLING YOU ON THAT PROMISE, NAMOR.
DON'T TELL ME YOU DON'T REMEMBER! THAT DAY...

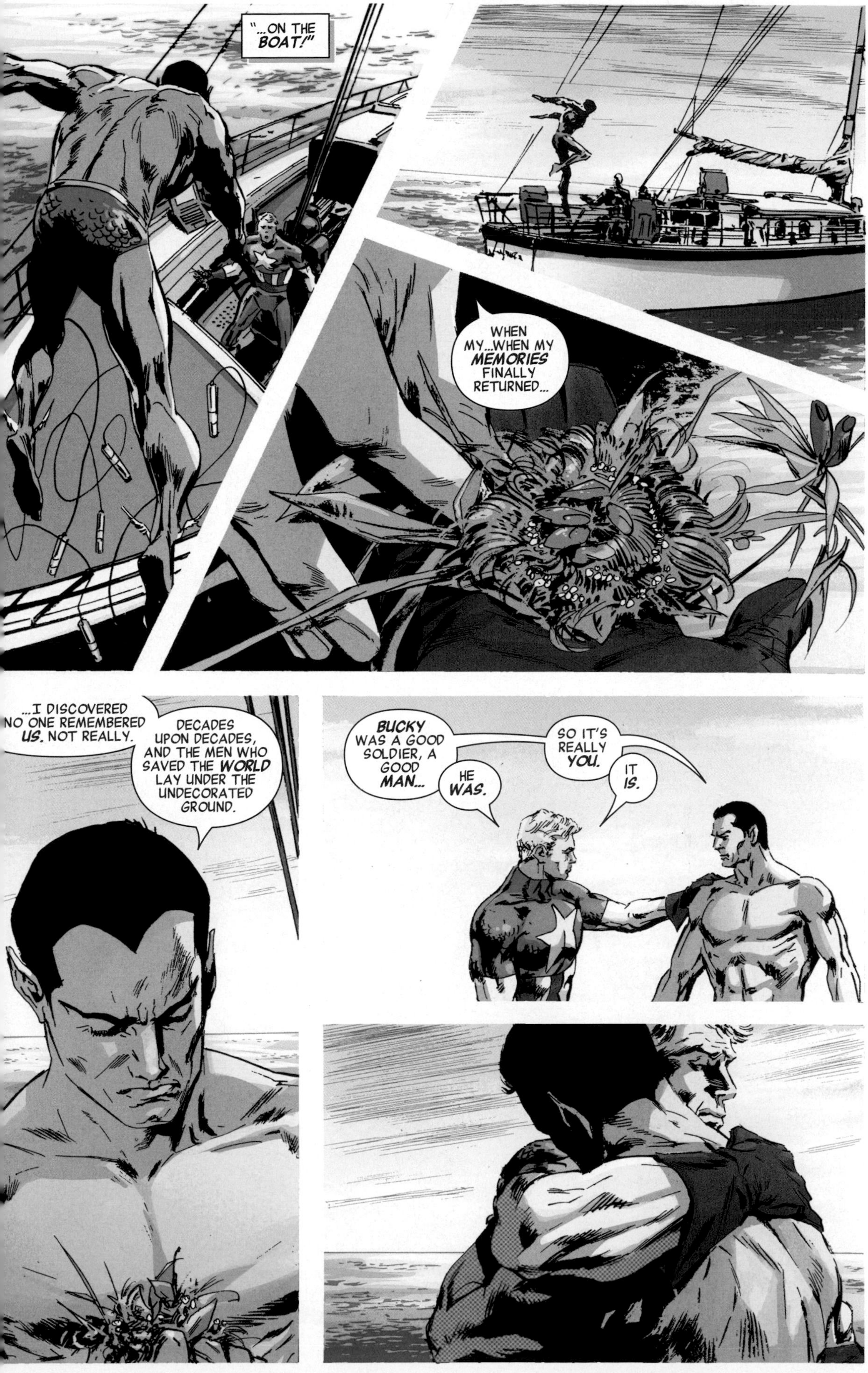
"...ON THE BOAT!"
WHEN MY...WHEN MY MEMORIES FINALLY RETURNED...
...I DISCOVERED NO ONE REMEMBERED US. NOT REALLY.
DECADES UPON DECADES, AND THE MEN WHO SAVED THE WORLD LAY UNDER THE UNDECORATED GROUND.
BUCKY WAS A GOOD SOLDIER, A GOOD MAN...
HE WAS.
SO IT'S REALLY YOU.
IT IS.

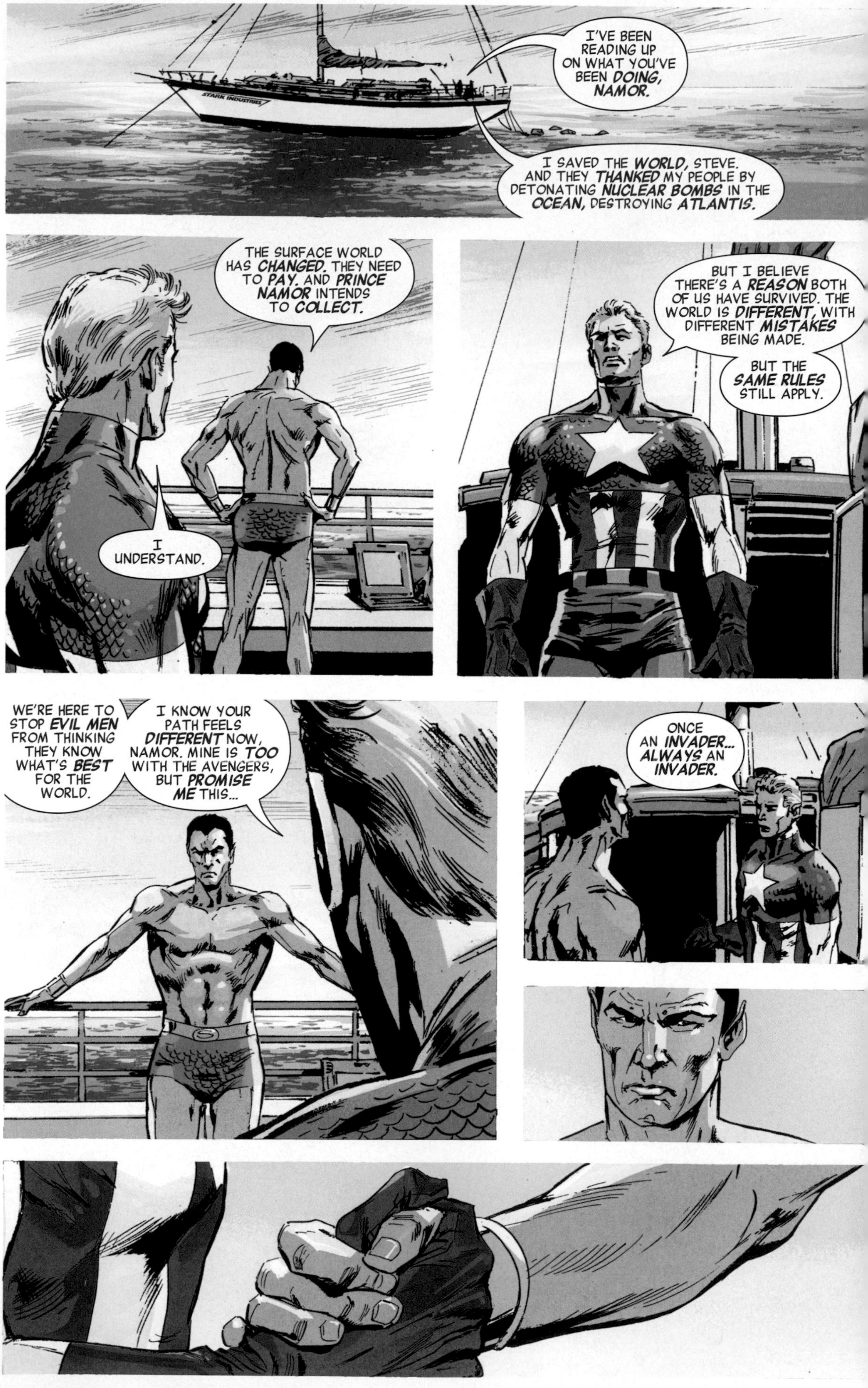
I'VE BEEN READING UP ON WHAT YOU'VE BEEN DOING, NAMOR.
I SAVED THE WORLD, STEVE. AND THEY THANKED MY PEOPLE BY DETONATING NUCLEAR BOMBS IN THE OCEAN, DESTROYING ATLANTIS.
STARK INDUSTRIES
THE SURFACE WORLD HAS CHANGED. THEY NEED TO PAY. AND PRINCE NAMOR INTENDS TO COLLECT.
I UNDERSTAND.
BUT I BELIEVE THERE'S A REASON BOTH OF US HAVE SURVIVED. THE WORLD IS DIFFERENT, WITH DIFFERENT MISTAKES BEING MADE.
BUT THE SAME RULES STILL APPLY.
I KNOW YOUR PATH FEELS DIFFERENT NOW, NAMOR. MINE IS TOO WITH THE AVENGERS, BUT PROMISE ME THIS...
WE'RE HERE TO STOP EVIL MEN FROM THINKING THEY KNOW WHAT'S BEST FOR THE WORLD.
ONCE AN INVADER... ALWAYS AN INVADER.

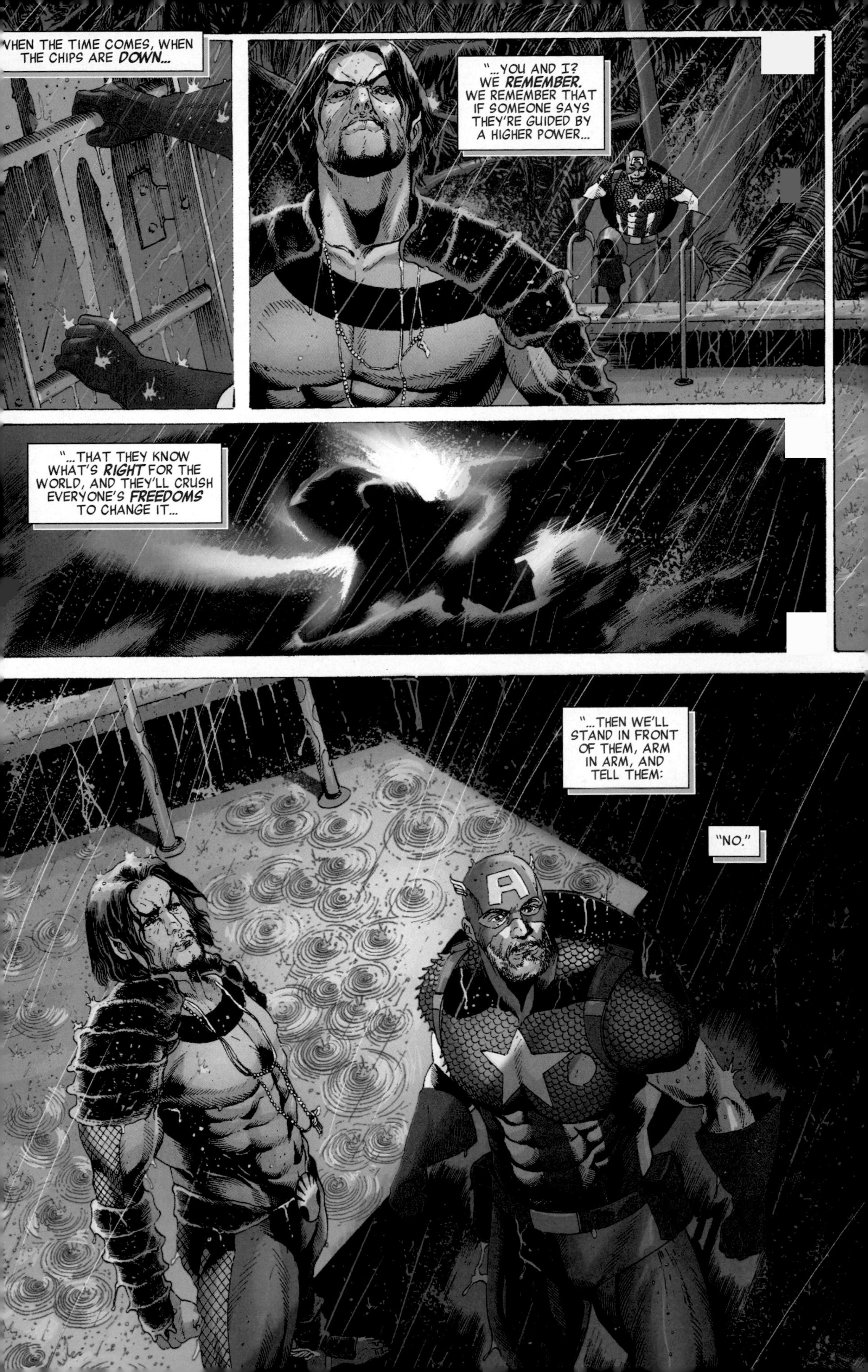

WHEN THE TIME COMES, WHEN THE CHIPS ARE DOWN...
"...YOU AND I? WE REMEMBER. WE REMEMBER THAT IF SOMEONE SAYS THEY'RE GUIDED BY A HIGHER POWER...
"...THAT THEY KNOW WHAT'S RIGHT FOR THE WORLD, AND THEY'LL CRUSH EVERYONE'S FREEDOMS TO CHANGE IT...
"...THEN WE'LL STAND IN FRONT OF THEM, ARM IN ARM, AND TELL THEM:
"NO."

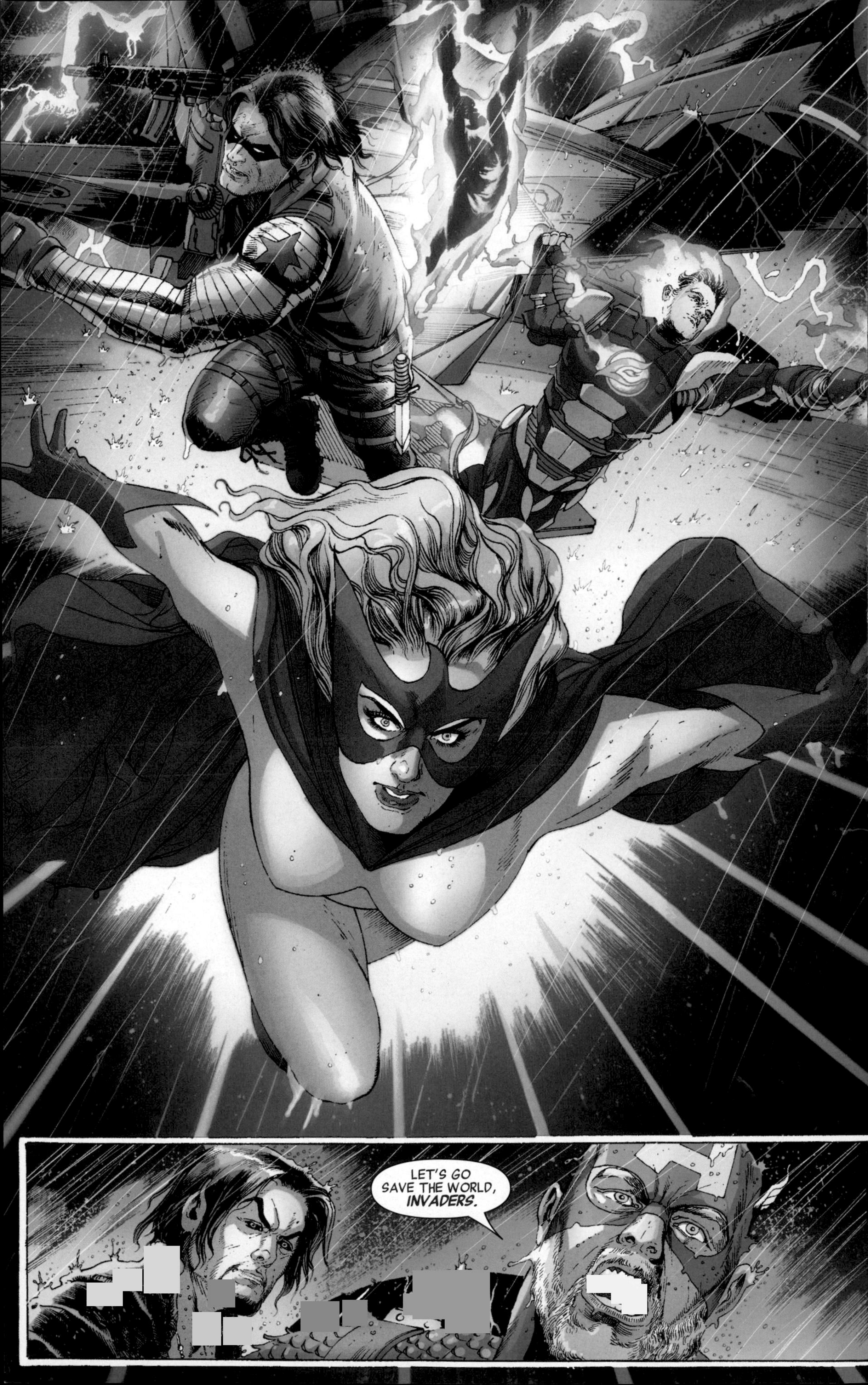
LET'S GO SAVE THE WORLD, **INVADERS.**

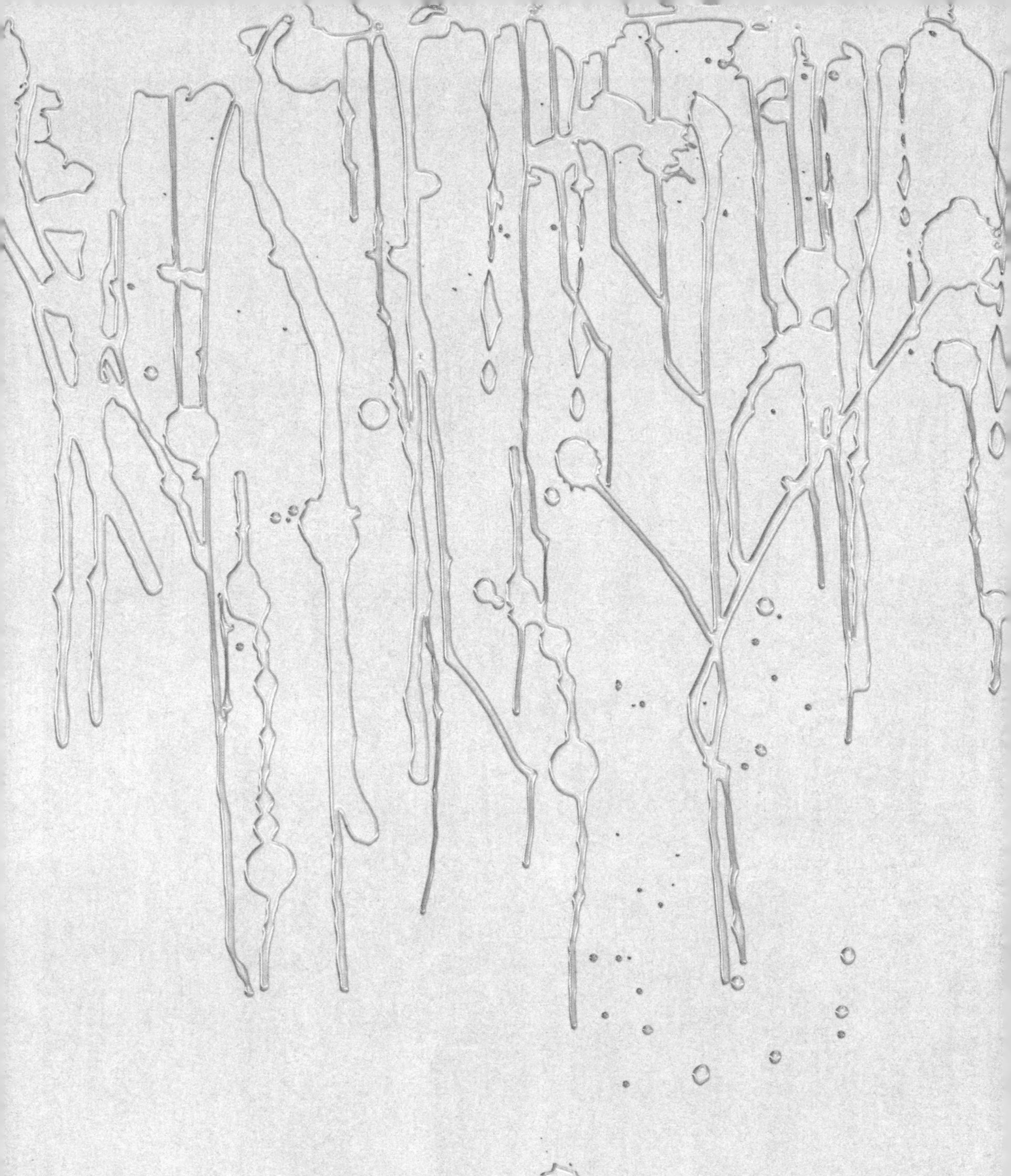

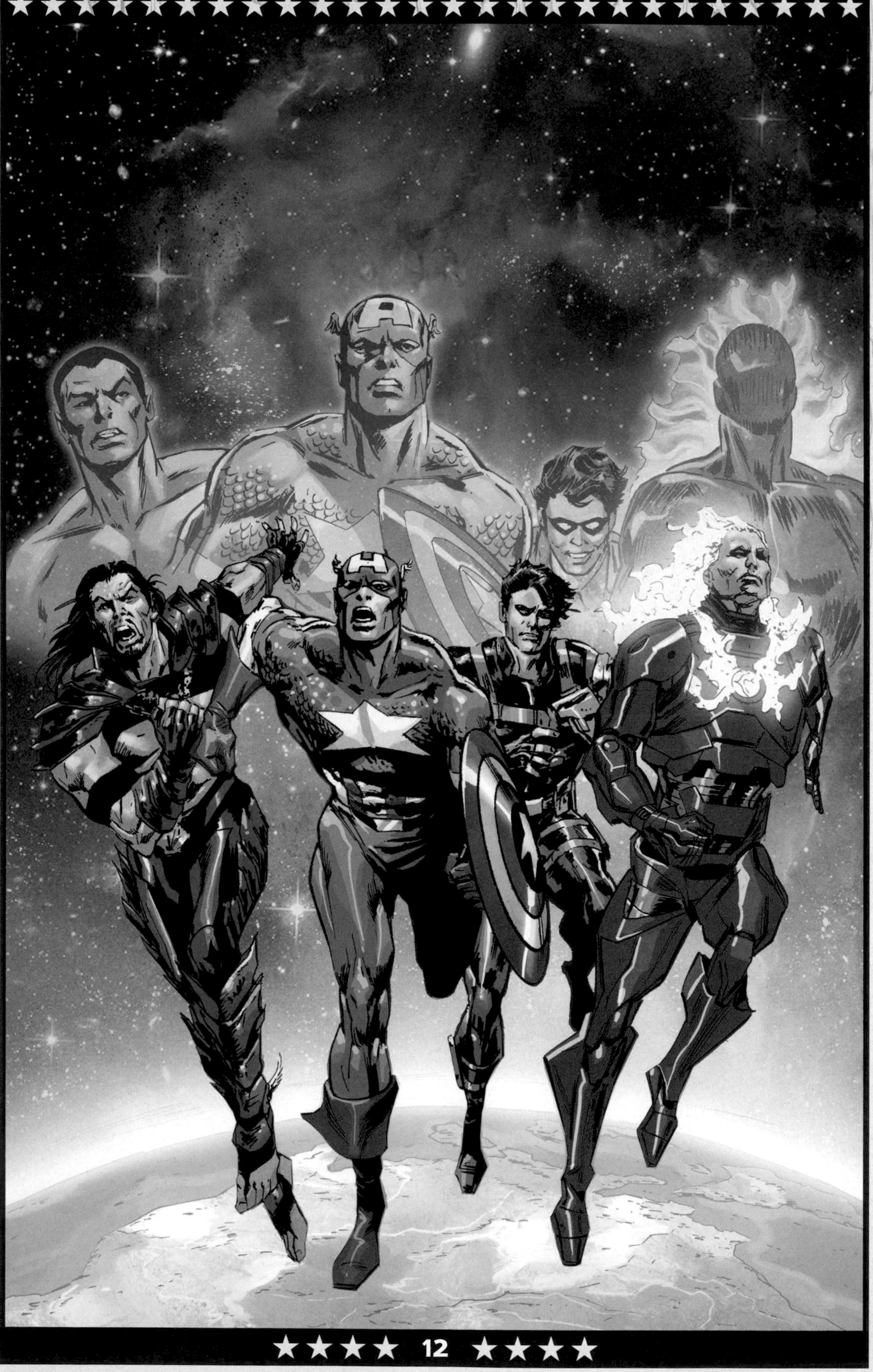

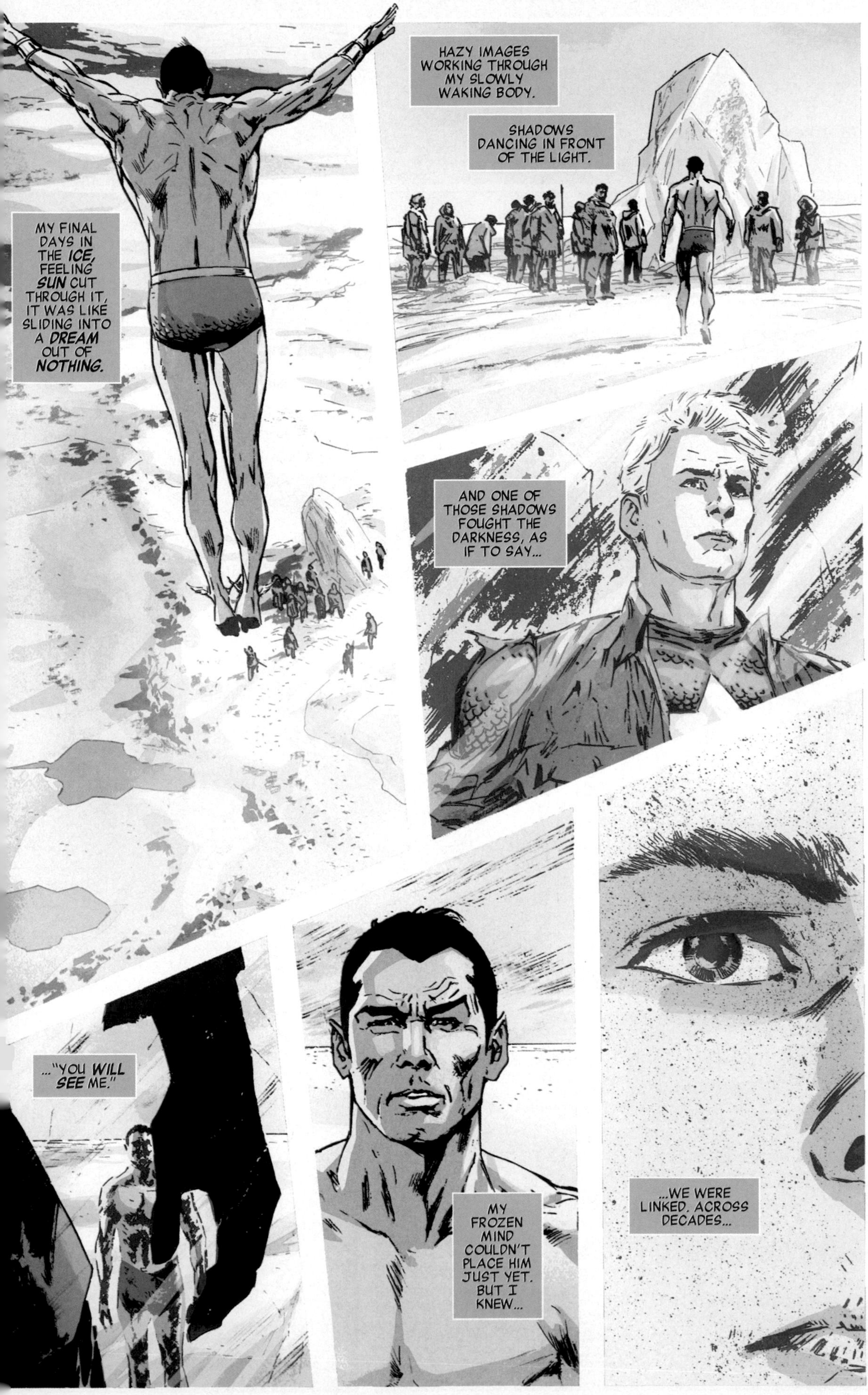
MY FINAL DAYS IN THE ICE, FEELING SUN CUT THROUGH IT, IT WAS LIKE SLIDING INTO A DREAM OUT OF NOTHING.
HAZY IMAGES WORKING THROUGH MY SLOWLY WAKING BODY.
SHADOWS DANCING IN FRONT OF THE LIGHT.
AND ONE OF THOSE SHADOWS FOUGHT THE DARKNESS, AS IF TO SAY...
..."YOU WILL SEE ME."
MY FROZEN MIND COULDN'T PLACE HIM JUST YET. BUT I KNEW...
...WE WERE LINKED. ACROSS DECADES...

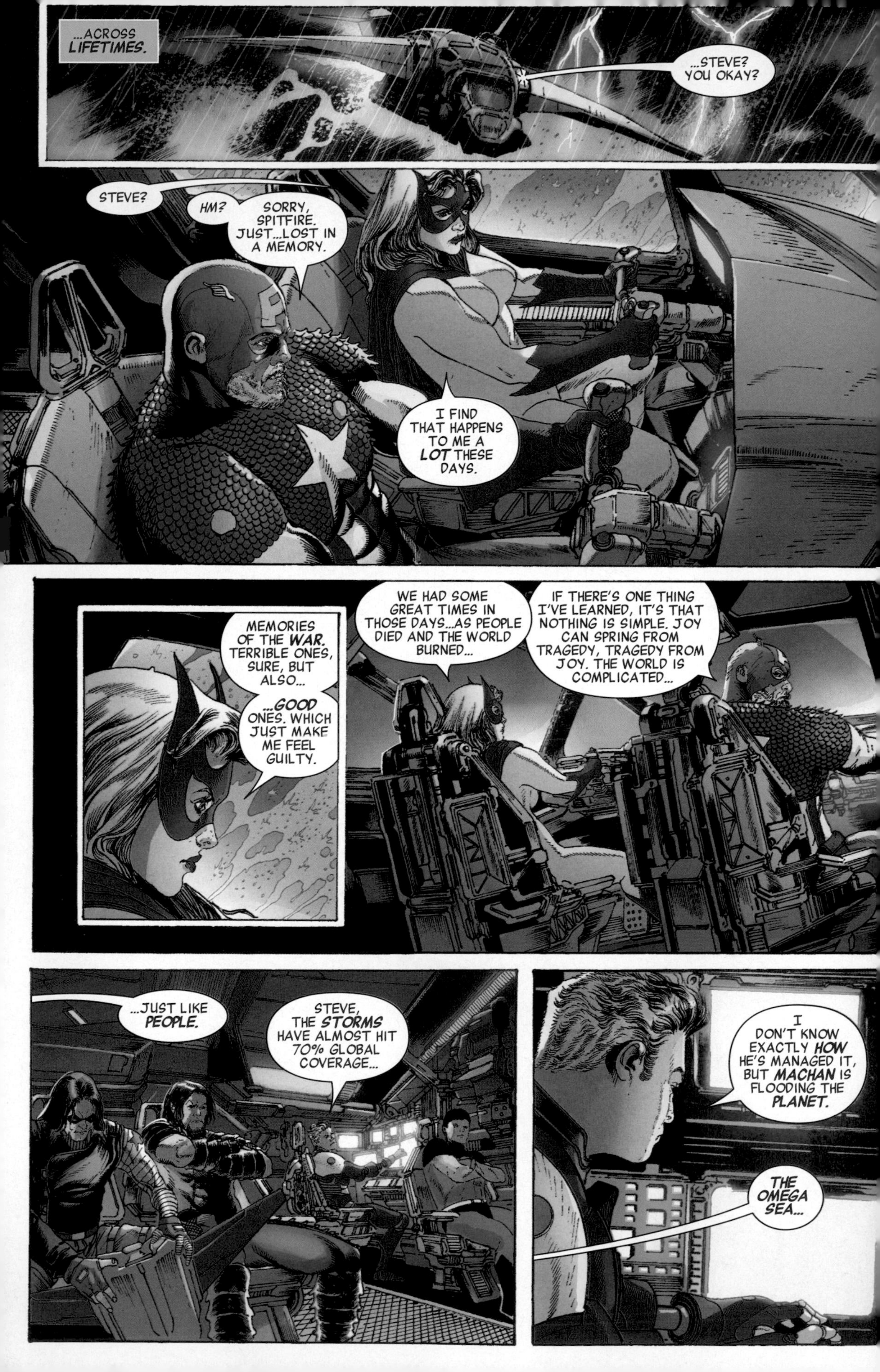
...ACROSS LIFETIMES.
...STEVE? YOU OKAY?
STEVE?
HM?
SORRY, SPITFIRE. JUST...LOST IN A MEMORY.
I FIND THAT HAPPENS TO ME A LOT THESE DAYS.
MEMORIES OF THE WAR. TERRIBLE ONES, SURE, BUT ALSO...
...GOOD ONES. WHICH JUST MAKE ME FEEL GUILTY.
WE HAD SOME GREAT TIMES IN THOSE DAYS...AS PEOPLE DIED AND THE WORLD BURNED...
IF THERE'S ONE THING I'VE LEARNED, IT'S THAT NOTHING IS SIMPLE. JOY CAN SPRING FROM TRAGEDY, TRAGEDY FROM JOY. THE WORLD IS COMPLICATED...
...JUST LIKE PEOPLE.
STEVE, THE STORMS HAVE ALMOST HIT 70% GLOBAL COVERAGE...
I DON'T KNOW EXACTLY HOW HE'S MANAGED IT, BUT MACHAN IS FLOODING THE PLANET.
THE OMEGA SEA...

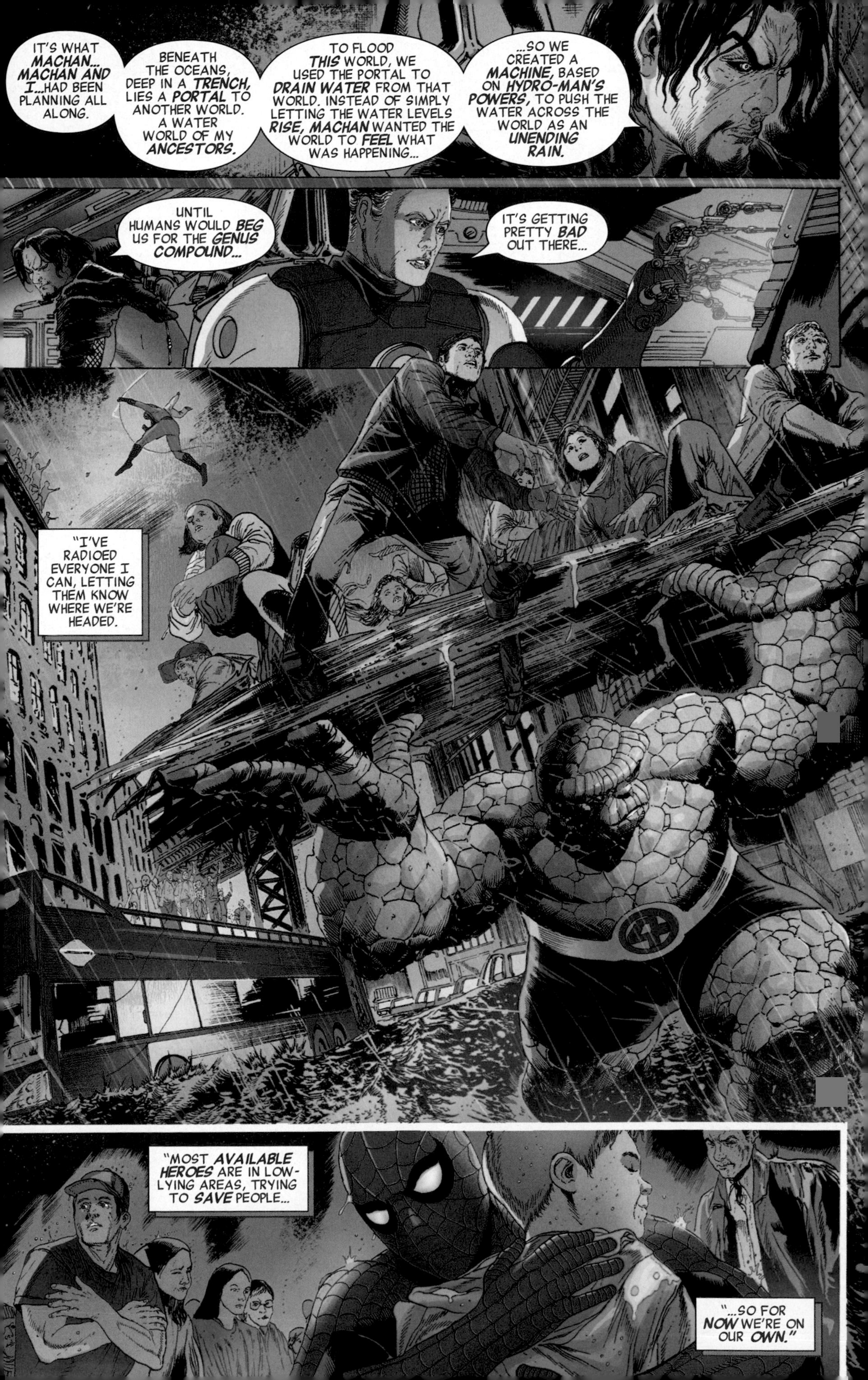
IT'S WHAT MACHAN... MACHAN AND I...HAD BEEN PLANNING ALL ALONG.
BENEATH THE OCEANS, DEEP IN A TRENCH, LIES A PORTAL TO ANOTHER WORLD. A WATER WORLD OF MY ANCESTORS.
TO FLOOD THIS WORLD, WE USED THE PORTAL TO DRAIN WATER FROM THAT WORLD. INSTEAD OF SIMPLY LETTING THE WATER LEVELS RISE, MACHAN WANTED THE WORLD TO FEEL WHAT WAS HAPPENING...
...SO WE CREATED A MACHINE, BASED ON HYDRO-MAN'S POWERS, TO PUSH THE WATER ACROSS THE WORLD AS AN UNENDING RAIN.
UNTIL HUMANS WOULD BEG US FOR THE GENUS COMPOUND...
IT'S GETTING PRETTY BAD OUT THERE...
"I'VE RADIOED EVERYONE I CAN, LETTING THEM KNOW WHERE WE'RE HEADED.
"MOST AVAILABLE HEROES ARE IN LOW-LYING AREAS, TRYING TO SAVE PEOPLE...
"...SO FOR NOW WE'RE ON OUR OWN."

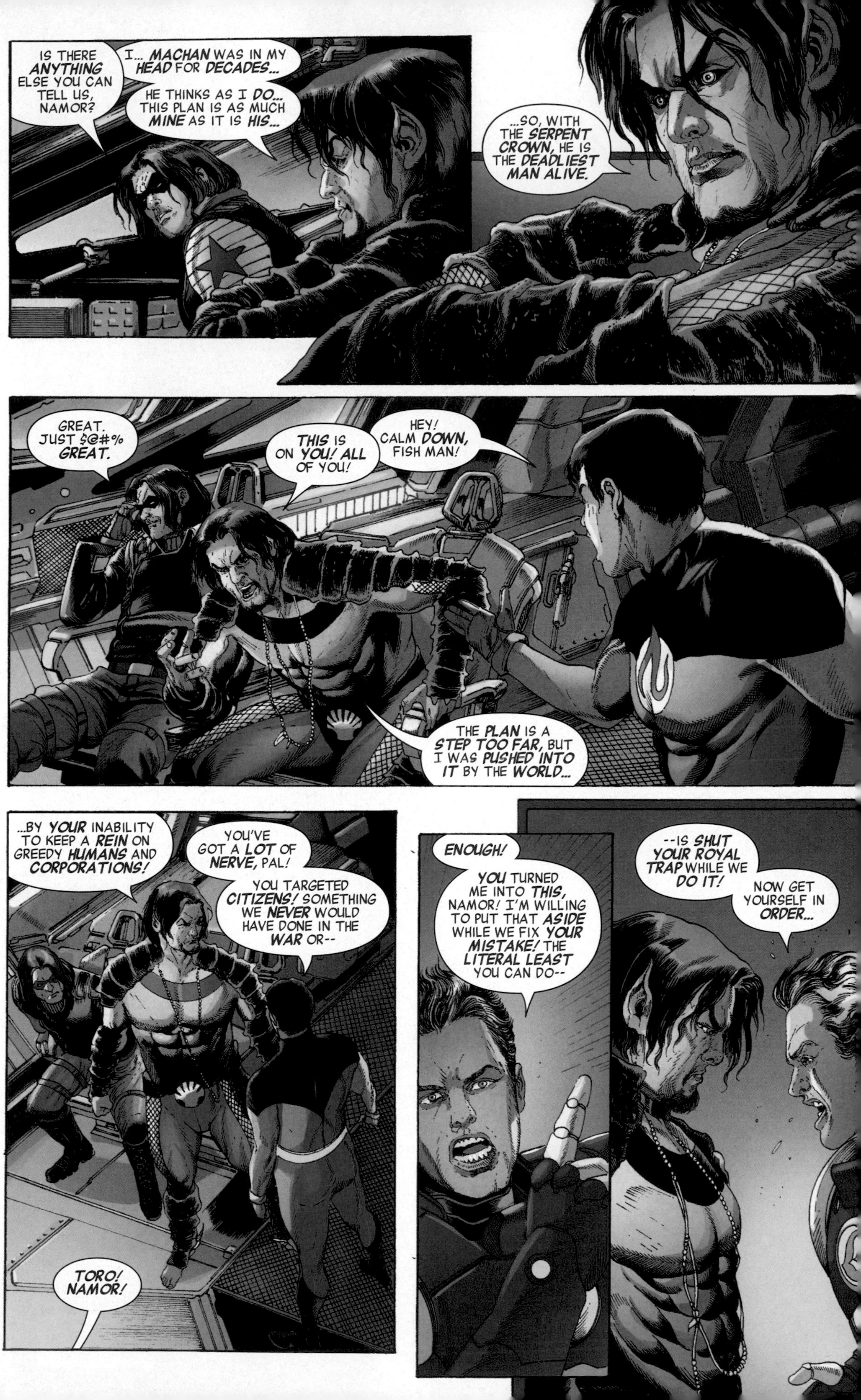
IS THERE ANYTHING ELSE YOU CAN TELL US, NAMOR?
I... MACHAN WAS IN MY HEAD FOR DECADES...
HE THINKS AS I DO... THIS PLAN IS AS MUCH MINE AS IT IS HIS...
...SO, WITH THE SERPENT CROWN, HE IS THE DEADLIEST MAN ALIVE.
GREAT. JUST $@#% GREAT.
THIS IS ON YOU! ALL OF YOU!
HEY! CALM DOWN, FISH MAN!
THE PLAN IS A STEP TOO FAR, BUT I WAS PUSHED INTO IT BY THE WORLD...
...BY YOUR INABILITY TO KEEP A REIN ON GREEDY HUMANS AND CORPORATIONS!
YOU'VE GOT A LOT OF NERVE, PAL!
YOU TARGETED CITIZENS! SOMETHING WE NEVER WOULD HAVE DONE IN THE WAR OR--
TORO! NAMOR!
ENOUGH!
YOU TURNED ME INTO THIS, NAMOR! I'M WILLING TO PUT THAT ASIDE WHILE WE FIX YOUR MISTAKE! THE LITERAL LEAST YOU CAN DO--
--IS SHUT YOUR ROYAL TRAP WHILE WE DO IT!
NOW GET YOURSELF IN ORDER...

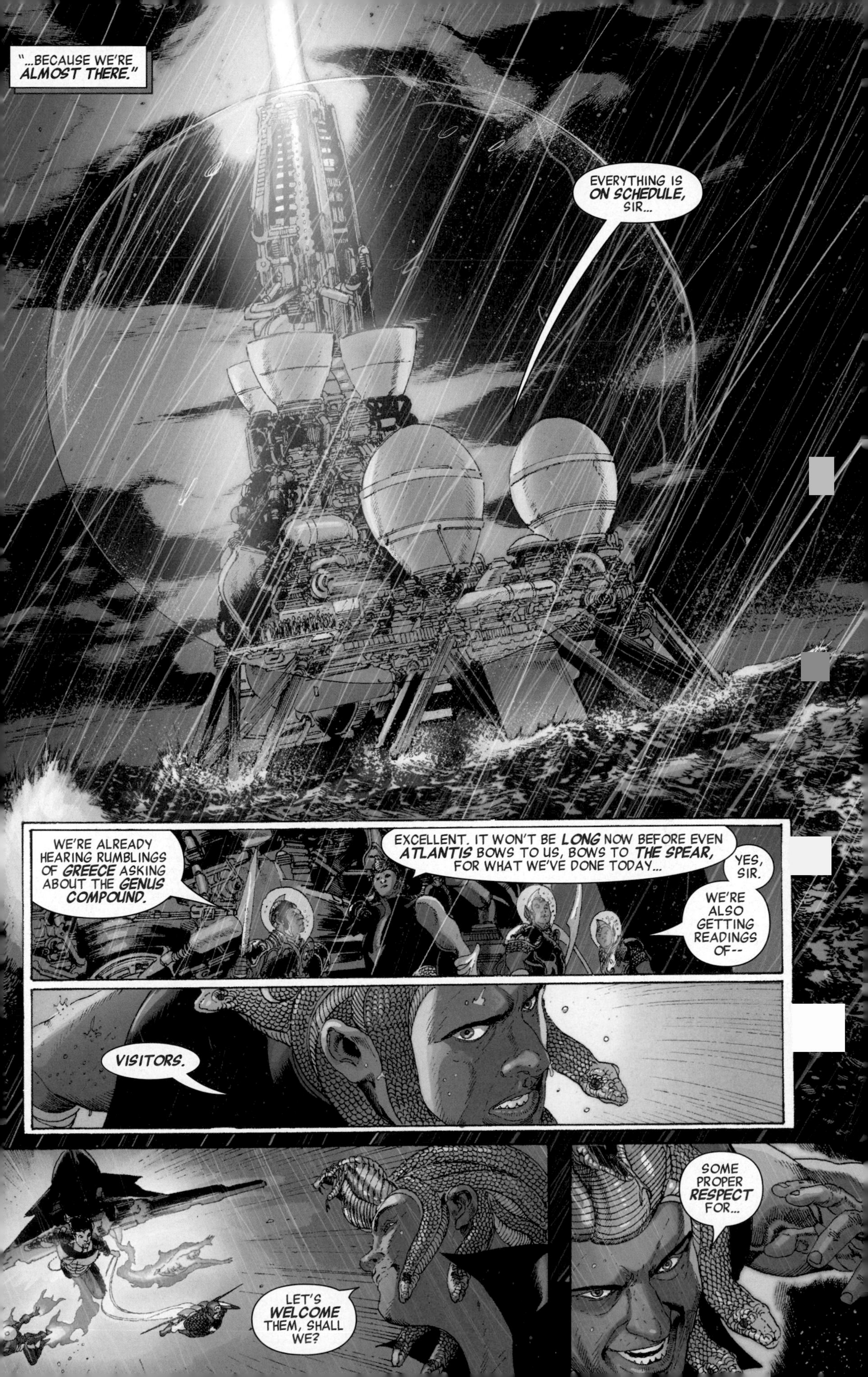
"...BECAUSE WE'RE ALMOST THERE."
EVERYTHING IS ON SCHEDULE, SIR...
WE'RE ALREADY HEARING RUMBLINGS OF GREECE ASKING ABOUT THE GENUS COMPOUND.
EXCELLENT. IT WON'T BE LONG NOW BEFORE EVEN ATLANTIS BOWS TO US, BOWS TO THE SPEAR, FOR WHAT WE'VE DONE TODAY...
YES, SIR.
WE'RE ALSO GETTING READINGS OF--
VISITORS.
LET'S WELCOME THEM, SHALL WE?
SOME PROPER RESPECT FOR...

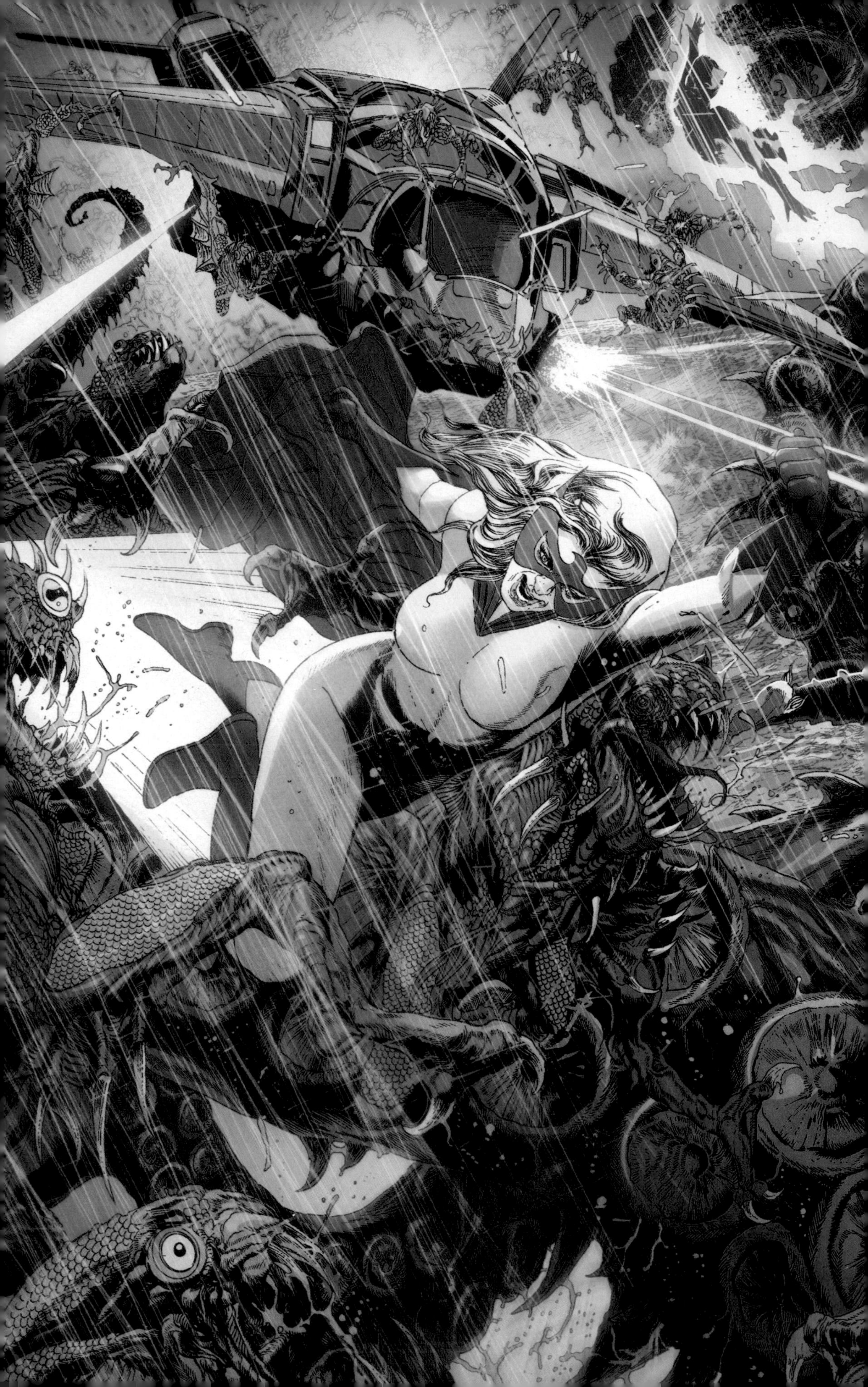

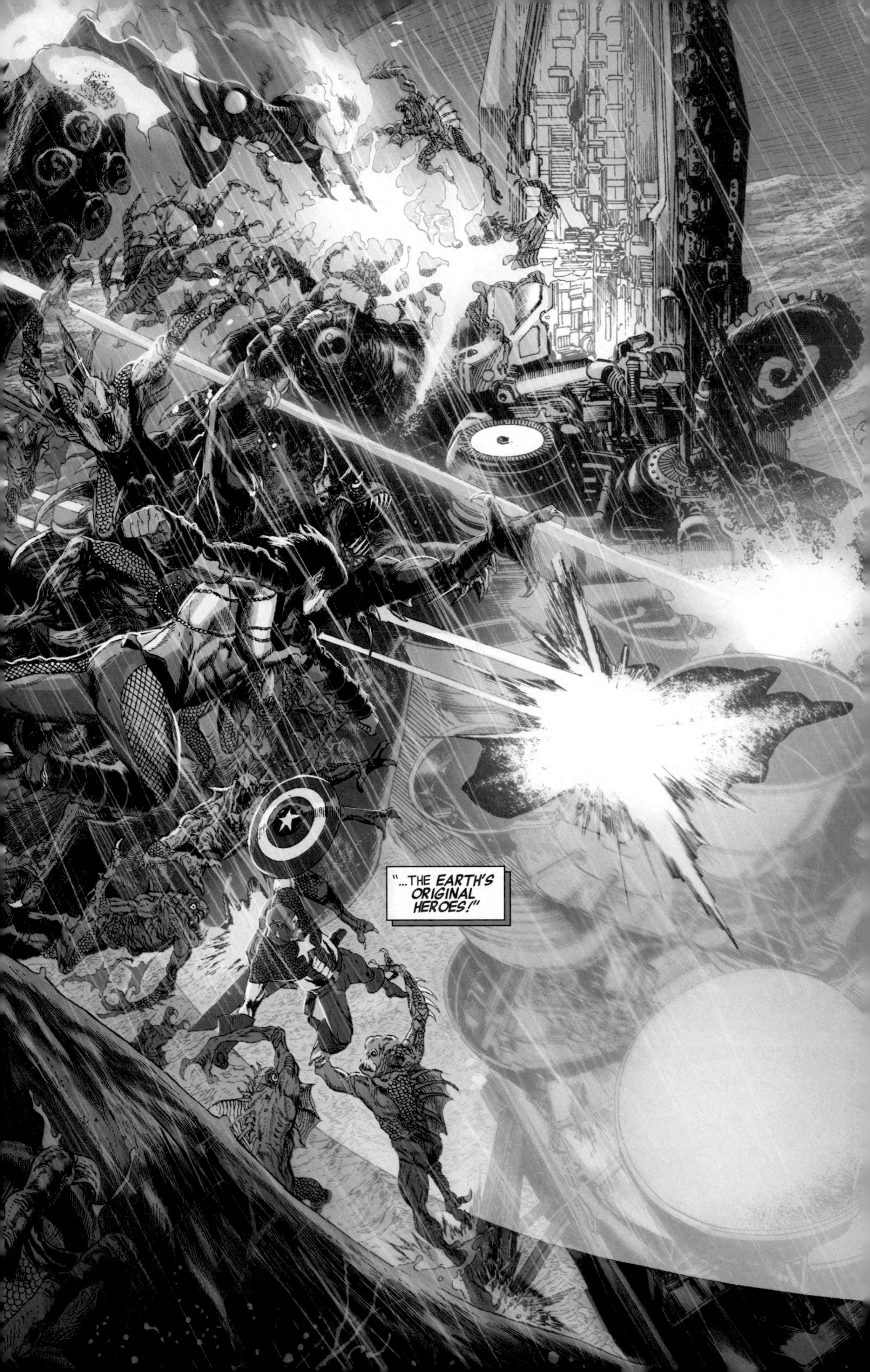
"...THE EARTH'S ORIGINAL HEROES!"

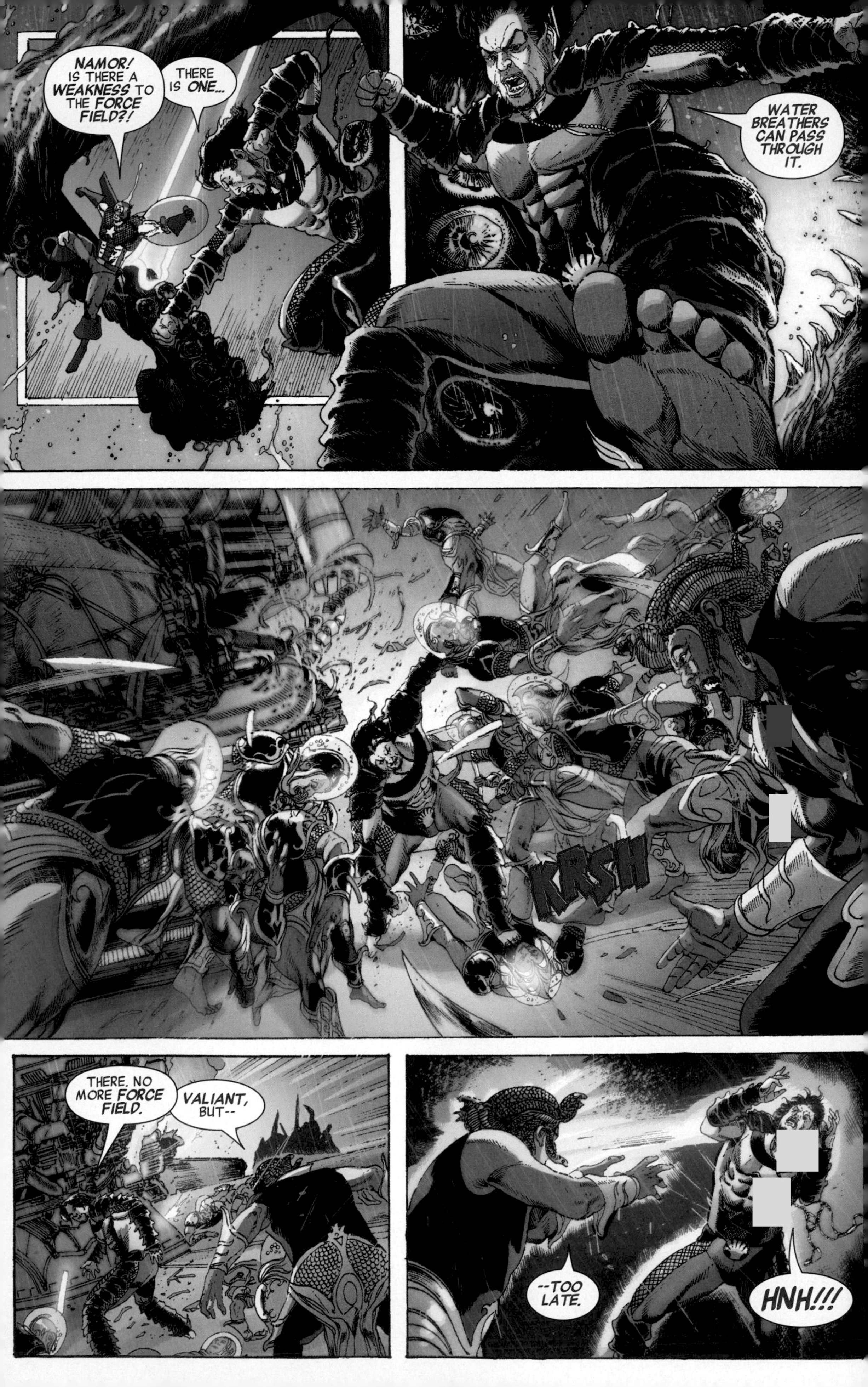
NAMOR! IS THERE A WEAKNESS TO THE FORCE FIELD?!
THERE IS ONE...
WATER BREATHERS CAN PASS THROUGH IT.
KRSH
THERE. NO MORE FORCE FIELD.
VALIANT, BUT--
--TOO LATE.
HNH!!!

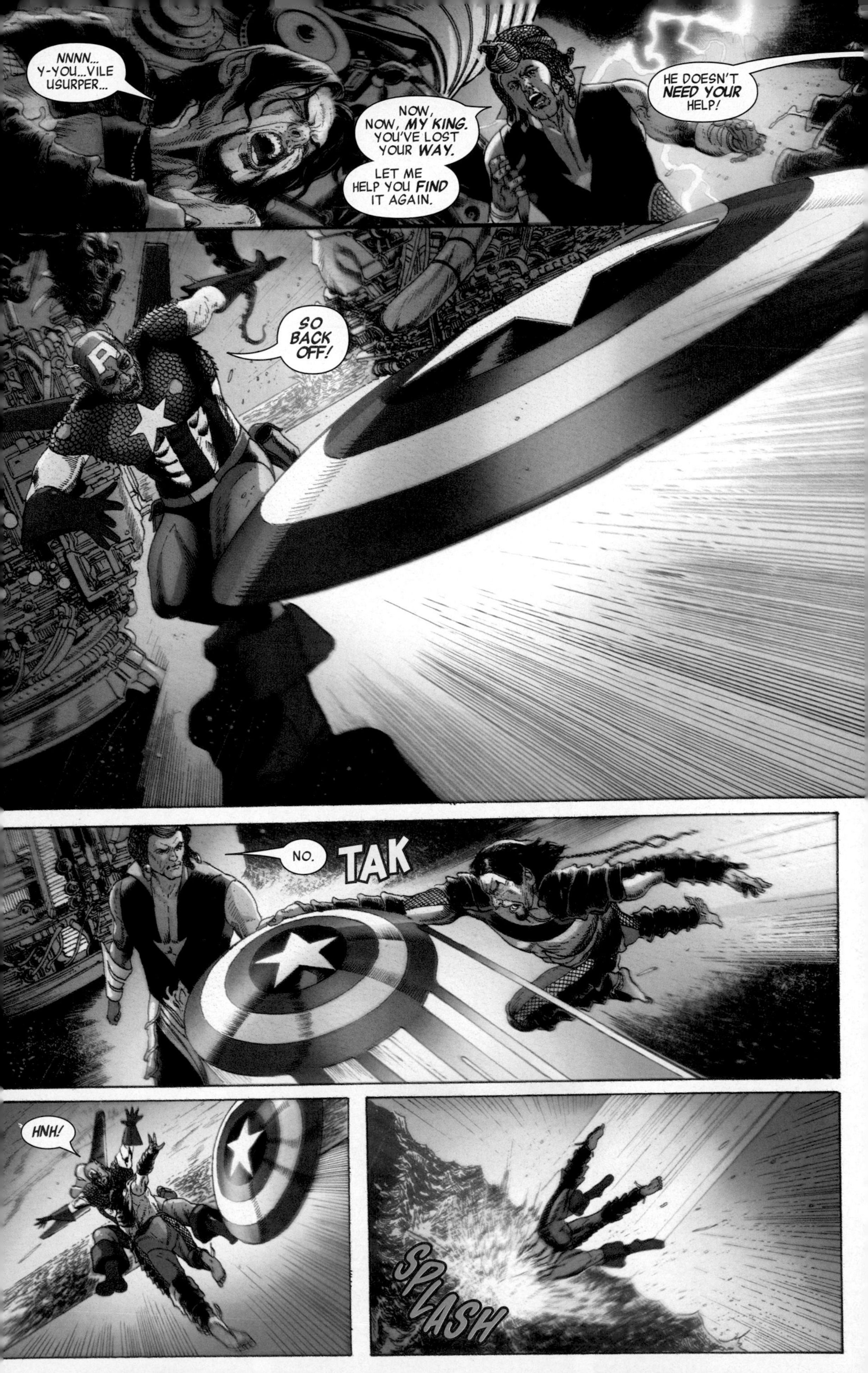
NNNN... Y-YOU...VILE USURPER...
NOW, NOW, MY KING. YOU'VE LOST YOUR WAY.
LET ME HELP YOU FIND IT AGAIN.
HE DOESN'T NEED YOUR HELP!
SO BACK OFF!
NO.
TAK
HNH!
SPLASH

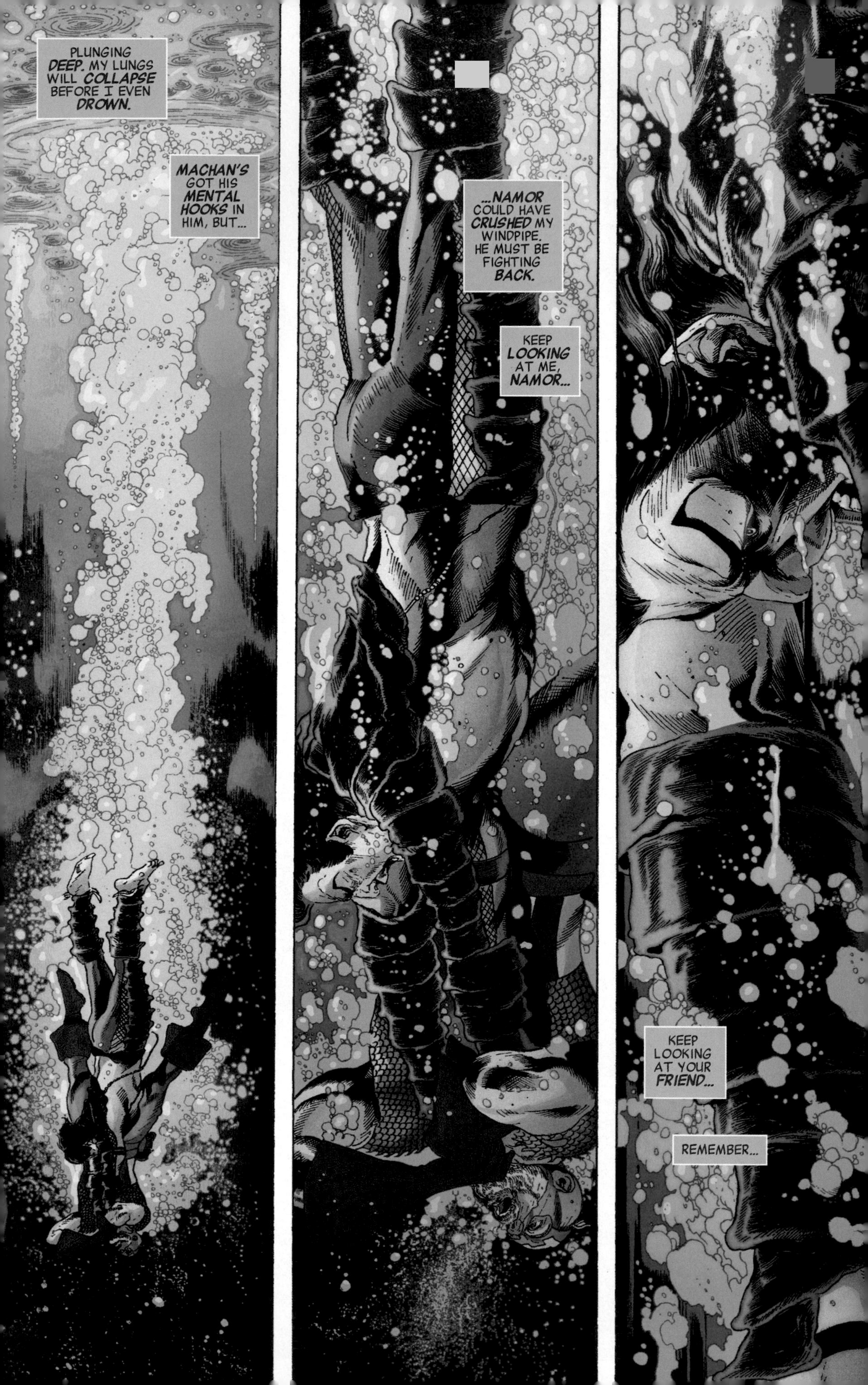
PLUNGING DEEP. MY LUNGS WILL COLLAPSE BEFORE I EVEN DROWN.
MACHAN'S GOT HIS MENTAL HOOKS IN HIM, BUT...
...NAMOR COULD HAVE CRUSHED MY WINDPIPE. HE MUST BE FIGHTING BACK.
KEEP LOOKING AT ME, NAMOR...
KEEP LOOKING AT YOUR FRIEND...
REMEMBER...

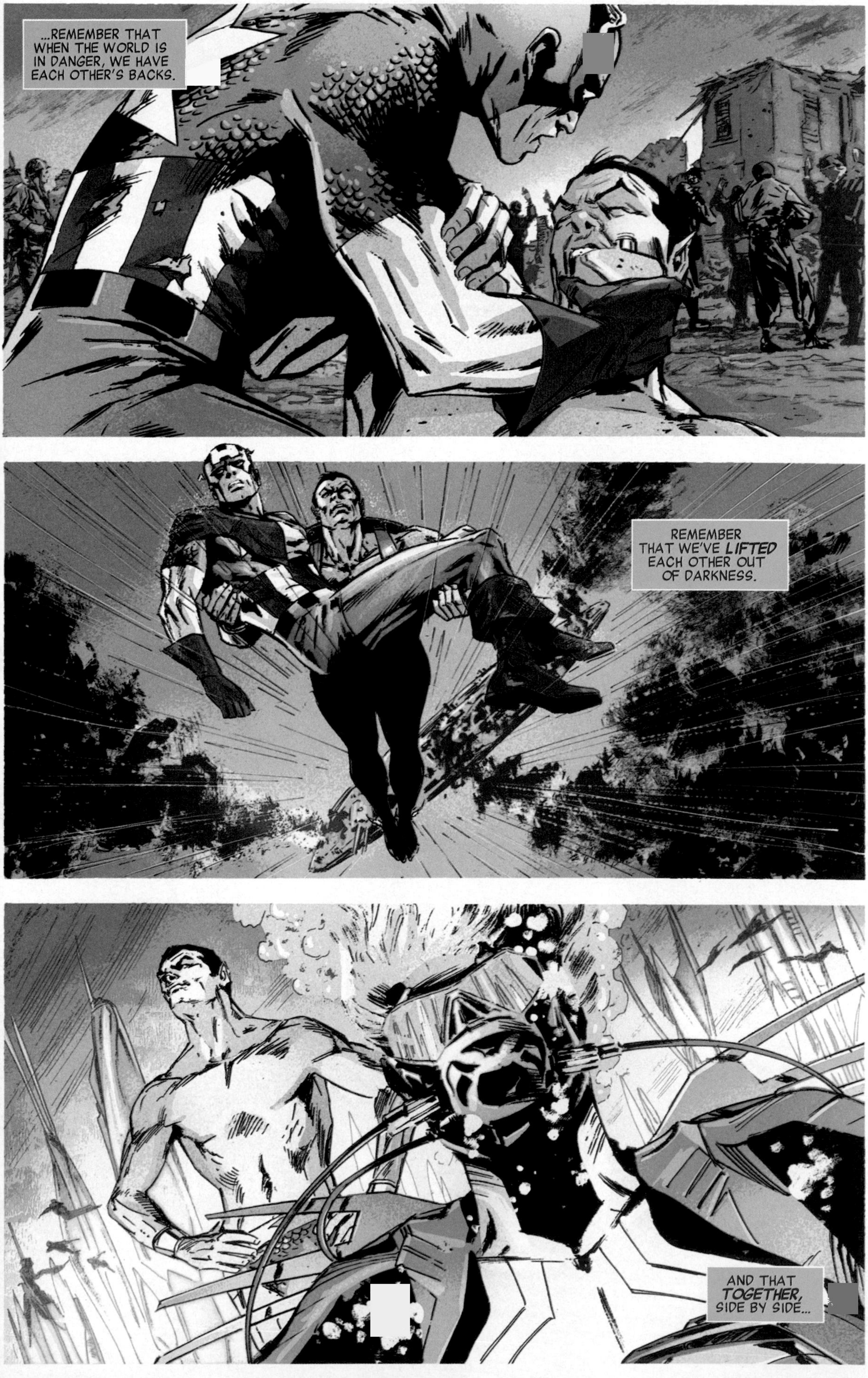
...REMEMBER THAT WHEN THE WORLD IS IN DANGER, WE HAVE EACH OTHER'S BACKS.
REMEMBER THAT WE'VE LIFTED EACH OTHER OUT OF DARKNESS.
AND THAT TOGETHER, SIDE BY SIDE...

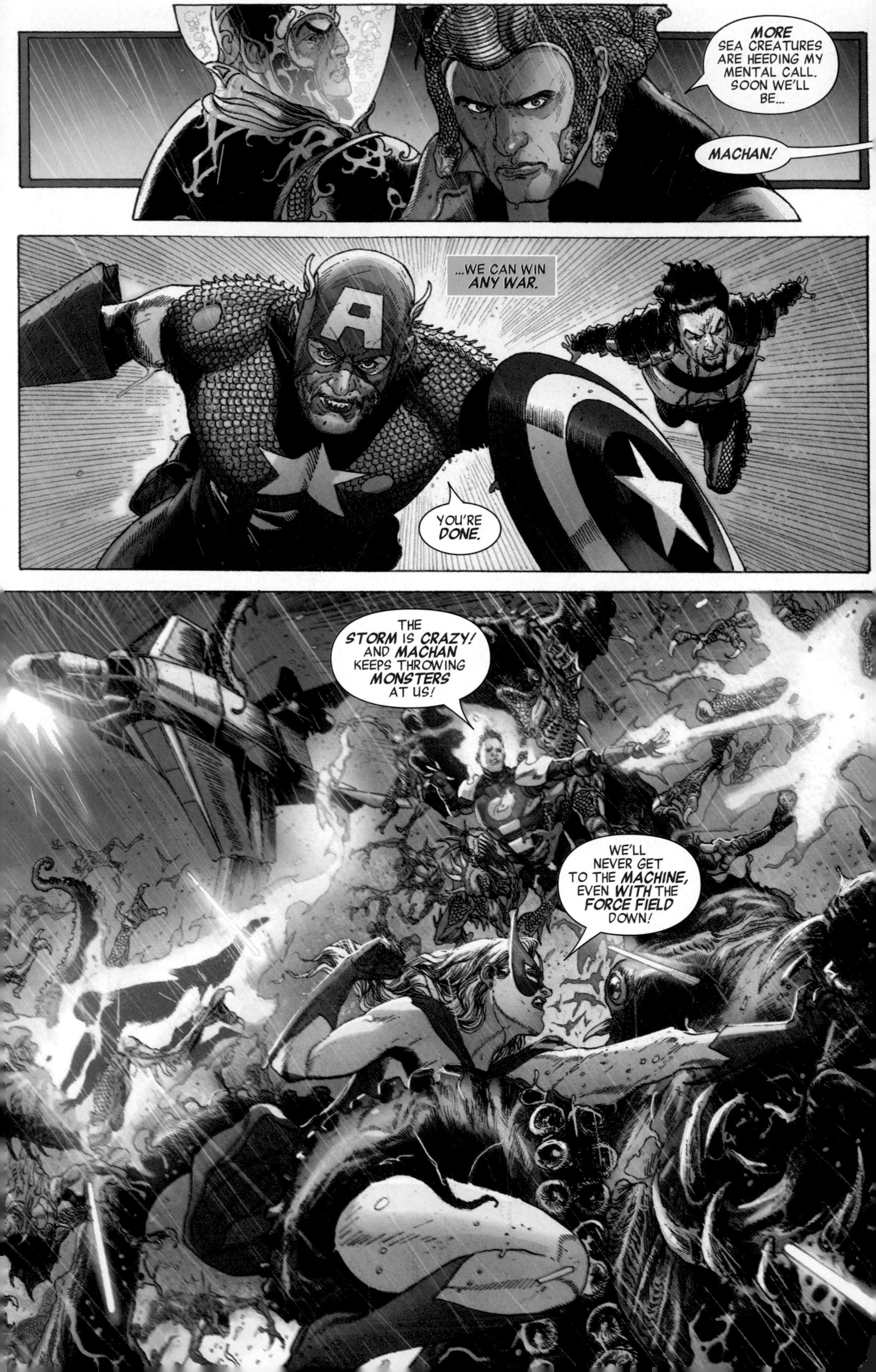
MORE SEA CREATURES ARE HEEDING MY MENTAL CALL. SOON WE'LL BE...
MACHAN!
...WE CAN WIN ANY WAR.
YOU'RE DONE.
THE STORM IS CRAZY! AND MACHAN KEEPS THROWING MONSTERS AT US!
WE'LL NEVER GET TO THE MACHINE, EVEN WITH THE FORCE FIELD DOWN!

I LOST VISUALS ON *CAP* AND *NAMOR!* WE NEED TO--

SKRAK

BUCKY! NO!

FASTER, COME ON, COME--

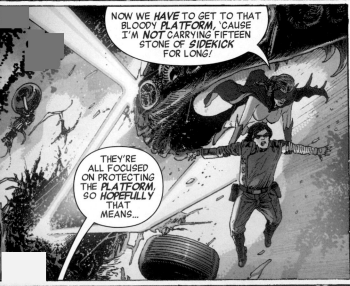

NOW WE *HAVE* TO GET TO THAT BLOODY *PLATFORM*, 'CAUSE I'M *NOT* CARRYING FIFTEEN STONE OF *SIDEKICK* FOR LONG!

THEY'RE ALL FOCUSED ON PROTECTING THE *PLATFORM*, SO *HOPEFULLY* THAT MEANS...

...THERE'S *LESS* RESISTANCE *BELOW!*

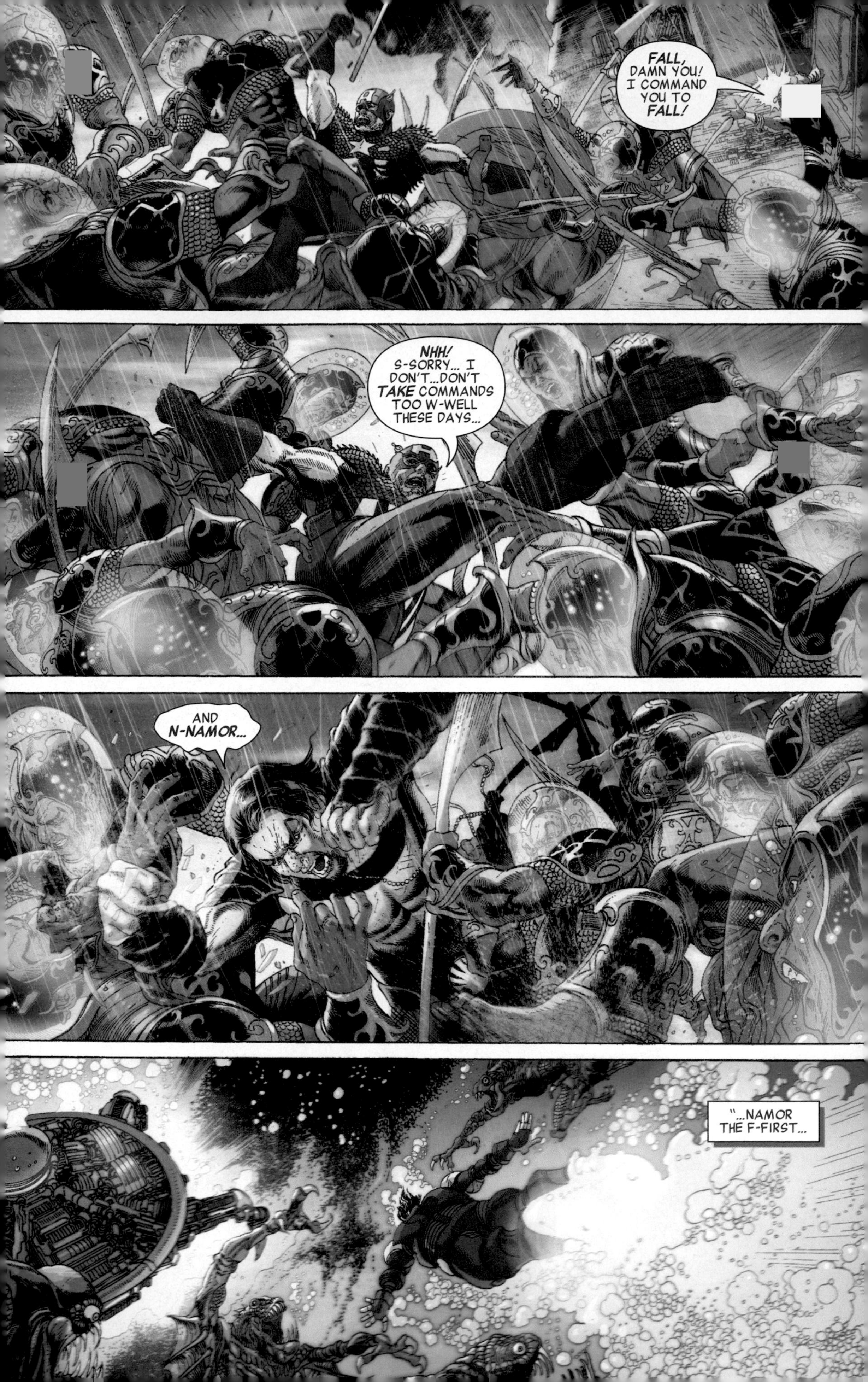
FALL, DAMN YOU! I COMMAND YOU TO FALL!
NHH! S-SORRY... I DON'T...DON'T TAKE COMMANDS TOO W-WELL THESE DAYS...
AND N-NAMOR...
"...NAMOR THE F-FIRST...

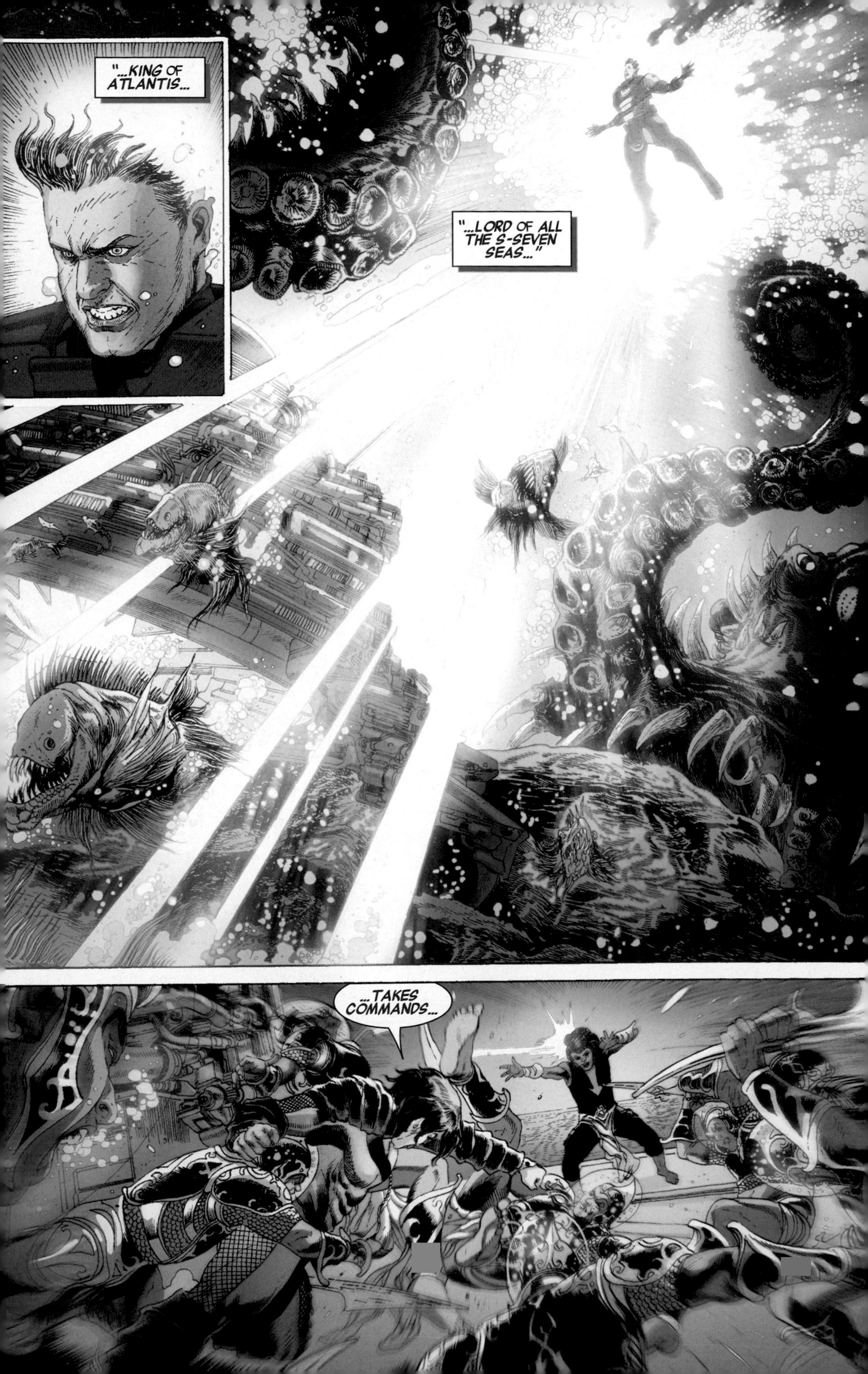
"...KING OF ATLANTIS...
"...LORD OF ALL THE S-SEVEN SEAS..."
...TAKES COMMANDS...

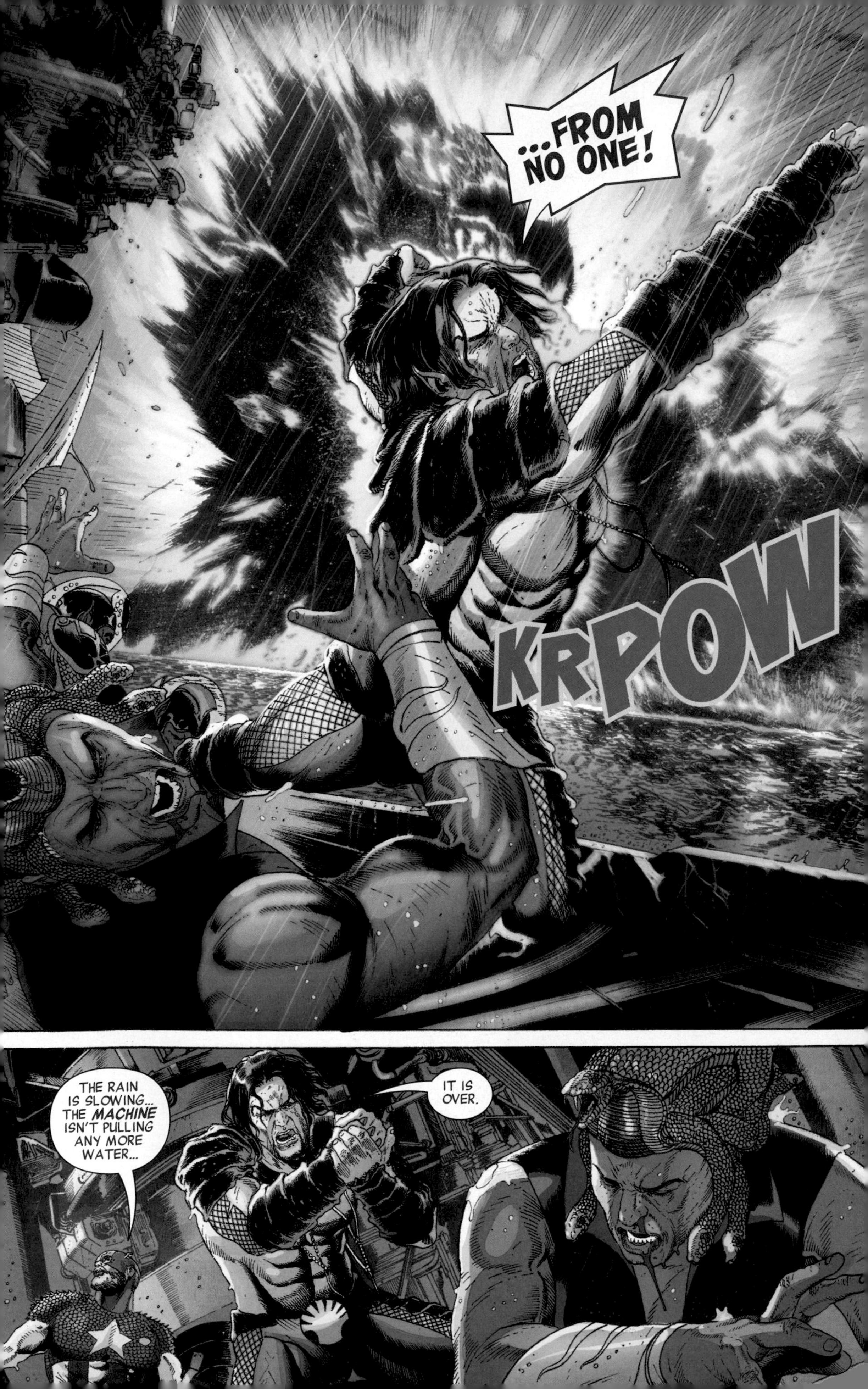
...FROM NO ONE!
KRPOW
THE RAIN IS SLOWING... THE *MACHINE* ISN'T PULLING ANY MORE WATER...
IT IS OVER.

I WILL REBUILD THE **MACHINE** TO **VODAN,** SEND THE **EXCESS OCEAN** BACK TO WHERE IT CAME FROM.

AND **THIS MAN**... THIS MAN WHO **TORTURED** ME AND THE **WORLD**...

NHH-HK!

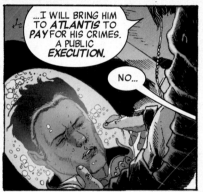

...I WILL BRING HIM TO **ATLANTIS** TO **PAY** FOR HIS CRIMES. A PUBLIC **EXECUTION.**

NO...

...YOU **WON'T.**

YOU ONCE LECTURED ME ABOUT THE **SACRIFICES** OF A KING.

PUTTING THE NEEDS OF A **NATION** ABOVE YOUR OWN, TAKING ON **BURDENS.**

WELL...

...**THIS** IS YOUR BURDEN.

IF YOU **DON'T** LET US LEAVE WITH **MACHAN,** THE WORLD WILL STILL THINK **YOU** DID THIS AND RAIN DOWN FIRE ON **ATLANTIS.**

SO, YOUR **SACRIFICE**...

...IS YOUR **BLOODLUST.** YOUR PERSONAL NEED FOR **VENGEANCE.**

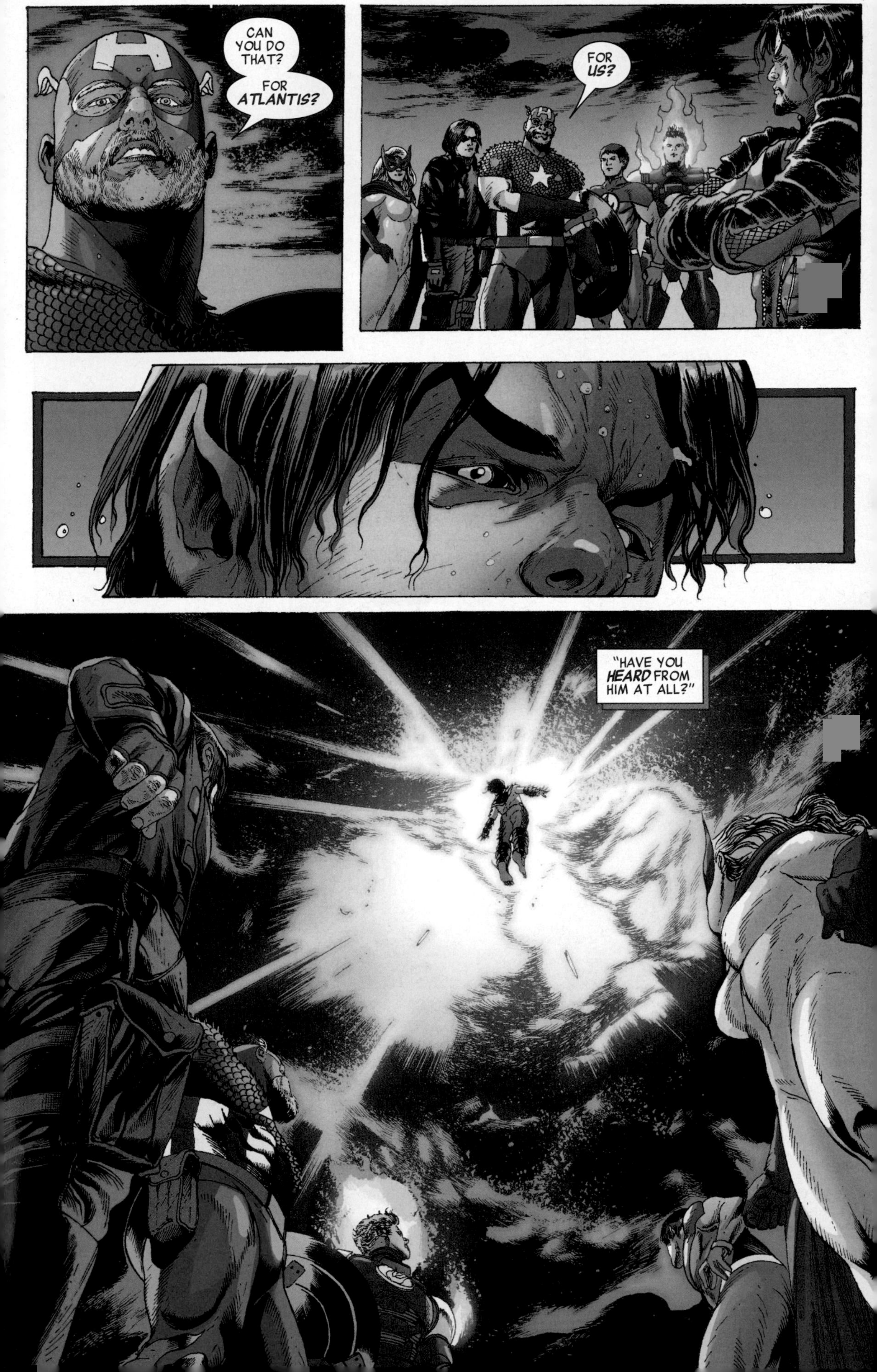
CAN YOU DO THAT?
FOR ATLANTIS?
FOR US?
"HAVE YOU HEARD FROM HIM AT ALL?"

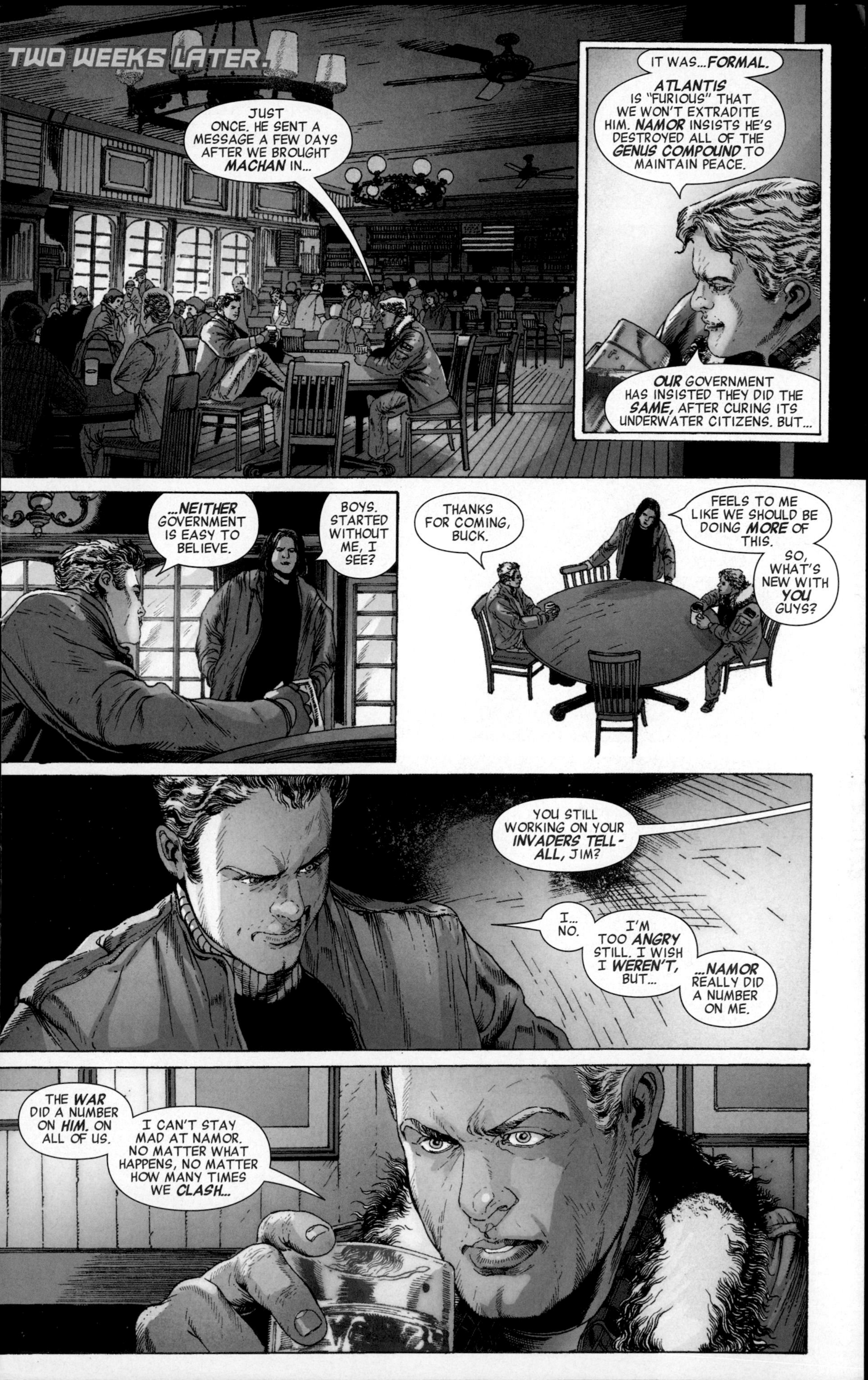
TWO WEEKS LATER.
JUST ONCE. HE SENT A MESSAGE A FEW DAYS AFTER WE BROUGHT MACHAN IN...
IT WAS...FORMAL.
ATLANTIS IS "FURIOUS" THAT WE WON'T EXTRADITE HIM. NAMOR INSISTS HE'S DESTROYED ALL OF THE GENUS COMPOUND TO MAINTAIN PEACE.
OUR GOVERNMENT HAS INSISTED THEY DID THE SAME, AFTER CURING ITS UNDERWATER CITIZENS. BUT...
...NEITHER GOVERNMENT IS EASY TO BELIEVE.
BOYS. STARTED WITHOUT ME, I SEE?
THANKS FOR COMING, BUCK.
FEELS TO ME LIKE WE SHOULD BE DOING MORE OF THIS.
SO, WHAT'S NEW WITH YOU GUYS?
YOU STILL WORKING ON YOUR INVADERS TELL-ALL, JIM?
I... NO.
I'M TOO ANGRY STILL. I WISH I WEREN'T, BUT...
...NAMOR REALLY DID A NUMBER ON ME.
THE WAR DID A NUMBER ON HIM. ON ALL OF US.
I CAN'T STAY MAD AT NAMOR. NO MATTER WHAT HAPPENS, NO MATTER HOW MANY TIMES WE CLASH...

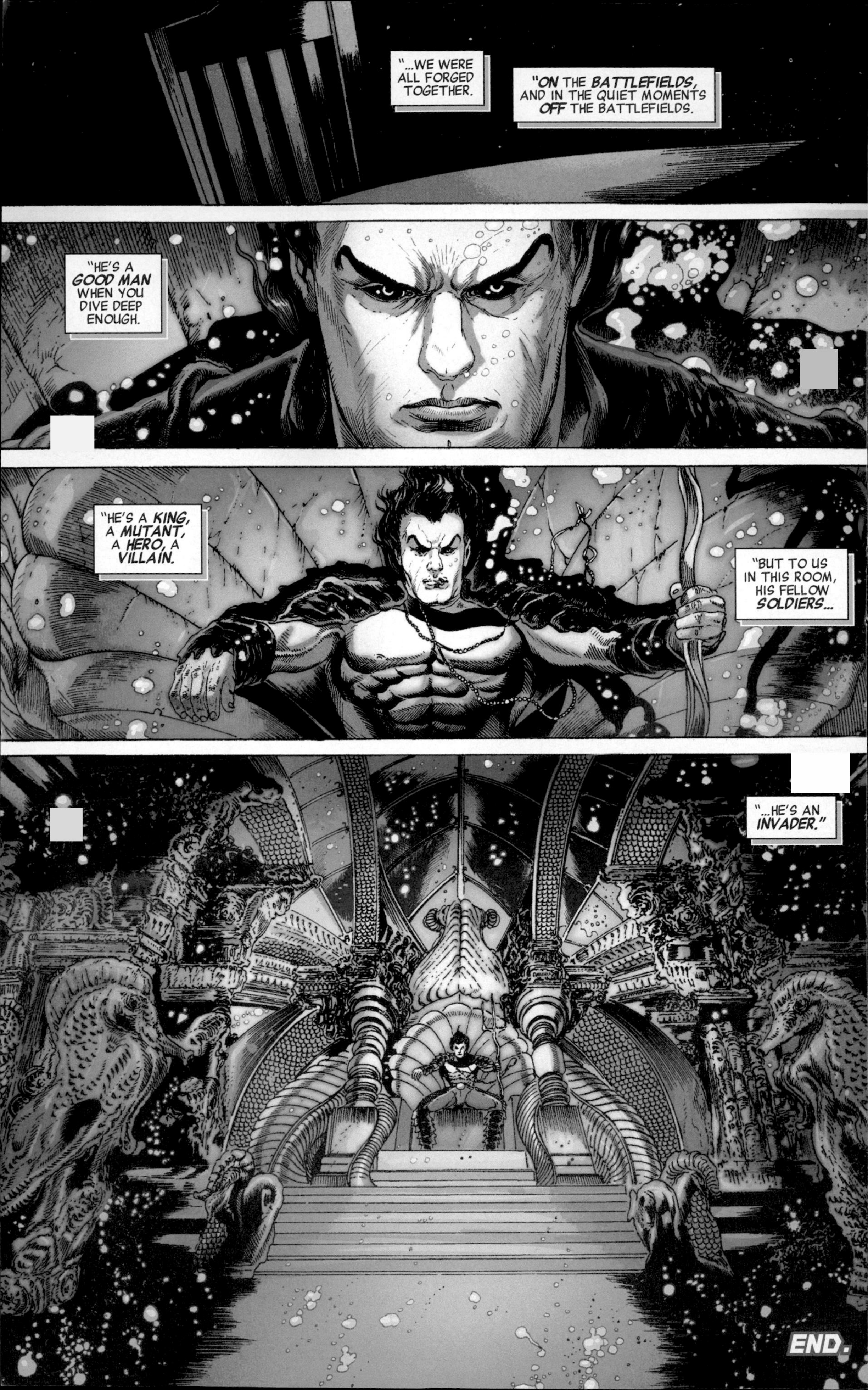
"...WE WERE ALL FORGED TOGETHER.
"ON THE BATTLEFIELDS, AND IN THE QUIET MOMENTS OFF THE BATTLEFIELDS.
"HE'S A GOOD MAN WHEN YOU DIVE DEEP ENOUGH.
"HE'S A KING, A MUTANT, A HERO, A VILLAIN.
"BUT TO US IN THIS ROOM, HIS FELLOW SOLDIERS...
"...HE'S AN INVADER."
END.

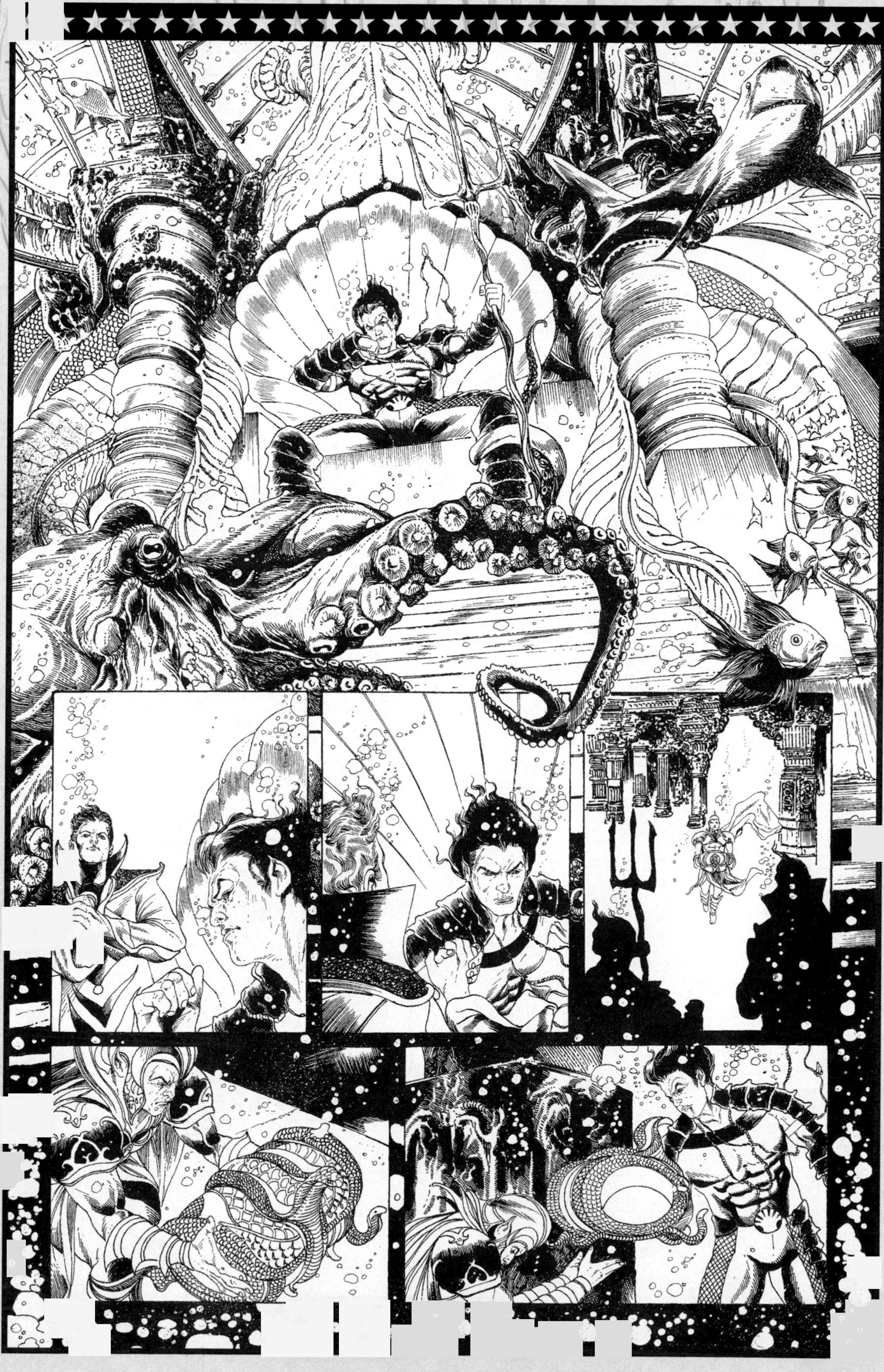

#7, PAGE 19 ART BY **CARLOS MAGNO**

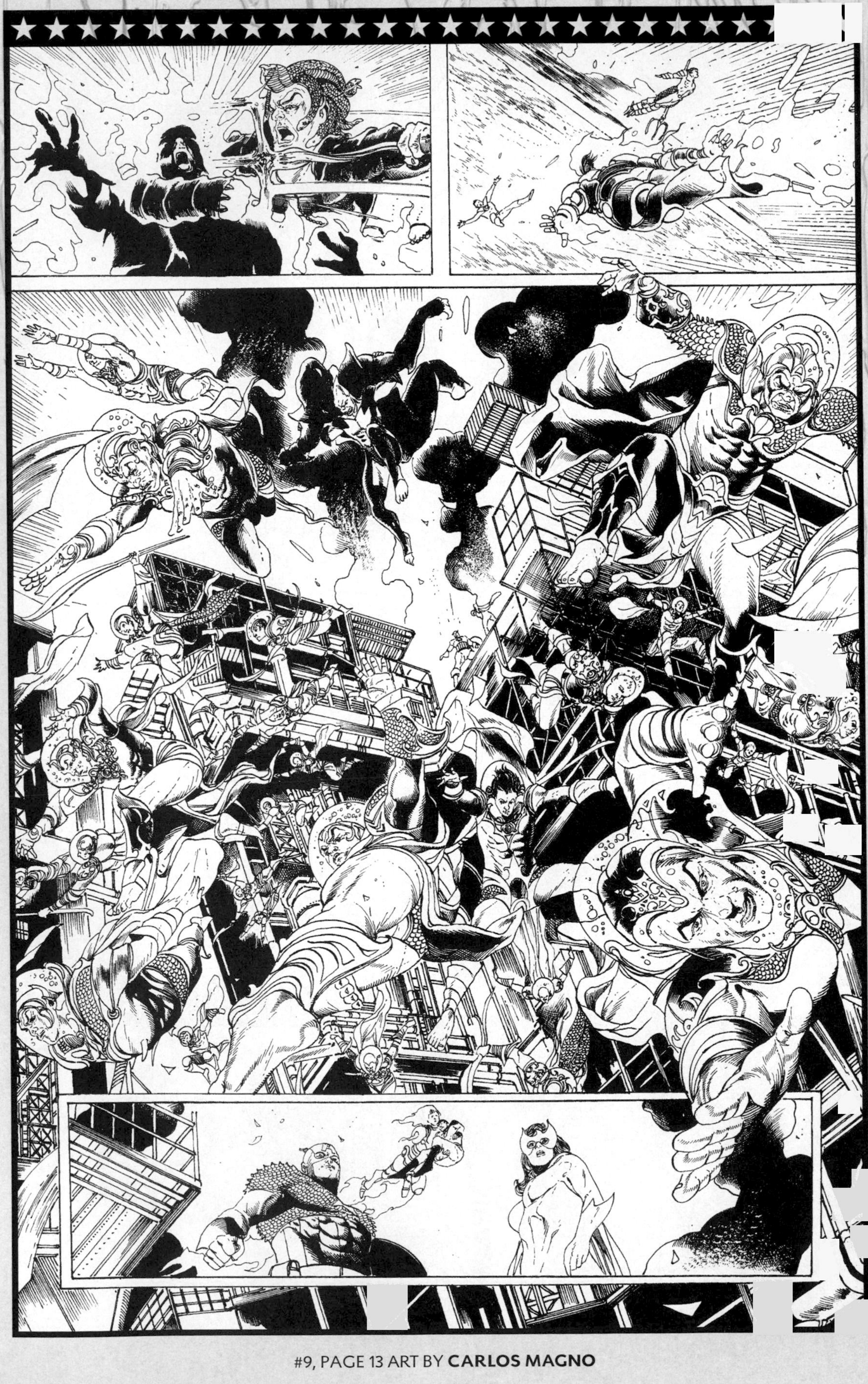

#9, PAGE 13 ART BY **CARLOS MAGNO**

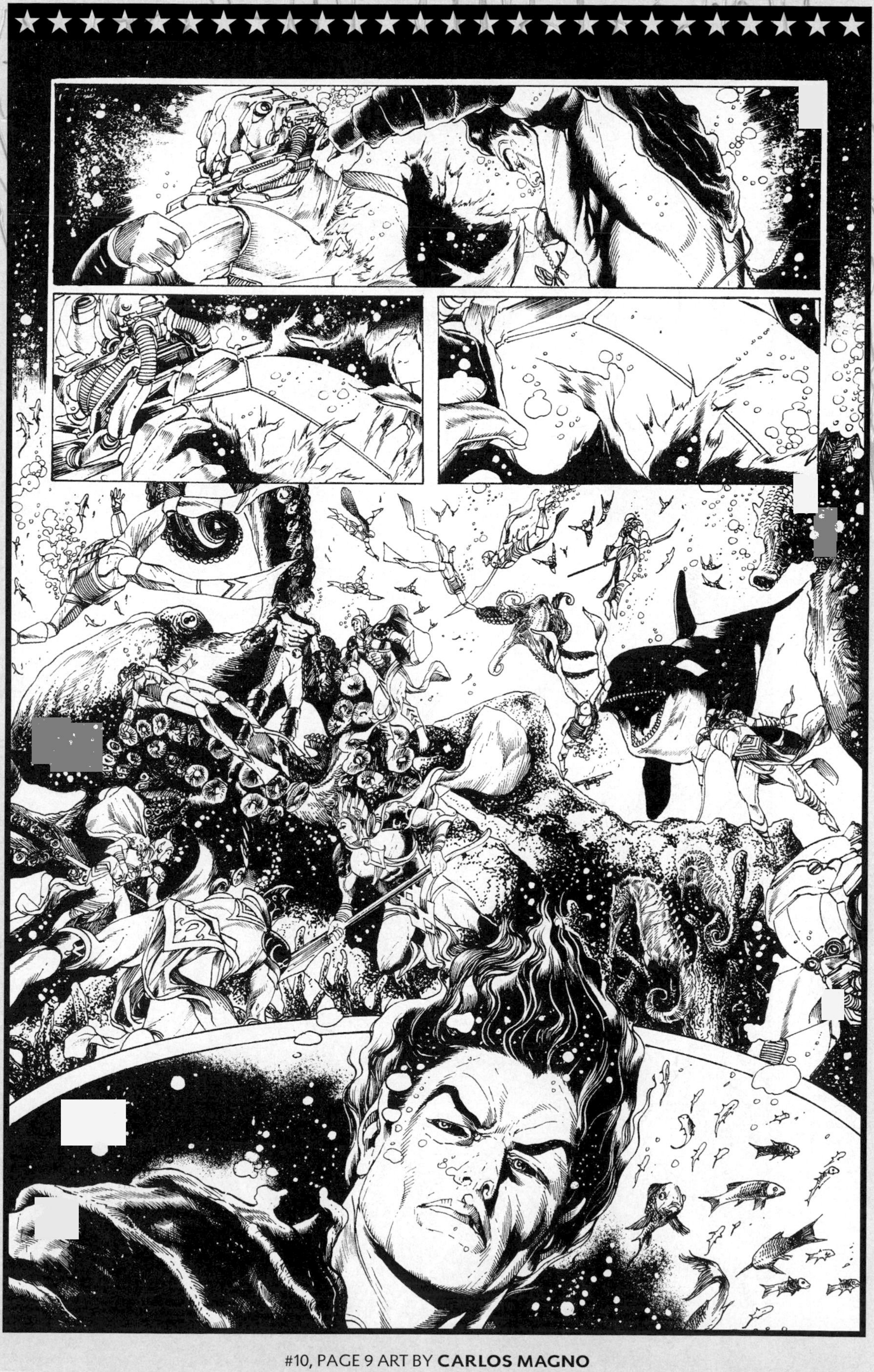

#10, PAGE 9 ART BY **CARLOS MAGNO**

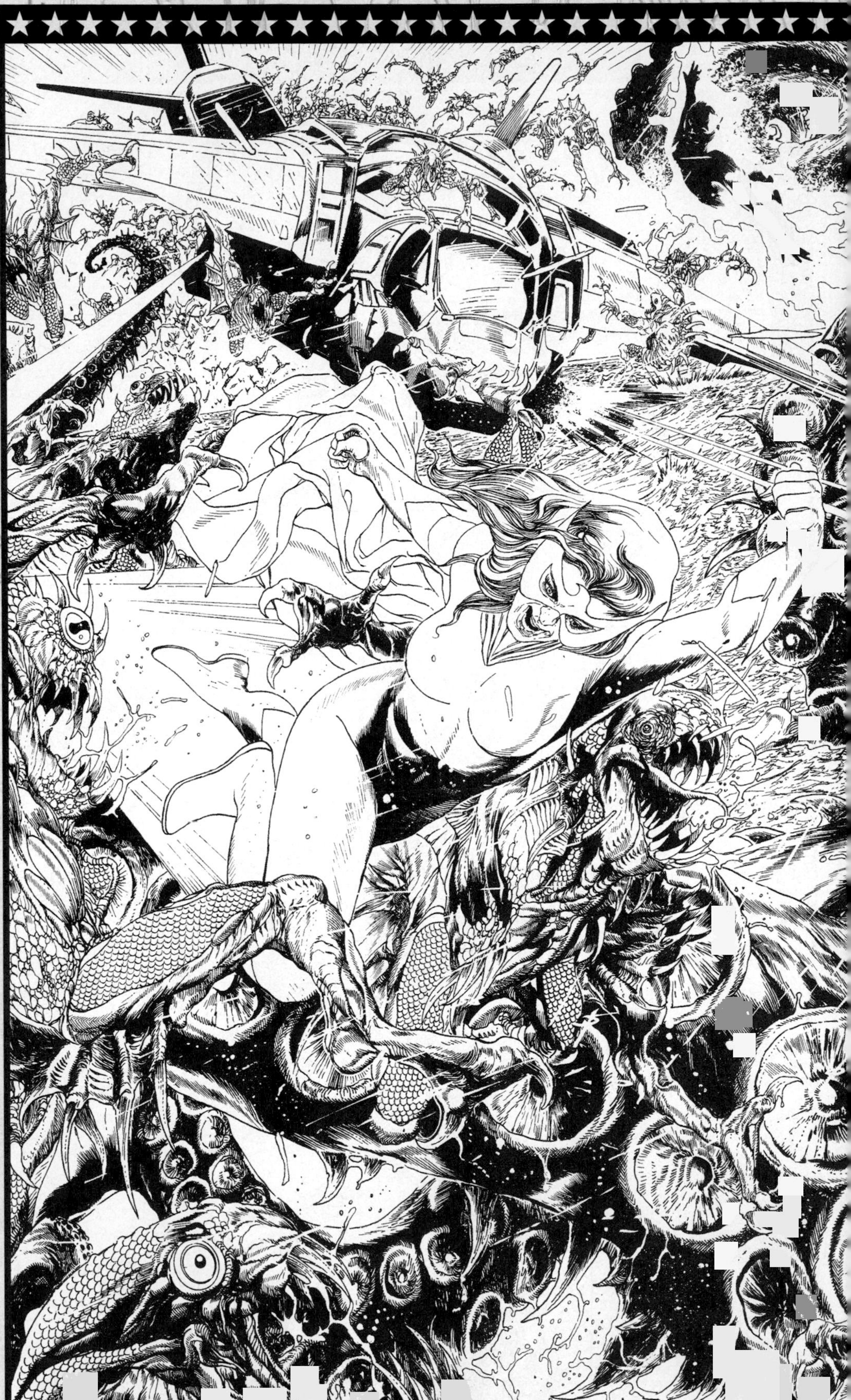

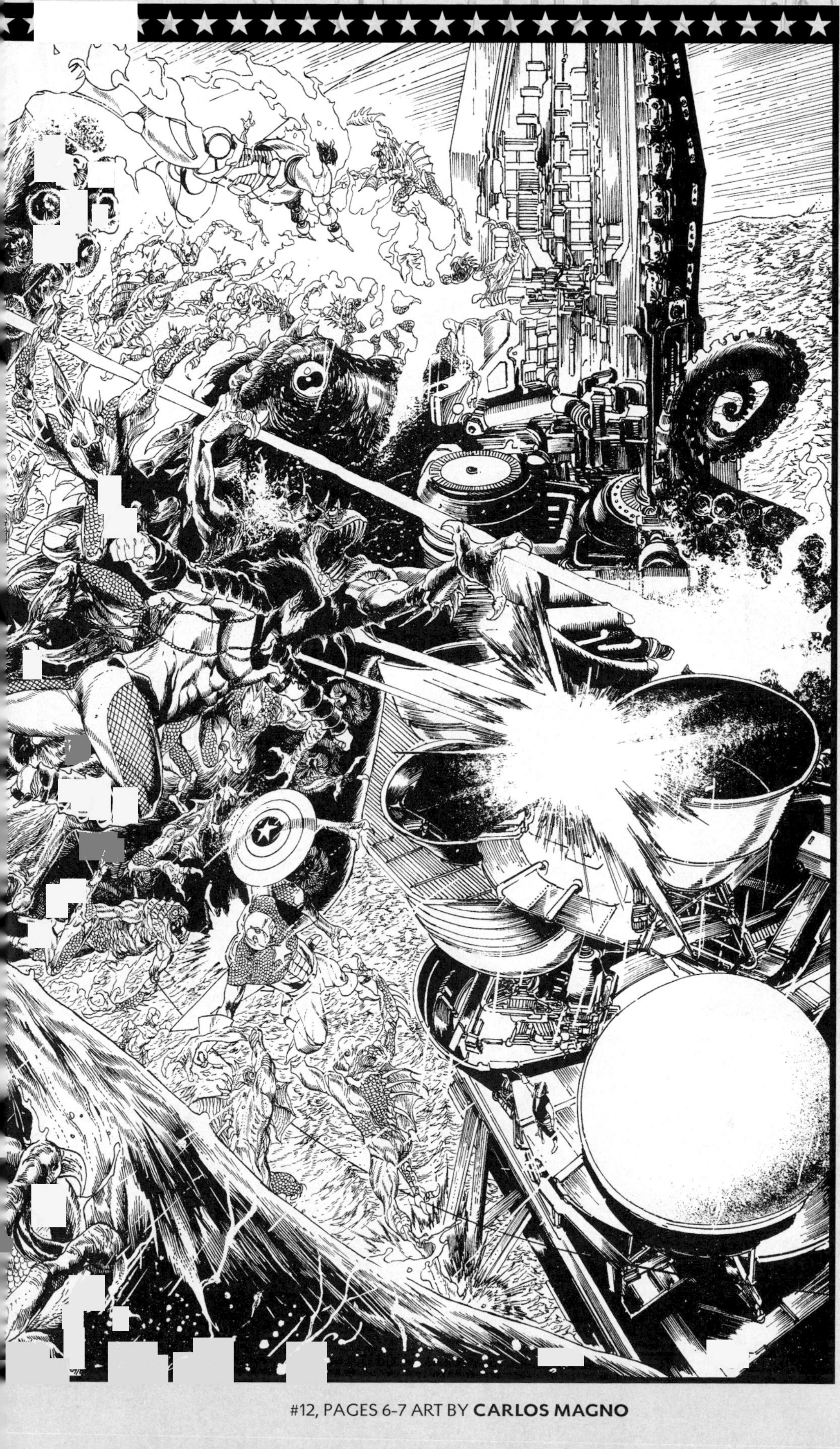

#12, PAGES 6–7 ART BY **CARLOS MAGNO**

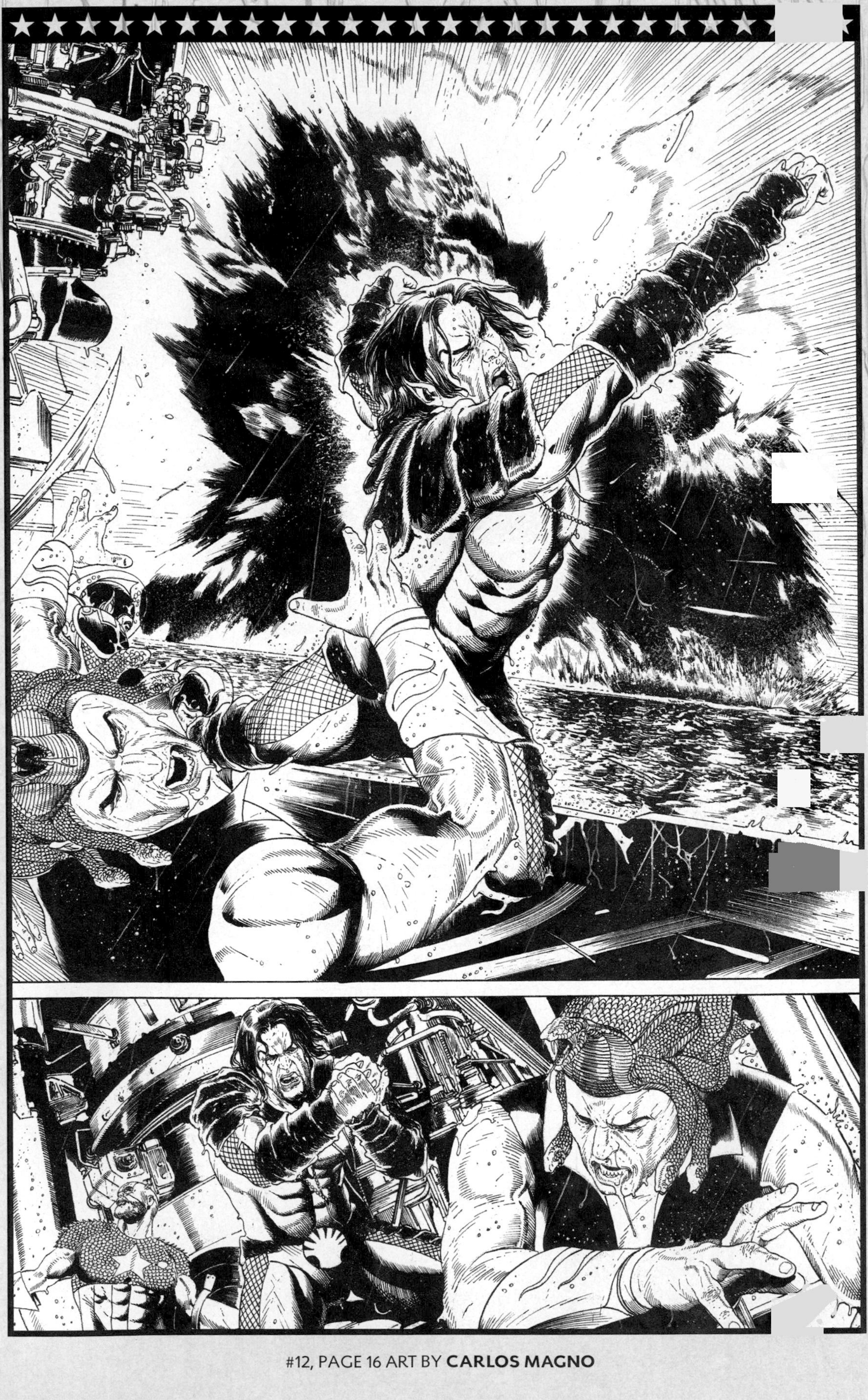

#12, PAGE 16 ART BY **CARLOS MAGNO**